Building Agents with OpenAI Agents SDK

Create practical AI agents and agentic systems through hands-on projects

Henry Habib

‹packt›

Building Agents with OpenAI Agents SDK

Portfolio Director: Gebin George
Relationship Lead: Vignesh Raju
Project Manager: Prajakta Naik
Content Engineer: Aditi Chatterjee
Technical Editor: Rahul Limbachiya
Copy Editor: Safis Editing
Indexer: Manju Arasan
Proofreader: Aditi Chatterjee
Production Designer: Ajay Patule
Growth Lead: Nimisha Dua

First published: October 2025

Production reference:1260922

Published by Packt Publishing Ltd.
Grosvenor House
11 St Paul's Square
Birmingham
B3 1RB, UK.

ISBN 978-1-80611-201-2

www.packtpub.com

To Soniya, Booboo, Mom, Dad, Maheen, Karan, Riri, and Cece.

– Henry

Contributors

About the author

Henry Habib advises F500 companies on analytics and operations, with a particular focus on building intelligent AI-driven solutions, tools, and agents to create impact and improve productivity.

He teaches online courses on how to build AI agents and automations for work, as well as other Gen AI topics, amassing a network of more than 400K students. He also facilitates technical programs at businesses and governmental organizations. A proponent of the no-code and Gen AI revolution, he believes that anyone can now create powerful and intelligent applications to automate their work without any deep technical skills.

He also runs **The Intelligent Worker**, a platform for teaching working professionals how to be more productive with Gen AI, no-code, automation, and other technologies, with courses and a free newsletter. He is also a speaker on Gen AI to many large F500 organizations.

As an instructor, Henry is passionate about teaching students how to succeed on any topic related to Gen AI, automation, no-code, data, and productivity. He does this by creating courses with engaging and helpful content and always being around to answer any questions.

Henry resides in Toronto, Canada, with his wife, and enjoys building random AI apps and playing tennis in his free time.

About the reviewer

Sankara Reddy Thamma is a seasoned solutions architect, technical delivery specialist, and AI innovator with over 15 years of experience in driving large-scale enterprise modernization, cloud migration, and AI-powered automation initiatives across industries, including banking, healthcare, utilities, and manufacturing. His technical expertise spans legacy mainframe, IBM DataStage, big data ecosystems, Snowflake, Databricks, agentic AI, and multi-cloud platforms (AWS, Azure, and GCP), coupled with deep proficiency in cloud modernization and legacy modernization, making him a trusted leader in transforming complex enterprise landscapes.

At the core of his contributions is a transformative vision of agentic AI. Beyond enterprise outcomes, Thamma plays an active role in advancing the AI and technology community. He is a senior member of IEEE, where he contributes as a peer reviewer across domains including AI, machine learning, generative AI, and data engineering. His contributions extend into technical publishing, serving as a technical book reviewer for Packt Publishing and Manning Publications, while also supporting leading AI journals and editorial boards. His expertise is recognized globally, with patents granted in the UK and India for intelligent code transformation leveraging agent-based accelerators.

As a published researcher, he has authored works in IEEE, Springer, and Scopus journals, covering themes such as secure prompt engineering, neurovisualization, and applied AI in healthcare. His ability to bridge cutting-edge research with applied enterprise solutions positions him uniquely at the intersection of theory and practice.

Subscribe for a free eBook

New frameworks, evolving architectures, research drops, production breakdowns—*AI_Distilled* filters the noise into a weekly briefing for engineers and researchers working hands-on with LLMs and GenAI systems. Subscribe now and receive a free eBook, along with weekly insights that help you stay focused and informed.

Subscribe at `https://packt.link/80z6Y` or scan the QR code below.

Table of Contents

Chapter 6: Multi-Agent Systems and Handoffs 131

Chapter 7: Model and Context Management 165

Preface

Building Agents with OpenAI Agents SDK comes at a time when there is a major shift in AI and how we work. The first wave came with ChatGPT, a **large language models (LLM)** in a consumer application, which gave everyone powerful new ways to generate and work with natural language. Now, we are moving into the next phase: AI agents. Unlike traditional software, which is built around rigid, deterministic rules, such as "if X, then Y," agents can handle ambiguity, can adapt to changing goals, and can reason through steps to accomplish tasks. They are not limited to answering questions; they can plan, orchestrate workflows, retrieve and synthesize information, use external tools, and even collaborate with one another. In doing so, they are beginning to take on work that once seemed possible only for humans. This transformation is still in its early days.

OpenAI Agents SDK is at the center of this change. It provides a practical and the best framework for building, deploying, and managing agents, from simple assistants to complex multi-agent systems. Just as Microsoft PowerPoint is a platform to build slide deck presentations, OpenAI Agents SDK is poised to become the way developers and tech enthusiasts build AI agents and agentic systems.

This book is your guide to mastering that skill. It takes a hands-on, example-based approach. We start in the beginning by learning the anatomy of an agent, its strengths and weaknesses, and how OpenAI Agents SDK works. We then deep dive into each of the SDK's capabilities, such as tools, memory, knowledge, multi-agent handoffs, and guardrails. We then take everything we've learned and build a full end-to-end practical AI agent solution.

By the end, you won't just understand AI agents in theory; you'll have built full, end-to-end agentic systems with OpenAI Agents SDK. You'll be equipped not only to answer the question, "What is an AI agent?", but also to design and implement AI agents in practice. The best way to learn is by building, and this book is written to get you building AI agents.

The book is structured into three parts:

- *Part 1, AI Agents*, lays the conceptual and practical groundwork for the rest of the book. We start by defining what an agent is, how it differs from a traditional chatbot or API client, and why agents have become a compelling pattern for automating work across software, data, and business processes. We will then build a mental model of an AI agent that you can use throughout the book: the brain of an agent (the model), the hands and eyes of an agent (the tooling interface), and the reference textbook (memory and knowledge), all under explicit constraints and guardrails. We will then learn about the core primitives of the best framework to build AI agents – OpenAI Agents SDK.

- *Part 2, OpenAI Agents SDK*, is the technical core of the book. Here, we move from "agent as an idea" to "agent as an engineered system," using OpenAI Agents SDK as our primary vehicle. Each chapter deepens one specific capability and the primitives set of OpenAI Agents SDK. For each component, we discuss the theory and then apply it to examples and demos as we build practical AI agents and agentic systems. Specifically, we will extend your agent with tools (from simple functions to hosted tools and agents-as-tools), add memory and knowledge retrieval, compose multi-agent systems with deliberate handoffs, and learn how to manage agentic systems.

- *Part 3, Build AI Agents*, is the key part of the book. Here, we will assemble an end-to-end agentic system using OpenAI Agents SDK, not as isolated features but as a coherent application. We will take the components introduced earlier (tools, memory and retrieval, sessions, model and context management, guardrails, multi-agent orchestration, etc.) and integrate them into production-shaped applications and workflows with clear inputs and outputs.

Who this book is for

If you are a software developer, consultant, or tech professional eager to harness the power of AI agents, this book is designed for you. Whether you are a Python developer exploring the latest in AI frameworks, a business analyst curious about automating workflows, or a productivity enthusiast looking to build practical AI-driven solutions, this book will give you the skills to turn ideas into working AI agents and agentic systems.

We assume you have a basic understanding of programming concepts in Python and a general comfort with technical tools such as APIs, development environments, and cloud-based services. You do not need prior experience with AI or machine learning to follow along as these concepts are introduced progressively.

By the end of this book, you will have both the conceptual grounding and the hands-on experience to design, implement, and scale AI agents using OpenAI Agents SDK, moving from simple agents to sophisticated, multi-agent systems capable of real-world impact.

What this book covers

Chapter 1, Introduction to AI Agents, explains what AI agents are and why they represent such a powerful paradigm for automating tasks. It sets the stage for understanding their role in modern workflows.

Chapter 2, Introduction to OpenAI Agents SDK, introduces the architecture, core concepts, and primitives of OpenAI Agents SDK, giving you a foundation to work with agent-based systems.

Chapter 3, Environment Setup and Developing Your First Agent, walks through setting up your development environment and building a simple agent from scratch, providing a practical first step into agent development.

Chapter 4, Agent Tools and MCPs, demonstrates how to extend agents with tools, from custom Python functions to OpenAI-hosted tools, while also covering how agents can interact through the **Model Context Protocol (MCP)**.

Chapter 5, Memory and Knowledge, shows how to give agents memory and retrieval abilities by integrating conversation history and vector databases, enabling them to use past context and external documents effectively.

Chapter 6, Multi-Agent Systems and Handoffs, explores collaboration between agents, including how they can hand off tasks to specialized sub-agents to solve complex, multi-step problems.

Chapter 7, Model and Context Management, covers techniques for customizing the underlying LLMs and their settings to fine-tune agent behavior.

Chapter 8, Agent System Management, focuses on operational practices such as monitoring, observability, guardrails, and policy enforcement to ensure agents run reliably and securely.

Chapter 9, Building AI Agents and Agentic Systems, brings everything together by guiding you through the construction of complete, real-world agent solutions that combine tools, memory, handoffs, and system management into cohesive applications.

To get the most out of this book

Following along will be easier if you bear the following in mind:

- **Theory**: We will generally start by explaining the theory behind particular concepts and primitives

- **Examples**: We will illustrate each concept with full end-to-end examples to make sure you can effectively use all the concepts learned

- **Projects**: At the end of the book, we take everything that we have learned and apply it to a full end-to-end AI agent and agentic system builds

- **Think beyond**: Reflect on how AI agents and OpenAI Agents SDK can be used to solve your problems

Here is a list of software/hardware you need to have:

Software/Hardware covered in the book	System requirements
Python 3.10 or higher	Windows, macOS, or Linux
OpenAI API key	

Download the example code files

The code bundle for the book is hosted on GitHub at `https://github.com/PacktPublishing/Building-Agents-with-OpenAI-Agents-SDK`. We also have other code bundles from our rich catalog of books and videos available at `https://github.com/PacktPublishing`. Check them out!

Download the color images

We also provide a PDF file that has color images of the screenshots/diagrams used in this book. You can download it here: `https://packt.link/gbp/9781806112012`.

Conventions used

There are a number of text conventions used throughout this book.

`CodeInText`: Indicates code words in text, database table names, folder names, filenames, file extensions, pathnames, dummy URLs, user input, and X handles. For example, "We then call the `Runner.run_sync` function, passing the newly created agent object as well as `input_context`, which, in this case, is a question that a customer may ask"

A block of code is set as follows:

```python
from agents import Agent, Runner, CodeInterpreterTool
from agents.tool import CodeInterpreter

# Instantiate the tool
tool_config = CodeInterpreter(
    container={"type":"auto"},
    type="code_interpreter"
)
codetool = CodeInterpreterTool(tool_config=tool_config)
```

Bold: Indicates a new term, an important word, or words that you see on the screen, for example, in menus or dialog boxes. For example: "Typically, you have one agent that controls the workflow (often called the **orchestrator**) and a set of agents that are called to fulfill certain tasks (often called the **workers**)."

Warnings or important notes appear like this.

Tips and tricks appear like this.

Disclaimer on AI usage

The author acknowledges the use of cutting-edge AI, such as ChatGPT, with the sole aim of enhancing the language, brainstorming ideas, refining clarity, and generally aiding within the book, thereby ensuring a smooth reading experience for readers. It is important to note that the content itself has been crafted by the authors and edited by a professional publishing team.

Get in touch

Feedback from our readers is always welcome!

General feedback: Email feedback@packtpub.com and mention the book's title in the subject of your message. If you have questions about any aspect of this book, please email us at questions@packtpub.com.

Errata: Although we have taken every care to ensure the accuracy of our content, mistakes do happen. If you have found a mistake in this book, we would be grateful if you reported this to us. Please visit http://www.packtpub.com/submit-errata, click **Submit Errata**, and fill in the form.

Piracy: If you come across any illegal copies of our works in any form on the internet, we would be grateful if you would provide us with the location address or website name. Please contact us at copyright@packtpub.com with a link to the material.

If you are interested in becoming an author: If there is a topic that you have expertise in and you are interested in either writing or contributing to a book, please visit http://authors.packtpub.com/.

Share your thoughts

Once you've read *Building Agents with OpenAI Agents SDK*, we'd love to hear your thoughts! Scan the QR code below to go straight to the Amazon review page for this book and share your feedback.

https://packt.link/r/1806112000

Your review is important to us and the tech community and will help us make sure we're delivering excellent quality content.

Join our Discord and Reddit spaces

You're not the only one navigating fragmented tools, constant updates, and unclear best practices. Join a growing community of professionals exchanging insights that don't make it into documentation.

Stay informed with updates, discussions, and behind-the-scenes insights from our authors. Join our Discord space at `https://packt.link/z8ivB` or scan the following QR code:	Connect with peers, share ideas, and discuss real-world GenAI challenges. Follow us on Reddit at `https://packt.link/0rExL` or scan the following QR code:

Your Book Comes with Exclusive Perks - Here's How to Unlock Them

---

Unlock this book's exclusive benefits now   **UNLOCK NOW**

Scan this QR code or go to `https://packtpub.com/unlock`,
then search this book by name. Ensure it's the correct
edition.

Note: Keep your purchase invoice ready before you start.

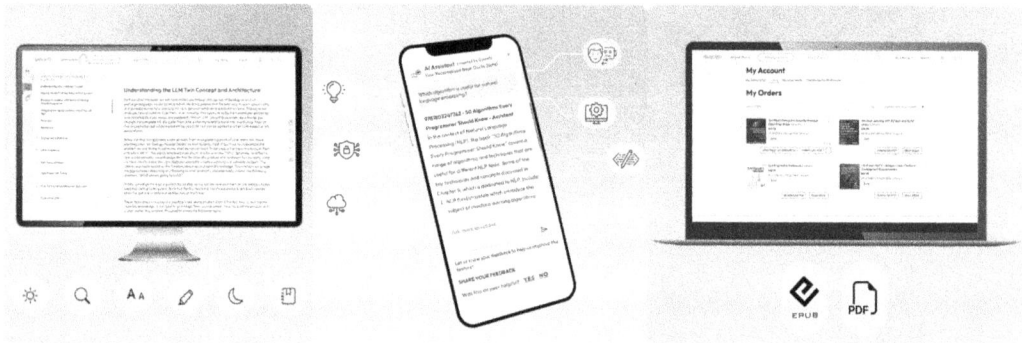

Enhanced reading experience with our Next-gen Reader:

⌒ **Multi-device progress sync**: Learn from any device with seamless progress sync.

▦ **Highlighting and notetaking**: Turn your reading into lasting knowledge.

◫ **Bookmarking**: Revisit your most important learnings anytime.

✸ **Dark mode**: Focus with minimal eye strain by switching to dark or sepia mode.

Learn smarter using our AI assistant (Beta):

✦ **Summarize it**: Summarize key sections or an entire chapter.

✦ **AI code explainers**: In the next-gen Packt Reader, click the **Explain** button above each code block for AI-powered code explanations.

Note: The AI assistant is part of next-gen Packt Reader and is still in beta.

Learn anytime, anywhere:

Access your content offline with DRM-free PDF and ePub versions—compatible with your favorite e-readers.

Unlock Your Book's Exclusive Benefits

Your copy of this book comes with the following exclusive benefits:

- Next-gen Packt Reader
- AI assistant (beta)
- DRM-free PDF/ePub downloads

Use the following guide to unlock them if you haven't already. The process takes just a few minutes and needs to be done only once.

How to unlock these benefits in three easy steps

Step 1

Keep your purchase invoice for this book ready, as you'll need it in *Step 3*. If you received a physical invoice, scan it on your phone and have it ready as either a PDF, JPG, or PNG.

For more help on finding your invoice, visit https://www.packtpub.com/unlock-benefits/help.

Note: Did you buy this book directly from Packt? You don't need an invoice. After completing Step 2, you can jump straight to your exclusive content.

Step 2

Scan this QR code or go to `https://packtpub.com/unlock`.

On the page that opens (which will look similar to *Figure 0.1* if you're on desktop), search for this book by name. Make sure you select the correct edition.

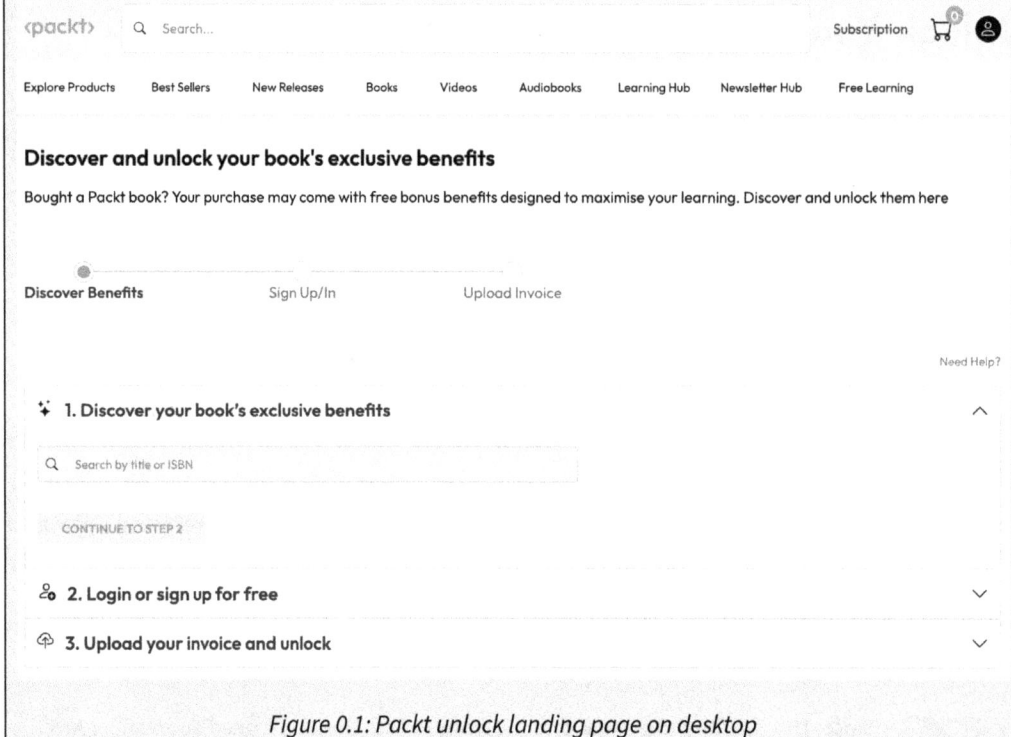

Figure 0.1: Packt unlock landing page on desktop

Step 3

Sign in to your Packt account or create a new one for free. Once you're logged in, upload your invoice. It can be in PDF, PNG, or JPG format and must be no larger than 10 MB. Follow the rest of the instructions on the screen to complete the process.

Need help?

If you get stuck and need help, visit https://www.packtpub.com/unlock-benefits/help for a detailed FAQ on how to find your invoices and more. The following QR code will take you to the help page directly:

Note: If you are still facing issues, reach out to customercare@packt.com.

Part 1

AI Agents

Part 1 lays the conceptual and practical groundwork for the rest of the book. We start by defining what an agent is, how it differs from a traditional chatbot or API client, and why agents have become a compelling pattern for automating work across software, data, and business processes. We will then build a mental model of an AI agent that you can use throughout the book: the brain of an agent (the model), the hands and eyes of an agent (tooling interface), and the reference textbook (memory and knowledge), all under explicit constraints and guardrails. We will then learn about the core primitives of the best framework to build AI agents: OpenAI Agents SDK.

This part is deliberately pragmatic. After establishing the "why" and "what," we get you hands-on quickly. You'll install the prerequisites, scaffold a minimal project, and stand up your first working agent.

This part contains the following chapters:

- *Chapter 1, Introduction to AI Agents*
- *Chapter 2, Introduction to OpenAI Agents SDK*
- *Chapter 3, Environment Setup and Developing Your First Agent*

1

Introduction to AI Agents

AI agents are changing the way we work. Software has typically created deterministic (if X, then Y) and rigid systems that cannot address ambiguity or adapt to different goals – but this is changing. With the advancements of **large language models (LLMs)**, intelligent systems are being created that can independently reason through steps and take actions to complete a goal. These AI agents are taking a larger share of work previously thought only a human could do, and it's just beginning.

By the end of this book, you will become a master at creating AI agents through OpenAI Agents SDK. The best way to learn this is to get your hands dirty and start building AI agent systems using that framework. Before we do this, however, we need to start at the most basic level, which is answering the question, "What is an AI agent?".

This chapter goes through everything you need to know to answer that question and, more importantly, lays the foundation we'll build in the rest of the book. We will explain *exactly* what an AI agent is and how it differs from traditional systems. This is important as many readers often confuse AI agents with sophisticated applications, such as chatbots or fraud detection systems. It's important to understand how AI agent systems work before we start building them. We will explore AI agents' practical applications beyond productivity. Finally, we will go through the different design patterns and frameworks available when building an AI agent, and understand why OpenAI Agents SDK is the pragmatic choice for most production systems.

Here is what we will cover in this first chapter:

- Overview of the AI agent system and its strengths and weaknesses compared to more traditional systems
- Practical applications of AI agents

- How AI agents are built, by understanding their anatomy and different design/framework patterns used to build them

By the end of this opening chapter, we will have a strong mental blueprint for how every real-world AI agent is assembled, which will serve as our compass for when we start building our own.

Technical requirements

This chapter will be an overview of AI agents from a theoretical point of view to set a good foundation before we start building them. As a result, we will not be writing any code or developing any applications in this chapter. However, to follow along and complete the exercises and projects discussed throughout the rest of the book, make sure you have the following set up in your development environment:

- **Operating system**: Windows 10/11, macOS, or Linux-based distribution (Ubuntu recommended).
- **Python version**: Python 3.8 or later. You can verify your Python version by running `python --version` in your terminal or Command Prompt.
- **OpenAI account**: Sign up at `https://platform.openai.com/signup`.
- **OpenAI API key**: Obtained by creating an account with OpenAI. You will require this to utilize OpenAI Agents SDK.
- **Code editor**: VS Code, PyCharm, or any IDE/editor you prefer.

Throughout this book, practical examples and the complete code from each chapter will be made available via the accompanying GitHub repository at `https://github.com/PacktPublishing/Building-Agents-with-OpenAI-Agents-SDK`.

You are encouraged to clone the repository, reuse and adapt the provided code samples, and refer to it as needed while progressing through the chapters.

Overview of AI agents

Before exploring AI agents in depth, we must first establish an intuitive understanding of what an AI agent actually is, how it fundamentally differs from traditional software, and what advantages and disadvantages this brings. This is difficult as there are varying definitions that often evolve with technological advancements. By clearly defining the key concepts upfront – including its benefits such as intelligent autonomy, reasoning abilities, and adaptive problem-solving – we can set the stage for understanding its practical applications and building approaches.

What is an AI agent?

An **AI agent** is an *intelligent system that can operate independently to accomplish a specific goal by perceiving the world around it and taking action.* Key distinguishing features of an AI agent include its ability to think and reason from a broad and sometimes ambiguous goal, its ability to create a plan to accomplish that goal, and its ability to autonomously complete that goal using a set of tools at its disposal that interact with the world.

This is in direct contrast to other conventional software systems that are deterministic (i.e., they follow a strict set of instructions based on a predefined plan) and cannot reason if situations outside of that plan are encountered. AI agents, on the other hand, can **observe** their environment, **reason** about what needs to be done, and **act** upon it in a continuous manner.

AI agents achieve this by combining the intelligence and reasoning abilities of LLMs with actions through standardized API calls. Let's explore the concepts and strengths of AI agents through a simple analogy to cement our understanding and differentiate it from classical software automation frameworks.

Understanding AI agents with a simple analogy

Imagine you are the head chef of a five-star restaurant, and you need to train two junior chefs, *Carlos* and *Adam*. Carlos is like a conventional automation software system or model, whereas Adam is like an AI agent. The way you would *train* these two chefs and the way that these two chefs *operate* are completely different.

Carlos requires you to teach him exactly what to do to prepare every dish. If you're teaching him to make an omelet, you must teach him how to open the fridge, take an egg, turn on the stove, pour some oil, crack the egg, and so on. Each step must be meticulously defined and shown to Carlos. When asked to make an omelet, Carlos performs the task exactly as-is, to perfection.

Adam works a different way, more like a human. Instead of giving him predefined steps, you show him how to perform actions around the kitchen – this is how you grab ingredients from the fridge, this is how you operate a stove, these are the basics of gastronomy, and so on. When asked to make an omelet, Adam relies on his reasoning ability and the set of tools/knowledge he's been given to accomplish that task, rather than following predefined steps.

Both Carlos and Adam are amazing chefs but have different strengths and weaknesses. In particular, Adam can embrace complexity and ambiguity. Because he can reason and is taught how to perform general actions, he can cook more than just an omelet – he can theoretically cook all kinds of foods as they all use the same actions.

This acts as the perfect analogy between AI agents and classical automation software/models. In short, *the intelligent autonomy afforded to an AI agent enables it to perform a diverse set of ambiguous tasks that just cannot be replicated.*

> **Note**
>
> It's important to mention that intelligent autonomy comes with the need for safe-guards. An autonomous agent might make a poor decision if its "brain" (the AI model) is misinformed. We will later discuss how to guide and constrain agents (through prompt instructions and guardrails) to ensure their autonomy is exercised respon-sibly. The key takeaway here is that AI agents bring a level of smart, goal-directed independence that sets them apart from traditional automated systems.

Strengths and weaknesses of AI agents versus traditional systems

The preceding analogy describes the key differences and advantages that AI agents have over other systems in addition to their ability to **embrace complexity**. Adam has **goal-directed autonomy**, which enables him to cook more than just an omelet; he can make scrambled eggs, poached eggs, and even sunny-side-up eggs. In fact, Adam can create new/novel creations that he has not been explicitly trained on as long as his set of actions is sufficient to perform that task. Adam can also complete tasks in another order if appropriate.

Adam exhibits reasoning, which means he can perform **adaptive problem-solving**, which enables him to do the following, which would be impossible for Carlos:

- Vary his cooking style to meet customer requests – Adam can cook an omelet more or less runny because he knows that leaving food on the stovetop for longer will make them more dry.
- If there is an ingredient missing, Adam can compromise and see whether there are any substitutions that he can make. He can handle real-world ambiguity and thrive on it.

Carlos would find these tasks impossible as he has been taught and can only cook one single way and cannot reason otherwise. If there are any externalities that prevent him from opening the fridge or turning on the stove, Carlos cannot proceed and stalls, whereas Adam could adapt.

There are, however, weaknesses with the AI agent model that, for certain use cases, may be so large and impactful that they are not the best options. Adam's brain is powered by an LLM, which is prone to **hallucinations**, which means the AI agent may hallucinate and perform nonsensical actions. This can resonate in, for example, Adam creating a steak dish but confidently claiming that it's tofu (which could cause awful outcomes for vegetarians). Adam may take novel and unseen approaches to accomplish the task (**reckless improvisation**), sometimes to the detriment of its purpose. For example, he may find that keeping the stove continuously on results in faster cooking but fails to realize it's dangerous and may burn the restaurant down. AI agents generally choose their own path to achieving their objectives, which may not be the most optimal or desired path.

Adam must also take time to reason, which means that he is inherently slower and expends more energy. In fact, an AI agent can be up to 100 times **more resource-intensive** and longer than its conventional software counterpart. Finally, Adam may also struggle with communicating his reasoning for taking certain actions (**lack of explainability**), a weakness common in many deep learning models.

Now that we understand what an AI agent is and its strengths and weaknesses, we can reason its practical applications over other traditional systems.

Practical applications of AI agents

AI agents are more than just a trendy idea – they are becoming central to how companies are leveraging AI to solve real problems. In particular, early adopters of AI agents are using them at all levels of their organizations, from customer-facing roles with AI agents that sell products and resolve issues to internal productivity such as software development or research.

Productivity gains

The most obvious and immediate motivation for AI agents is improved productivity, primarily through replacing or augmenting human work that traditional software systems cannot replace or augment. By handling these tasks autonomously, AI agents free up humans to focus on higher-level, more strategic work and creativity.

Consider customer support as an example. Traditionally, a customer support center might require dozens or hundreds of human agents to handle queries. Traditional software systems may replace this with automated chatbots that serve answers from a tree-like hierarchy of question-answer combinations, but their impact is limited as they cannot take action and they struggle with ambiguity. A traditional system may be able to answer *How do I reset my password?* but struggles with *Can you look at my most recent transaction and tell me where I bought that, and then process a return for me while sending a confirmation email to my accountant?* AI agents, with the right architecture and tooling, can easily address these queries and can even loop in humans when necessary. In fact, it is projected that AI will handle 95% of customer service in the near future (`https://www.tidio.com/blog/ai-customer-service-statistics/`).

Software development is also a typical function where AI agents are swarming. It is well known that AI coding assistants such as GitHub Copilot have been proven to help developers complete tasks 55% faster and help developers *stay in the flow*, and they've reported that they are 60% less frustrated when coding (`https://github.blog/news-insights/research/research-quantifying-github-copilots-impact-on-developer-productivity-and-happiness`). AI agents take this one step further. There are now several companies creating fully autonomous AI agents that can resolve errors and build new features in your code base through the entire development life cycle (understanding user requirements, writing code, testing code, managing pull requests, updating Jira, and communicating with managers). Examples beyond GitHub Copilot include Devin and Cursor.

There are also domain-specific AI agents that are meant to improve the productivity of particular tasks (such as HR, law, etc.) or industries (banking, retail, etc.). For example, in HR, AI agents can automate candidate screening, predict employee attrition, and personalize onboarding processes. In the legal sector, firms such as MinterEllison have deployed AI tools such as Lantern to expedite document review, processing thousands of documents per hour – significantly faster than human reviewers. In banking, institutions such as JPMorgan Chase utilize AI agents to enhance client services by automating personalized investment advice and related research.

Overall, AI agents serve as a catalyst for productivity by performing or augmenting human tasks.

Better interactivity

AI agents are fundamentally changing the way we interact with computers. Traditionally, most interactions followed rigid patterns that had to be performed by experts familiar with that field. For example, consider a manager working in retail. Analyzing their store sales compared to other stores over time required a dedicated data analyst who could translate the manager's request into a SQL query that could be run against a database. Alternatively, this type of request could be performed through a higher abstraction of the same task, such as interacting with Power BI or Excel, but this still requires the manager to be familiar with those tools (and all the related menus, forms, etc.)

AI agents, however, fully remove this barrier. AI agents receive user requests through natural language and contain the necessary tooling to perform SQL queries. The LLM can fully translate the user request into the required SQL query and can also explain the results to the user. In this way, the manager can directly interact with the data.

This is not only limited to text; AI agents are continuously becoming more multi-modal, being able to interact with voice and vision. For example, voice-enabled AI agents enable doctors to dictate notes and automatically write prescriptions that are sent to the patient's pharmacy. Retailers are using vision capabilities to audit shelves and automatically order more inventory and instruct associates to fill those shelves when the shelves are empty.

Overall, AI agents are driving a shift from *tools* to *partners*. Instead of requiring users to adapt to software (learning its interface and entering data in rigid ways), the software adapts to the user, and the entire learning barrier and its related friction is removed.

New businesses

AI agents are not just improving productivity and interactivity; entire new businesses and strategies are being built from AI agents. A good analogy is the internet. The internet made certain tasks faster – for example, writing emails is far faster than sending physical letters through the mail. It also created entire new business models such as e-commerce, digital marketplaces, online-based services, and more.

For example, businesses such as **Jasper.ai** and **Copy.ai** have emerged, providing AI-agent-driven platforms specifically designed to autonomously produce marketing content, social media posts, and sales copy. These AI-driven solutions enable companies to drastically accelerate content creation, reduce marketing expenses, and scale their messaging efforts far beyond what traditional approaches could achieve.

Build methodology of AI agents

Now that we understand an AI agent conceptually and its practical applications, we will discuss the anatomy of an AI agent as well as explain the step-by-step approach to designing and building them. Understanding this anatomy will help us design and implement agents systematically, so we can ensure each component is accounted for and functioning properly.

Anatomy of an AI agent

AI agents follow a typical pattern and can be broken down into three fundamental components. Specifically, the anatomy of an AI agent comprises the following:

- **Model:** This is the *brain* of the operations. It interprets input, reasons about actions, and generates outputs. Typically, this is an LLM with system instructions and a control logic framework that enables it to reason and iterate.

- **Tooling interface:** This is the *hands and eyes*. It provides the agent with the ability to act, such as sending emails or searching the web via APIs or local function calls.

- **Memory and knowledge:** This is the *reference textbook*. It contains information that helps the AI agent perform its tasks, such as databases, documents, and so on.

Model

All intelligent AI agents are powered by an **underlying model** that enables them to understand inputs, create a plan of action, generate action inputs, review action responses, and iterate that process until its goal is achieved. The core model does not technically need to be an LLM – it can be any system that can follow the *observe*, *reason*, and *act* tenets we described previously. In practice, however, this typically is a powerful LLM such as OpenAI's *GPT-4o* model or Google Gemini's *2.5 Pro* model.

The model acts as the brain of the AI agent, which means that the importance of choosing the right LLM cannot be overstated. There are several factors to consider when determining which model to use. These trade-offs exist when attempting to use an LLM for any task. They include the following:

- **Cost:** LLMs vary significantly in their cost, typically expressed as a dollar amount per number of tokens (or word blocks) processed. Foundational models are a lot cheaper than specialized fine-tuned heavy-reasoning models.

- **Latency:** LLMs vary in their speed to respond, which is not only based on the LLM's architecture but also on where and how the LLM is hosted.

- **Performance**: This factor is certainly the most diverse. Because of the proliferation of LLMs, there is a wide array of strengths that differ based on the use case. Certain LLMs are great at coding tasks, while others perform much better at creative exercises. Certain LLMs are multi-modal – they can input and output not only text but also images, video, and audio. LLMs also differ in their context window, which determines how much they can read or write at a time.

- **Bias**: LLMs also differ in their knowledge and leanings, which need to be understood when determining what model to choose for your AI agent. Many models have knowledge cut-off dates (i.e., they only "know" about events up to a particular date), which could pose trouble if we are creating an AI agent that recalls recent events. Additionally, LLMs can have political or informational leanings that might unintentionally (or sometimes intentionally) skew their responses. An example is *DeepSeek*, which has a notable pro-Chinese bias, according to the Guardian (`https://www.theguardian.com/technology/2025/jan/28/we-tried-out-deepseek-it-works-well-until-we-asked-it-about-tiananmen-square-and-taiwan`).

> **Note**
>
> Certain aspects of performance and bias, such as knowledge cut-off dates and political leanings, can be resolved by tactics such as **retrieval augmented generation (RAG)**, nuanced prompting, or post-train refinements. These will be covered later.

Note that models used to power AI agents are not purpose-built or trained for each AI agent. Instead, these are general-purpose pre-trained models that are just given special instructions to behave like agents. In other words, the underlying model between ChatGPT, a travel planner AI agent, GitHub Copilot, and a customer service AI agent may all share the same underlying model, *OpenAI GPT-4o*. What differs between these applications is not the model but the instructions provided to the model and how the model interacts with other components.

These "instructions" are provided to the model by defining a **system prompt**. A system prompt tells the model how to act and drives its underlying behavior. Most debugging with the performance of AI agents occurs by adjusting its system prompt to lead to a more desired result. A good analogy is when you write a system prompt, you are defining the model's identity and purpose. As a result, providing accurate and well-nuanced system prompts is very important.

Control logic framework

Another key aspect of an AI agent is the **control logic framework**, which is its ability to observe, reason, and act iteratively until a desired goal is achieved. This loop is not necessarily done by the model itself; instead, it's the agentic framework code that forces the model to run this loop. This is typically incorporated into the AI agent's model component, which can be summarized in pseudocode as follows:

```
Read user's goal and create action plan


For each step in action plan:
    Create action inputs
    Execute action
    Get result
    Add result to memory
    Modify action plan if necessary or if goal not achieved
    If goal is achieved:
        Return output to user
```

Agentic frameworks differ on the actual approach and there are several variations, but most follow the preceding structure of high-level planning and execution. Common ones include **chain-of-thought (CoT)** and **ReAct**. In fact, some frameworks even have the agent generate an answer and then a second pass, where the agent (as a judge) evaluates the first agent's answer and logic.

Tooling interface

A critical requirement for an AI agent that we previously discussed is its ability to interact with the *outside world*, which is called its **tooling interface**. Normally, an LLM interacts with a user through text, image, and audio outputs, producing tokens from its vast deep learning neural network. The *outside world* refers to the environment beyond it, which typically refers to other applications such as email, searching the web, or controlling your computer. This enables AI agents to *do stuff* and serves as its hands and eyes.

The mechanism of how an AI agent interacts with other applications is by providing the AI agent with a *framework for how and when to execute actions* within these applications. For example, the framework for an AI agent that assists with email tools may include the following actions (again, in pseudocode):

```
Action #1: Send an email
    Description: Sends an email to a user
    Parameters: to_email_address, email_subject, email_body
```

```
Action #2: List all emails
    Description: Lists all emails, including email_id
    Parameters: search_term (optional)


Action #3: Read an email
    Description: Returns the content of an email
    Parameter: email_id
```

When an AI agent is created with these tools, its model and control logic framework decides when to use these actions and determines the correct inputs for these actions.

For example, an AI agent may be given the task of finding all emails related to the *coffee expansion proposal*, summarizing them, and sending the summary to the user's manager. In that case, the AI agent would first call the List all emails action with the search term coffee expansion proposal or something similar, use the Read an email action to read them, summarize them using the LLM, and then use the Send an email action to send the summary.

The act of registering these tools with the AI agent differs based on the agentic framework that is being used. In all cases, however, the AI agent can do the following:

- **Show an awareness of the existence of these tools** – Typically, by automatically adding the tool names, definitions, and parameters into the system prompt of the model.
- **Execute the tool actions** – Typically done automatically through the agentic framework that is chosen. These can either be in the form of **function calls** on the client machine (i.e., the machine that runs the AI agent also contains the logic of the tool actions) or **API calls** on a server-side machine (a server contains the logic of the tool actions and the AI agent simply makes calls to the server to perform those actions).
- **Receive output from tool actions and pass it to the model** – Again, this is typically done automatically through the agentic framework that is chosen.
- We defined AI agents earlier as being able to interact with the outside world iteratively to achieve a goal. Inherently, this means that the tooling interface (i.e., how the AI agent interacts with the outside world) is a critical component. Because of this, the act of writing tools (writing the logic, providing detailed instructions and input parameters, registering them to AI agents, determining the right selection and granularity of actions, error handling, how to expose them to AI agents, etc.) is a key module in the book, for which an entire chapter is dedicated.

Memory and knowledge

Recall that we referred to AI agents as intelligent systems.

Memory and knowledge with respect to AI agents are separate but related concepts. The purpose of both is to provide the relevant context to the model in light of the user's overall request. This improves the AI agent's intelligence and effectiveness. Let's talk about each concept and how it's used mechanically to provide more context to the AI agent.

Memory refers to the AI agent *remembering relevant information from current and previous interactions with the user*. There are typically two types of memory, as discussed in the following subsections.

Working memory

Working memory is the information stored in the interaction history in the *current sessions* of the AI agent. It's best to think about this in a traditional chat context. Let's assume you ask ChatGPT *How hot is the sun?* and it replies with its answer. Your next message, in the same conversation, is *How big is it?*. ChatGPT is intelligent enough to understand that your subsequent request is related to the sun because it has your previous interactions/chats in its working history.

Mechanically, recent chats are retained in the prompt that is sent to the model so that the LLM can always refer back and understand the context of the user's request. This is why you can ask follow-up questions and these chat-based systems can respond to them correctly. Note that it is also very common for working memory to be injected into the system instructions.

Working memory has a limit. For example, GPT-4o might handle 128K tokens only, and beyond that, earlier messages drop out new ones are added. Strategies such as context windows or sliding windows are used to keep the most relevant recent information, depending on the agentic framework being used.

Long-term memory

Long-term memory is information stored from the interaction history of previous sessions of the AI agent. This enables an AI agent to go from a classically *stateless* experience (where each request is handled independently of prior interactions) to a *stateful* experience (each request is colored by information retrieved from previous interactions). AI agents that are deemed to be intelligent from a consumer point of view typically have some implementation of long-term memory. For example, consider an AI agent that helps you write emails.

Mechanically, this is done by the AI agent storing information from interactions in a database, which it can then read later, both of which can be done through a tool interaction. For example, the AI agent may have the following tooling, which enables it to store and recall memories:

```
Action #1: Store information
    Description: Stores important information about the user
    Parameters: information


Action #2: Read information
    Description: Retrieves important information about the user
```

The implementation of memory and knowledge differ based on the agentic framework and the model chosen. In most circumstances, working memory and training knowledge are typical – no extra functionality is required to enable these components. Long-term memory or relevant knowledge, however, does require dedicated tooling, which can increase the complexity of AI agents. These aspects will be discussed in a dedicated chapter.

Knowledge refers to the AI agent **recalling relevant information** from a stored knowledge base. Unlike memory, the information that is recalled is not generated from previous interactions with the user but, instead, from sources of knowledge. These include documents, databases, files, text corpus, and so on. There are typically two types of knowledge. as discussed in the following subsections.

Training knowledge

Training knowledge refers to information that is inherently stored in the model through its training data. For example, all LLMs can easily answer the question *How big is the sun?* as the information to answer that question exists in the corpus of text on which the LLM was trained. This is also referred to as **general knowledge**. It's the "baked-in" knowledge that an LLM has consequent to how it was trained.

An LLM's training knowledge is often its source of greatest benefit – being able to recall terabytes of useful general knowledge in a few seconds and adapt it to the user's request is powerful. From an AI agent's point of view, however, this is not that helpful. An AI agent is typically not meant to recall general knowledge; an LLM connected to a chat interaction can serve that purpose much better. In addition, an LLM cannot recall information past its training knowledge cut-off date, nor can it recall information that is not publicly available – two elements that are needed to build effective and impactful AI agents. In fact, we generally purposely instruct the model to ignore any of its training knowledge when generating a response.

Instead, an AI agent should be able to retrieve specific contextual information relevant to the user's request in real time. This is where the other type of knowledge is helpful.

Retrieved knowledge

Retrieved knowledge refers to information that is retrieved in real time from a knowledge store based on the user's request. Unlike training knowledge, which is static and fixed at the time the model was trained, retrieved knowledge is dynamic and adaptable. The knowledge store can be documents, databases, and more. The important factor here is that only the relevant information based on the user's context is retrieved and added to the model during the AI agent runtime.

Mechanically, this is achieved through tooling similar to long-term memory. The tooling enables the AI agent with retrieval mechanisms such as a vector database (using the RAG pattern), structured APIs, file repository searches such as SharePoint or Google Drive, and web search. The AI agent uses the user's input to search these sources for relevant documents or records, which are then supplied as context to the model for response generation.

There are many benefits to integrating retrieved knowledge into an AI agent. In particular, an AI agent can do the following:

- Answer questions with up-to-date or proprietary content
- Provide citations or references for traceability (whereas it's extremely difficult for an LLM to provide a source with its trained knowledge)

This type of relevant knowledge is crucial for making AI agents useful and impactful. Consider an AI agent that serves as the HR role for an organization. The only way it can answer questions about the organization's vacation policy, benefits, sick time, and so on is by a method of knowledge retrieval. A sales AI agent may search through a company's **customer relationship management (CRM)** system to find notes on a customer the user is asking about.

Now that we understand the anatomy of an AI agent, we can distinguish between different design and implementation patterns in terms of how they tackle the model, the tooling interface, and the memory and knowledge components.

Design patterns

All AI agent design patterns contain the core three components but have variations in how they implement the components. In particular, they differ based on how they control the control logic framework (which we discussed earlier) and its tooling sophistication. These include ReAct, CoT, planner-executor, and hierarchical/multi-agent.

CoT

CoT simply encourages the model to produce a step-by-step reasoning trace before generating a final answer. A literal interpretation of it would be to tell someone to think about a problem, create a plan on how they are going to solve it, and then take the steps to solve it. One limitation of CoT is that it's unable to take action and, more importantly, unable to adapt its plan based on the results of actions.

ReAct (Reasoning + Acting)

ReAct is a pattern that we mentioned and described in pseudocode earlier. This design pattern enforces an AI agent to iteratively reason about the problem and choose a tool or action to take, feeding the result back into the continuous loop until its goal is achieved. The difference between ReAct and CoT is in its ability to act and then adjust its plan based on the results of that action. This is best for real-world agents that need to reason and interact with tools to solve complex tasks. This pattern is most often the go-to for most traditional AI agents.

Planner-execution

The **planner-execution** pattern separates the system performing the planning from the system performing the execution. An agent first generates a high-level plan and then another agent (or multiple agents) executes each task in that plan. This pattern works well for very long-term complex tasks or tasks that can easily be modularized and delegated to sub-agents.

Hierarchical/multi-agent

A **hierarchical/multi-agent** pattern divides tasks among multiple specialized agents that are experts in that particular domain or task. This pattern can also perform work in a distributed nature, meaning that the system can finish tasks simultaneously rather than sequentially. This system is akin to a normal company, which contains a manager (a CEO) who delegates tasks to specialized workers with their own domain (CMO, COO, CFO, etc.).

For example, if we build an AI agent that resolves customer complaints, there may be an agent that receives the complaint and produces an action plan, and then specialized agents to perform those tasks, each with their own model, tooling infrastructure, and memory and knowledge (such as a customer agent that can look up customer information, a compliance agent that reviews policies, and a response agent that drafts a reply to the customer).

Note

These patterns are not mutually exclusive. In fact, most real-world agents, especially those built with the frameworks briefly discussed next, tend to blend these approaches depending on the complexity of the task and the tools available. The OpenAI Agents SDK framework, for example, combined ReAct and hierarchical/multi-agent patterns.

In addition to the design patterns, companies have built different frameworks to develop and deploy AI agents, which differ based on the design pattern used and based on its feature set. These include OpenAI Agents SDK, LangChain, LangGraph, AutoGen, AutoGPT, and Crew AI.

Overall, **OpenAI Agents SDK** stands out because of its minimalism and flexibility. It contains a powerful agnostic architecture that can combine both powerful OpenAI components (such as *web search* or *computer use*) and custom-made tooling. It has very useful integrated tracing, guardrails, and other enterprise-ready security and observability features that other frameworks do not have. Finally, it's an open source project that continues to receive lots of focus and growth – an example is that it added the **Model Context Protocol** (**MCP**) integration weeks after the module's release.

Summary

In this chapter, we learned about AI agents, their practical applications, and their build methodology.

AI agents are intelligent systems capable of independently achieving goals by reasoning, planning, and interacting with the world through tools. Unlike traditional automation systems that require rigid, predefined instructions, AI agents can handle ambiguity and dynamically adjust their steps and actions based on the overall goal.

AI agents help organizations work faster by augmenting or replacing work traditionally done by humans. They also enable individuals to directly interact with tools and data without friction. Finally, organizations are creating entirely new businesses by leveraging the AI agent architecture.

The core anatomy of an AI agent consists of the following: the model, the tooling interface, and its memory and knowledge component. Design patterns guide how these components work together. For instance, ReAct allows agents to reason and adapt with each action step, while multi-agent systems distribute tasks across specialized sub-agents for efficiency. Various frameworks implement these concepts differently.

Among these frameworks, OpenAI Agents SDK stands out for its minimal, extensible architecture, built-in observability, and enterprise-grade features, making it a robust choice for building production-grade AI agents.

In the next chapter, we'll take a deep dive into the OpenAI Agents SDK framework.

Unlock this book's exclusive benefits now

UNLOCK NOW

Scan this QR code or go to `https://packtpub.com/unlock`, then search this book by name.

Note: Keep your purchase invoice ready before you start.

2

Introduction to OpenAI Agents SDK

An **SDK**, or **Software Development Kit**, is a curated collection of libraries, tools, and documentation that lets developers stand on the shoulders of someone else's hard work. I really like this (cheeky) definition, as it states in plain terms what every developer wants with an SDK: to write fewer lines of code. Good SDKs remove the drudgery of wiring, configuration, and boilerplate so that developers can focus on what makes their application unique.

OpenAI Agents SDK is used to build AI agents and is beautiful in its simplicity. Instead of confronting you with custom configuration languages or labyrinthine class hierarchies, it ships a handful of clear-cut primitives—agents, runners, tools, handoffs, guardrails, and tracing—implemented in idiomatic Python. With those six building blocks (you could even call them LEGO blocks), you can spin up a single-agent or multi-agent prototype within minutes.

Here is what you will learn as part of this second chapter:

- **Design principles of OpenAI Agents SDK**, including minimal abstraction and frameworks for multi-agent orchestration—Pythonic, flexible, and extensible
- **Core primitives** that make up the SDK, with detailed examples of each primitive and how they are used

By the time you finish this chapter, you will not only know what each primitive does but also why the SDK's minimalist architecture is a pragmatic launchpad for building—quickly and reliably— the agentic systems that the rest of this book will guide you through.

Technical requirements

Throughout this book, practical examples and the complete code from each chapter will be made available via the accompanying GitHub repository at `https://github.com/PacktPublishing/Building-Agents-with-OpenAI-Agents-SDK`.

You are encouraged to clone the repository, reuse and adapt the provided code samples, and refer to it as needed while progressing through the chapters.

Design features of OpenAI Agents SDK

OpenAI Agents SDK was designed with a few key principles in mind, aimed at balancing ease of use with flexibility for developers. Understanding these design choices will help clarify why the SDK works the way it does (and how it differs from other solutions).

Framework for building AI agents

At a high level, OpenAI Agents SDK is used to build AI agents in the same way web frameworks (such as Django, Ruby on Rails, etc.) are used to build websites. These frameworks abstract the low-level parts of AI agent development and orchestration. This enables developers to focus on the higher-level impactful logic and deploy an agent as fast as possible without needing to worry about scaffolding.

With the SDK, we can create an agent with a few lines of Python code:

```
agent = Agent(name="Assistant", instructions="You are an AI agent",
    model="gpt-4o")

result = Runner.run_sync(agent, "Tell me a joke")

print(result.final_output)
```

This example instantiates a basic AI agent with the OpenAI GPT-4o model and with some basic system instructions. The control logic framework that enables the agent to think iteratively is already embedded within the agent itself as a direct result of the framework. We then run the agent on a user query and print the output from the model.

> **Note**
>
> At this point, we are introducing code as a way to understand the simplicity and ease of use of implementing the SDK. To actually run the code would require installing and importing the necessary libraries, which we will go through in detail in the next chapter.

Without the SDK, this would notably take thousands of lines of code to orchestrate, not to mention the additional thousands of lines of code to create a tracing and logging system that you get automatically with OpenAI Agents SDK.

OpenAI Agents SDK is engineered to address the inherent challenges in constructing LLM-driven processes that require more than just text generation. These challenges include enabling models to reason through multi-step problems, interact with external data sources and APIs (tool use), and coordinate actions among multiple AI entities.

Multi-agent orchestration

As a subset, this framework also enables developers to build multi-agent solutions. In fact, this was the original purpose of the framework's predecessor, **Swarm** (the idea being you can originate a series of agents in a swarm-like fashion to complete a task). The idea here is that for specific tasks, you can't have one agent do everything. Instead, you have a *team of agents*, each specialized in a particular task, that *hand off* the delegation to each other when necessary.

Imagine a customer-support workflow:

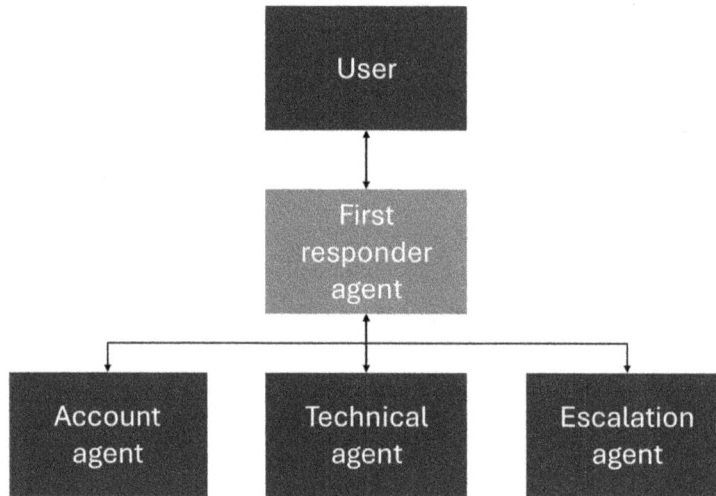

Figure 2.1: A customer support workflow

Let's break down and discuss the agentic workflow:

- **First responder agent**: Answers the calls, understands the issue, performs simple FAQ requests, and hands off to other agents as needed
- **Account agent**: Can look up customer orders and status
- **Technical agent**: Can fix user authentication bugs and set up new connection lines for the customer
- **Escalation agent**: Loops in a human as a last possible resort

Each agent focuses on its domain, yet to the end user, the experience feels like a single, coherent conversation. All the context-passing, role-switching, and error-handling happen inside the SDK's orchestration layer (done with a primitive called **handoffs**). You configure handoff routes once and let the framework do the choreography. This can be done with a few lines of code:

```
account_agent = Agent(name="Account agent")
technical_agent = Agent(name="Technical agent")
escalation_agent = Agent(name="Escalation agent")

first_responder_agent = Agent(
    name="First Responder Agent",
    handoffs=[account_agent, technical_agent, escalation_agent]
)
```

Minimal abstraction

One of the guiding philosophies behind OpenAI Agents SDK is "few enough primitives to make it quick to learn." Rather than introducing layers upon layers of new classes, the SDK gives us a short, memorable vocabulary. Realistically, if you can remember the core primitives and how they work, then you've already grasped 80% of the framework.

These primitives include: **agents**, **runner**, **tools**, **handoffs**, **guardrails**, and **tracing**. We will deep dive into each of these frameworks in the next section, and the structure of this book purposely mimics these primitives—as going through each one is the best way to learn the framework.

That is essentially it. There is no hidden meta-language and no opaque runtime generating code you cannot see. You wire an agent together with plain Python, decorate a few functions with @ function_tool, and click **run**. This is important as it provides a fast-onboarding experience: most developers can skim the docs or a sample notebook over lunch and build a working prototype by the afternoon.

This SDK is more like a lightweight library than a sprawling framework, but this characteristic does have some trade-offs. Unlike some other comprehensive frameworks such as LangChain, the OpenAI Agents SDK does not itself ship with hundreds of turnkey integrations such as document loaders or memory stores; these concepts instead need to be self-developed by the user.

Pythonic, extensible, and open sourced

The OpenAI Agents SDK is built in and speaks fluent Python. There are no YAML manifests to wrestle with, no proprietary scopes to memorize, and no metaprogramming magic hiding real work. An agent is just a Python object and a tool is an ordinary Python function with a special decorator. You orchestrate them with the same Python language constructs you already use every day. This makes it extremely useful and simple for Python developers, and shares similarities with other loved minimalist libraries such as *Flask* and *Pydantic*.

OpenAI Agents SDK is "ready to deploy" with default constructs but is also deliberately extensible. Any particular construct can be hot-swapped with your own component:

- The **model** used in the agent object can be swapped for any LLM, such as an on-premise LLAMA model (provided it complies with the *Chat Completions* standard, which is a standard protocol developed by OpenAI when interacting with foundational LLMs; we will discuss this in detail in *Chapter 10*). We have discussed before that this framework is completely model agnostic.

- The **tools** in this framework are just Python functions with added decorators, meaning they can easily be swapped at any time for another Python function or a hosted API call, including connecting to MCP servers.
- The **tracing** is, by default, sent to the **Traces** dashboard within OpenAI but can be hooked up to any telemetry tool such as *Azure Monitor Logs* or *DataDog*.

Technically, even the agent-execution loop is modular. The high-level runner handles retries, step limits, and concurrent calls, but advanced users can bypass it and drive lower-level primitives directly inside an existing event loop or task queue.

For example, rather than calling `Runner.run_sync(agent, input)`, an advanced user can manually step through the agent's execution logic using the `agent.run_step(...)` method or control the loop using `agent.get_initial_state()` and `agent.step(...)`. This is particularly useful in environments where you need to interleave agent execution with other async operations, such as within a FastAPI route, allowing for full control over timing, concurrency, or resource management.

Finally, the SDK is open sourced, which means this framework benefits from complete transparency and an ever-growing list of developers who are continually improving the framework and making it more resilient.

Overall, OpenAI Agents SDK provides a streamlined, Pythonic framework specifically designed to simplify and accelerate the creation and orchestration of sophisticated AI agents. By offering minimal yet powerful abstractions (agents, runners, tools, handoffs, guardrails, and tracing), the SDK empowers developers to quickly build complex, multi-agent solutions without wrestling with excessive boilerplate or hidden configurations. Its extensibility and compatibility with existing Python constructs enable both rapid deployment and deep customization when creating AI agents.

Core primitives

As we mentioned before, OpenAI Agents SDK introduces a handful of core concepts (normally called **primitives**) that we can use to build agent systems. These are the building blocks for any agent-driven application using the SDK.

To understand what primitives are, let's say you're designing a robot assistant to help manage a smart home. The assistant should be able to turn off lights, adjust the thermostat, respond to voice commands, and notify you if a window is left open. Instead of building everything from scratch, the SDK gives you a small set of foundational pieces: one for defining what the agent knows (state), one for what it can do (tools), one for how it thinks (policy), and so on. These are the **primitives**. You combine them like assembling distinct parts of a machine to create a functioning agent.

Think of primitives as LEGO bricks in a LEGO set. They're the smallest standard pieces you use to build anything. The SDK might later include prebuilt recipes (like a LEGO instruction manual), but the bricks themselves are the primitives.

Agent

The **agent** primitive is the most fundamental concept of OpenAI Agents SDK. It essentially serves as a highly configurable wrapper around an LLM to make it "agentic" (i.e., providing it with a persona or *system instructions*, a tooling interface, and other settings necessary for it to autonomously make decisions and pursue a goal). When an agent is instantiated with the agent primitive, it can have the following configuration:

- **Name:** The name of the agent, typically only used for identification purposes
- **Instructions:** These are identical to the system prompt that we discussed in the previous chapter; they provide the guidelines to the LLM on its role, objectives, behaviors, and personas
- **Model:** The underlying LLM that powers the agent's intelligence
- **Tools:** A list of tools that the agent can call to get answers
- **Handoffs:** A list of other agents to whom the agent can delegate tasks
- Here is an example of an instantiation of an agent:

```
Customer_service_agent = Agent(
    name="Customer Service Agent",
    model="gpt-4o",
    instructions="""
        You are an AI agent that helps resolve customer issues in a
positive cheerful manner.
    """,
    tools=[get_account_information, refund_customer_payment,
        track_customer_order],
)
```

> **Note**
>
> The Agent class can also take in other useful parameters such as guardrails, output type, and many more. These will be covered in subsequent chapters.

Unsurprisingly, most of these components match the anatomy of an AI agent that we discussed in the previous chapter. This configurability is what enables developers to quickly spin up specialized agents, tailored to a specific role or task within a larger application.

This agent can either respond with natural language or call one of the tools it's been given. It's worth mentioning that this SDK provides a single Agent class, unlike some frameworks that have different classes for each agent type. Here, the agent behavior simply depends on the preceding configurations, nothing else.

Runner

This primitive is the engine behind an agent. In the previous chapter, we discussed that a key element in a successful agentic application is its ability to iteratively and autonomously solve a problem (i.e., it can make decisions and vary based on further inputs it receives to achieve a goal). This agent loop functionality is baked into this primitive. The **Runner** (sometimes called the **Agent Loop**) is the cyclical process of interacting with the LLM, managing tool calls, determining what it should do next, and repeating the process.

Recall that we generalized this set of actions in the following pseudocode:

```
Read user's goal and create action plan


For each step in action plan:
    Create action inputs
    Execute action
    Get result
    Add result to memory
    Modify action plan if necessary or if goal not achieved
    If goal is achieved:
        Return output to user
```

By automating this core logic, the agent loop significantly simplifies the developer's task. It abstracts away the low-level orchestration of LLM interactions and tool use, allowing developers to concentrate on defining the agent's high-level behavior through instructions and the capabilities it needs via tools, rather than getting bogged down in the mechanics of the execution cycle. Managing this reasoning loop was historically one of the trickiest parts of building agentic AI (developers had to capture the model's chain of thought and implement the loop logic themselves).

To call the runner primitive, we can simply call the run method within the Runner class:

```
result = await Runner.run(agent, "My order number is XYZ - help me figure
out where my order is")
```

Note

Runner.run() has a useful argument called max_turns that caps how many cycles the agent may take. By bounding the loop, max_turns acts as a safety valve against endless spins caused by a bad configuration or an unsolvable task. We will go through this in detail in subsequent chapters.

Tools

The **tool** primitive is a core concept within OpenAI Agents SDK and is truly "well deployed" in terms of simplicity. In my opinion, it is one of the most "beautiful" aspects of this SDK. Any Python function can be turned into a tool by adding a specific tool decorator. This decorator enables the agent's LLM to understand the tool implicitly through its name, docstring, and arguments automatically. If the agent's LLM decides to invoke that tool, the LLM will automatically create the necessary arguments/schema needed to call it.

For example, we can create a Python function that returns the status of an order given an order ID and add it as a tool with the related decorator. This decorator will parse the docstring and arguments of the function automatically and provide them as system instructions to the LLM so that the agent knows what tools it has, what it can do, and what input arguments to provide. Here is the code to create a tool:

```
Customer_service_agent = Agent(
    instructions="""
        You are an AI agent that helps resolve customer issues in a
positive cheerful manner.
    """,
    tools=[get_order_status],
)


@function_tool
def get_order_status(order_id: str) -> str:
    """"Gets the order status based on order_id
    Args:
        order_id: the order_id of the order
    """

    # API call to get order status
    return order_status
```

Note that OpenAI Agents SDK also enables developers to instantiate other types of tools in addition to user-defined functions—hosted tools and agents as tools:

- **Hosted tools**: These are built-in tools specifically provided by and hosted in OpenAI. They include common tools that you may want your agent to have, such as the ability to search the web, search through files, generate an image, and so on. They also include the ability to connect to a local computer's shell/terminal or functionality via a hosted **Model Context Protocol** (**MCP**) server.

- **Agents as tools**: These are agents that you have previously instantiated that are then converted into tools. This, however, is rare in practice as calling agents are typically achieved through handoffs where they are more like context passing.

Handoff

The **handoff** primitive controls the mechanism by which agents delegate or transfer control to other agents. This enables multi-agent orchestrations and was one of the bedrock features of the SDK's predecessor, Swarm. Agents can be specialized for specific tasks, and handoffs allow you to have a system of specialized agents (each with its own persona and tools) to address a goal rather than one agent that controls everything.

Imagine you are creating an agent that creates research reports. Agent A specializes in outlining a research plan. It passes that plan to Agent B, which scours the web, distills the findings, and then hands the summary to Agent C, which is specialized to take in findings and create a final report based on desired specs. The Agents SDK manages each handoff smoothly. This architecture can easily be created with this primitive in the following way:

```
research_plan_agent = Agent(name="Research plan agent")
web_search_agent = Agent(name="Web search agent")
final_report_agent = Agent(name="Final report agent")

research_report_agent = Agent(
    name="Research report agent",
    handoffs=[research_plan_agent, web_search_agent, final_report_agent]
)
```

What's the difference between an agent handoff versus a tool calling?

- **Transfer of context**: During a handoff, the SDK transfers the necessary context, such as the conversation history (instead of pre-defined rigid arguments), to the next agent, letting the work proceed without interruption.

- **Transfer of control**: Handoffs put another "driver" in charge of the overall goal rather than "outsourcing" a particular sub-task. The agent that is "invoked" can call its own tools and then hand off to another agent as desired.

Guardrails

Guardrails are a primitive in the SDK that serve as safety mechanisms designed to perform validations on both the user input and agent output. They are instantiated in the same way as a tool (e.g., with a specified decorator on a custom Python function) and are triggered based on your defined logic. For example, we can set up a guardrail that ensures the user is asking our customer service agent about customer service issues and not something random.

```python
@input_guardrail
async def input_guardrail(
    ctx: RunContextWrapper[None], agent: Agent,
        input: str | list[TResponseInputItem]
) -> GuardrailFunctionOutput:
    # Logic to determine if input is related to a customer service query
    if is_customer_service_query:
        return GuardrailFunctionOutput(
        output_info = "This is a customer query question",
        tripwire_triggered = False,
    )
    else:
        return GuardrailFunctionOutput(
        output_info = "This is NOT a customer query question",
        tripwire_triggered = True,
    )
```

If the guardrail fails any validation, a "tripwire" is triggered, and a specific error type is raised in Python. This error can be handled in whatever way is desired. For example, you may want the error to trigger a message to the user to let them know that this is not a valid use of the agent, or to purposely halt any further execution and return an error code.

```python
try:
    await Runner.run(agent, "What is the meaning of the universe?")

    except InputGuardrailTripwireTriggered:
        print("Please enter a customer service related inquiry, not a
random question")
```

The concept of guardrails in AI agents is important yet barely discussed. For example, you may want to run the preceding guardrail as executing any agents or tools may be computationally or financially expensive. Any autonomous system that is not deterministic needs guardrails to ensure proper functioning, and this primitive makes it simple for developers to implement this mechanism.

Note

Guardrails usually take the form of decorated Python functions that embed the validation rules. These can be applied to either the initial input from the user or the output to the user. However, those functions can themselves call on another agent to inspect the candidate input or output and decide whether it meets the specified criteria. This means not only can you have agents as tools but also agents as guardrails.

Tracing

The **tracing** primitive allows developers to observe and debug the behavior of their agent systems by capturing and recording detailed execution flows during a run. Tracing acts like a flight data recorder for your agent's reasoning loop. This includes every decision made by the agent, tool invocations, intermediate messages, and handoffs between agents. Without tracing, understanding how and why an agent came to a particular result can be extremely difficult, especially in complex or multi-agent workflows.

The SDK provides a built-in tracing utility that can be used manually, but more commonly, tracing is enabled automatically through the SDK's integrated tracing system. This system can persist traces locally or send them to a remote tracing backend such as OpenAI's built-in UI or your own custom observability setup.

Let's look at a simple example. Imagine we want to debug the behavior of our customer service agent when it receives a user request:

```
From agents import Runner, enable_tracing
await Runner.run(agent, "Please cancel my last order.")
```

Once tracing is enabled, the SDK captures and logs the following:

- The initial user input and system instructions
- The model's internal reasoning (thoughts)

- Any tool calls made (with arguments and outputs)

- Any handoffs triggered (with full context)

- Final response returned to the user

These can all be viewed in the OpenAI Traces UI or your own preferred UI, such as DataDog:

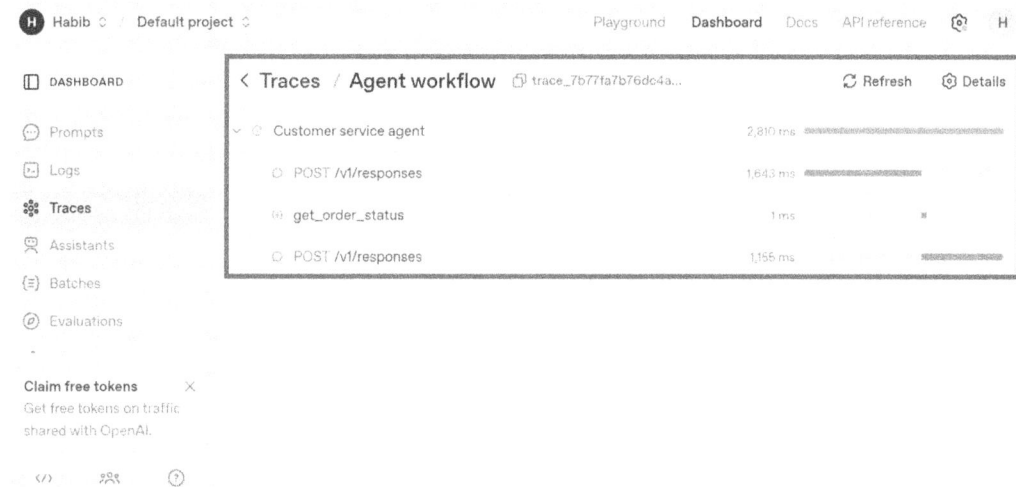

Figure 2.2: Capturing and recording detailed execution flows through tracing

Note

Tracing is especially powerful when paired with guardrails. For example, when a guardrail tripwire is triggered, tracing allows you to capture exactly what input caused the issue and what steps were taken up to that point. This makes it much easier to tune your agents or validate business logic in sensitive applications.

Summary

In this chapter, we conducted a deep dive into OpenAI Agents SDK and what makes it special. We saw how its minimalist abstraction philosophy strips away boilerplate, letting plain Python do the talking, while still being powerful enough to create sophisticated AI agents and multi-agent solutions. We also saw how it was completely open sourced, inviting community scrutiny and enabling tons of extensions.

We then looked at the core primitives that make up the SDK. In particular, we focused on the following:

- **Agent**: A thin wrapper that turns an LLM into an autonomous agent. It carries a name, system instructions, an optional tool belt, and a list of peer agents for potential handoffs.

- **Runner**: The execution engine that drives an agent's iterative reasoning loop, handles retries, and enforces safety limits to prevent infinite spins.

- **Tools**: Ordinary Python functions (or hosted APIs/agents) decorated so the model can discover their purpose, construct valid arguments, and invoke them exactly when needed.

- **Handoffs**: The orchestration mechanism that lets an agent delegate control (and the full conversational context) to another agent, enabling elegant multi-agent workflows.

- **Guardrails**: Policy checks that wrap every step of the loop, ensuring outputs, tool calls, and handoffs stay within business and compliance boundaries.

- **Tracing**: Automatic, structured logs of every prompt, response, and tool invocation— essential for debugging, observability, and post-mortem analysis.

Armed with these LEGO-brick primitives, we can quickly stand up useful agents in minutes with a few lines of code. In the next chapter, we will set up our environment and create our first agent, putting all these concepts into practice.

Subscribe for a free eBook

New frameworks, evolving architectures, research drops, production breakdowns—AI_Distilled filters the noise into a weekly briefing for engineers and researchers working hands-on with LLMs and GenAI systems. Subscribe now and receive a free eBook, along with weekly insights that help you stay focused and informed.

Subscribe at `https://packt.link/80z6Y` or scan the QR code below.

3

Environment Setup and Developing Your First Agent

It's time. We can start getting our hands dirty and start building our first AI agent. Although OpenAI Agents SDK is relatively straightforward, we first need to make sure our environment is properly configured and that we understand some basic Python concepts relevant to the SDK. A functioning environment is the launchpad for everything else in this book, from writing and running agents to testing tools, debugging traces, and orchestrating multi-agent workflows.

Here is what you will learn as part of this chapter:

- *Environment setup*: We will install Python, set up a virtual environment, install openai-agents SDK, and securely configure your OpenAI API key. We will also verify that your environment is ready by running a test script.

- *Development prerequisites*: The SDK is built around essential Python concepts that we need to be aware of, including type hints, docstring literals, decorators, asynchronous programming (async/await), and the Pydantic library for structured data validation. These are essential when we build tools and interact with data between agents.

- *Building your first AI agent*: With the setup complete, we will create our first real agent, which will be a customer service assistant, and then progressively enhance it. We will add a tool to handle order status lookups, and then introduce a handoff to a specialized agent for customer retention. This section puts the full development loop into action, covering the internals of the **control logic framework** we discussed previously.

In this chapter, we start coding. By the end of this chapter, you will have a fully functional SDK environment, a basic understanding of the Python concepts that the SDK relies on, and a real working AI agent that can take inputs, call tools, and hand off control to other agents. Let's get right into it.

Technical requirements

Throughout this book, practical examples and complete code from each chapter will be made available via the accompanying GitHub repository at `https://github.com/PacktPublishing/Building-Agents-with-OpenAI-Agents-SDK`.

You are encouraged to clone the repository, reuse and adapt the provided code samples, and refer to it as needed while progressing through the chapters.

Environment setup

The first step in using OpenAI Agents SDK is successfully setting up your environment, which includes installing the SDK and configuring your system to be able to run it. We will cover prerequisites, how to set up a project with a virtual environment, and how to install the SDK on both Windows and macOS. We will also need to obtain an OpenAI API key and ensure that it can be stored and accessed securely. Following these steps will help avoid common installation issues and will confirm that your environment is ready for development.

> **Note**
>
> This chapter walks through setting up your environment for the purposes of running the SDK locally. If you cannot run the SDK locally (perhaps due to missing prerequisites on your machine) or prefer not to, then most of what we will cover in the book can be run remotely using Google Colab. If you would like to take this approach, please skip to the section titled *Alternative methods: Google Colab*.

Python version and dependencies

As discussed previously, OpenAI Agents SDK is built on Python. This means that your machine must have Python installed, and specifically Python 3.9 or above. It is also useful to have your desired instance of Python available in your PATH variable (if you are on Windows) so that the Python command is available in your PowerShell/Command Prompt.

To verify the correct installation of Python on your machine, open the appropriate console environment based on your operating system. This is typically PowerShell or Command Prompt if you are on Windows 10 or Terminal if you are on Windows 11 or macOS. In the future, this will simply be referred to as your console.

Open your console and type in the following command. This should return the Python version. Verify that it is above 3.9. If it is not or the command returns an error, then follow the installation instructions for your operating system at `https://www.python.org/downloads/`. Type in this command:

```
$ python - version
>>> Python 3.10.6
```

Project directory, virtual environment, and installations

A clean and organized project structure is the first step toward building a maintainable application. In the book, each example will be in its own different project folder, organized within a chapter folder, and all within one central root folder. As our project grows in sophistication throughout this book, having a dedicated directory will be essential for managing agents, tools, and configuration files.

Create the required project folder so that it looks like the following configuration. This represents the folder path from the root directory down to the chapters:

```
Root
└ Chapter3
└ Chapter4
```

You can either create these folders manually or use the `mkdir` command in your console terminal.

Because we will be installing the `openai-agents` library, we must also create a virtual environment to isolate the SDK from your other Python projects. To create a virtual environment, ensure you are in your root folder, and enter the following command on your console terminal:

```
$ python -m venv .venv
```

This will create a new virtual environment, all housed within your `.venv` folder. Next, we must activate the virtual environment so that all our subsequent Python statements run through the Python interpreter within our virtual environment (along with its installed libraries).

On macOS, use the following:

```
source .venv/bin/activate
```

On Windows, use this:

```
.venv/Scripts/activate
```

After activation, your prompt will typically prepend the environment name (e.g., .venv). This indicates that any Python packages you install or commands you run will use this isolated environment. Note that you will need to activate the virtual environment in any new terminal session before running your code. Whenever this book tells you to *activate your virtual environment*, it means run these commands to put your terminal in this isolated environment.

Next, we will use Python's package manager, pip, to download and install OpenAI Agents SDK by running the following command in our console terminal:

```
$ pip install openai-agents
```

This command will download and install the SDK and all its requirements. You should see the console log output ending with Successfully installed openai-agents, notifying you that the library has been installed. At this point, you have Python, the virtual environment, and all the requisite libraries necessary to start building agents – the next step is to set up API access with OpenAI.

Registering for OpenAI API and setting up the API key

In order to use OpenAI's **large language models (LLMs)**, you need an OpenAI platform account with a positive credit balance and an OpenAI API key. The API key serves as the unique identifier that links your API requests to your account.

Follow these steps to generate an OpenAI API key:

1. Navigate to https://platform.openai.com/ and either sign up for an account or log in to an existing account. Note that you will need a valid email address.

2. Select **Settings** from the top-right menu and then select **Billing** from the left menu. Fill in your payment details and then select **Add to credit balance**. Type in $10 to add $10 to your OpenAI API credit balance.

3. Next, select **API keys** from the left menu and select **Create new secret key**. Give this API key a name such as OpenAIAgentsSDKKey and select the **Default** project. Then, select **Create secret key** to generate your private OpenAI API key.

4. At this point, you will see your OpenAI key and a **Save your key** prompt. Note that this is the only opportunity you have to see and copy your API key – after this, it cannot be retrieved ever again from OpenAI. Select the **Copy** button to copy your API key into your clipboard and then paste it somewhere on your machine (such as a .txt file) for now.

5. The following figure shows the API key management screen in the OpenAI platform dashboard:

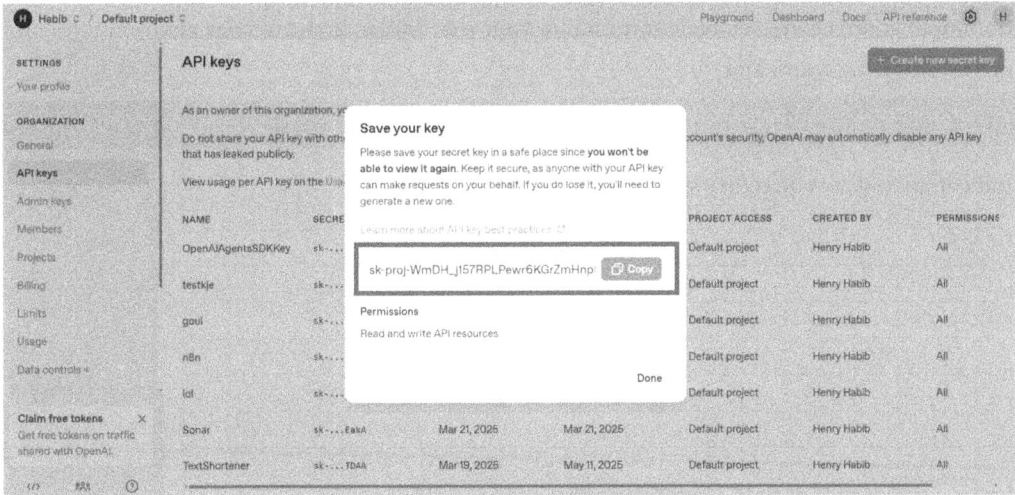

Figure 3.1: API screen in the OpenAI UI

After generating your key, the next step is to secure it. This is critical to protect your account from unauthorized use.

Note

This API key serves as an authentication layer to your OpenAI account. As such, you must treat this API key like a password and secure it accordingly. Do not share it or commit it to any open repositories. Technically, anyone with this API key can act on your behalf and spend your API credits. It is for this reason that we always use environment variables to handle the API key rather than writing it explicitly.

Because this API key ultimately grants access to your account, it must be protected even during local development. The best way to do that is to create a .env file within the root folder of your project, which will store the API key. Within the .env file, type in the following, replacing it with the OpenAI API key:

```
OPENAI_API_KEY="sk-..."
```

Next, you must install python-dotenv to load environment variables stored in your .env file into your application. Open a console terminal in your root folder, activate your environment, and run the following command:

```
$ pip install python-dotenv
```

Your completed root directory should look like the following:

```
Root
  └ .venv
  └ .env
  └ Chapter3
  └ Chapter4
  └ ...
```

Here is a screenshot of the CLI environment:

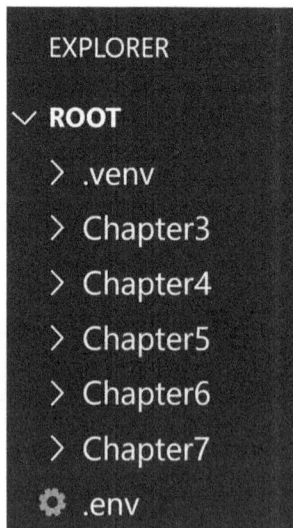

Figure 3.2: CLI environment

Note

You can always go back to OpenAI and revoke your key if you suspect someone else has it or if you have accidentally leaked it. Simply go back to your OpenAI account, go to **API keys**, and select **Revoke** near the API key that you would like to deactivate.

Verifying the environment setup

Let us now put everything together and verify that we can initialize and run an agent using the SDK. Create a new folder called Chapter3, create a new file called verify_environment_setup. py within that directory, and type in the following:

```python
import os
from dotenv import load_dotenv
from agents import Agent, Runner

# Load environment variables from the.env file
load_dotenv()

# Access the API key
api_key = os.getenv("OPENAI_API_KEY")

# Check to confirm API key is accessible:
if not api_key:
    print("Error: OPENAI_API_KEY not found. Please set it in your.env
file.")
else:
    print("API Key loaded successfully.")

#Create an agent and run it
agent = Agent(name="Echo Agent", instructions="Return the words 'Setup
successful'")
result = Runner.run_sync(agent, "Run setup")
print(result.final_output)
```

💡 **Quick tip**: Enhance your coding experience with the **AI Code Explainer** and **Quick Copy** features. Open this book in the next-gen Packt Reader. Click the **Copy** button

(1) to quickly copy code into your coding environment, or click the **Explain** button

(2) to get the AI assistant to explain a block of code to you.

```
function calculate(a, b) {
  return {sum: a + b};
};
```

Copy   Explain

(1)   (2)

📖 **The next-gen Packt Reader** is included for free with the purchase of this book. Scan the QR code OR go to packtpub.com/unlock, then use the search bar to find this book by name. Double-check the edition shown to make sure you get the right one.

This program verifies that the two required libraries (python-dotenv and openai-agents) are installed, that your OpenAI API key environment key is accessible, and that it can be used to create a basic AI agent. Then, run the Python program, and if you see the following outputs, then your environment has been successfully set up:

```
PS C:\Users\hasyh\OneDrive\Documents\1_Projects\30. Packt Publishing\
OpenAI Age nts SDK\Root> python .\Chapter3\verify_environment_setup.py
API Key loaded successfully.
Setup successful
```

Note that you can run Python files in different ways, depending on your operating system and your IDE. In VS Code, for example, you can run any Python program by selecting the **Play/Debug** button at the top right.

The most fundamental way to run a Python program, though, is from the console terminal. Activate your environment and then run the program by typing in Python followed by the location of your Python file:

```
python Chapter3\verify_environment_setup.py
```

You've now completed the essential setup steps for building with OpenAI Agents SDK: installing dependencies, managing your API key securely, and verifying that everything works.

In the next section, we'll explore an alternative remote environment.

Alternative methods: Google Colab

If you prefer not to set up a local development environment, or you're working on a device without administrative privileges, **Google Colab** provides a convenient and cloud-based alternative. It allows you to run Python code in a Jupyter Notebook-style environment, with zero setup on your part.

To use OpenAI Agents SDK in Colab, follow these steps:

1. Sign up for an account and start a new notebook at `https://colab.research.google.com/`:

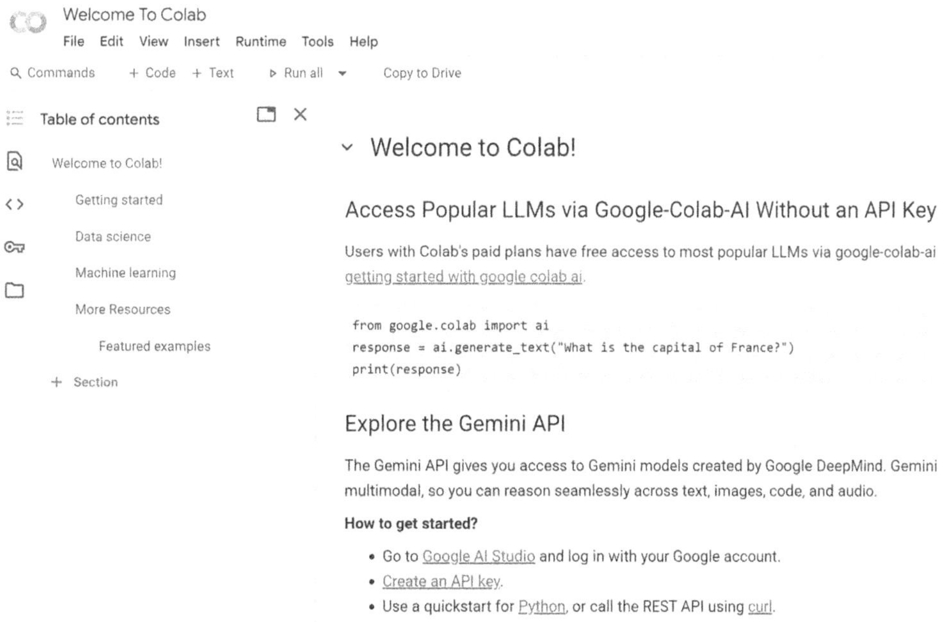

Figure 3.3: Google Colab UI

2. Python is already installed for you, but you still need to install OpenAI Agents SDK. At the top of the first code cell, install the SDK by running the following:

```
!pip install openai-agents
```

3. Set your OpenAI API key by storing it in an environment variable:

```
import os
os.environ["OPENAI_API_KEY"] = "your-api-key-here"
```

4. You can now import the SDK and begin using it. Follow the instructions in this section to import all required libraries.

5. If your notebook involves multiple files (e.g., loading tools or agents from separate Python modules), use Colab's **Files** pane to upload them.

Running the SDK in Colab supports nearly all of the workflows we cover in this book, with the added benefit of being easy to share and replicate. While there may be some limitations for advanced use cases involving local system resources or custom networking, Colab is sufficient for the majority of agent development scenarios.

In the next section, we'll explore how to create and structure your first real agent by diving into the core primitives that power the SDK.

Development prerequisites

To use OpenAI Agents SDK, you need more than just a working installation and environment. The SDK is designed with specific Pythonic architectural patterns in mind, and being familiar with these principles will make using the SDK a lot easier. In this section, we will go through a quick primer on three key Python principles needed to use the SDK.

Note that this is not an exhaustive Python tutorial. Learning Python fundamentals is outside the scope of this course. This section, though, will align you with the techniques used in the SDK examples throughout this book.

Python functions architecture

The SDK is used via Python code, so you'll be writing your own functions and maybe classes to extend agent capabilities. For example, the Agents SDK allows you to define tools as simple Python functions that the agent can call. As a result, you should be familiar with how to create and use Python functions:

```
# An example Python function
def echo(message):
    return f"Message: {message}"
```

Additionally, the most important concepts to master here are the architecture around the Python function, such as type hints, docstrings, and decorators – all of which are used extensively by OpenAI Agents SDK:

- **Type hints**: Python supports optional type hints (also known as type annotations), which can be used to specify the variable type of inputs and outputs to a Python function. OpenAI Agents SDK uses type hints as a functional part of the framework. When you create a custom tool, for example, the SDK inspects your function's type hints and passes them to the LLM, enabling it to understand exactly what arguments your tool expects and in what format. In the following example, type hints specify that the expected input to the function is an integer and that the output is a string.

- **Docstrings**: Docstrings are strings found directly after the definition of a function, the purpose of which is to document what the function does, its inputs, and its outputs. In the context of OpenAI Agents SDK, docstrings serve as metadata that can help the LLM better understand what the function (or tool) does. Note that this is technically not required, but it is helpful for proper AI agent interpretability.

- **Decorators**: Decorators are higher-order functions that wrap another function to modify or enhance its behavior. In the context of OpenAI Agents SDK, decorators are often used to mark a function as a tool (e.g., @function_tool) and to add metadata such as a tool name, description, or parameter schema.

The following code snippet demonstrates a complete example that brings all three elements (decorator, type hints, and docstring) together in a tool function compatible with OpenAI Agents SDK:

```
@function_tool # decorator
def get_order_status(orderID: int) -> str: # type hint
    """

    Returns the order status given an order ID
    Args:
        orderID (int) - Order ID of the customer's order
    Returns:
        string - Status message of the customer's order
    """
```

```
if orderID in (100, 101):
    return "Delivered"
elif orderID in (200, 201):
    return "Delayed"
elif orderID in (300, 301):
    return "Cancelled"
```

Understanding how to properly structure your functions with these elements will make your agent tools more readable, maintainable, and compatible with the SDK's built-in features.

Python asynchronous programming

Most modern Python programs are **synchronous**, meaning that each step in the program executes one at a time sequentially. In short, each step must be successfully completed before the next one can begin. This contrasts with **asynchronous** programming, which handles operations concurrently and which (thankfully) Python also supports with the asyncio library and async/await commands.

OpenAI Agents SDK provides both synchronous and asynchronous ways to run agents. However, the preferred way to run the agent is asynchronously, especially for more complex use cases (e.g., running multiple agents or tools in parallel). Agentic workflows are asynchronous, spending much of their time waiting for external operations such as API calls, tool executions, LLM responses, and so on. To manage this efficiently and enable your agent to do multiple things at the same time, OpenAI Agents SDK uses Python's asynchronous programming features without blocking the whole program.

The basics of Python's asynchronous programming can be summarized as follows:

- An async function is defined using async def instead of the traditional def statement
- async functions must be called by prepending the execution with await
- async functions can only be called by other async functions or an event loop
- An event loop can be created in Python using the asyncio.run() command

Note

For many of the examples covered in the book, a synchronous call is actually fine to use, as (at least in the beginning) we will not be handling multi-agent queries, multi-tool calls, or streaming output. However, it's still good to understand how async works and prioritize running async, as the SDK is built to take advantage of it.

As we progress through the chapters, you will encounter both synchronous and asynchronous patterns. Having a solid grasp of Python's async model will help you better understand how agent interactions are orchestrated under the hood and how to scale your workflows more efficiently.

Python Pydantic data validation

Pydantic is a comprehensive Python library used for data validation. In short, this library enables developers to define a data structure (called a model), and the library will automatically verify that a specific data input matches that data structure.

OpenAI Agents SDK uses Pydantic in several different ways:

- **Structured inputs into tools**: When building tools, you can define the expected input parameters not only using type hints as we discussed before, but also using a Pydantic data structure model. This allows the SDK to validate inputs before passing them to the function, and also provides a clear schema that the LLM can understand and follow when invoking the tool.

- **Structured outputs from agents**: You can define a data structure in Pydantic and set it as the desired outputs within an agent. In this way, you can be sure that any outputs received from an agent will always conform to your set Pydantic data model structure. This means your outputs adhere to a consistent, structured format, which is ideal for downstream processing or API responses.

- **Guardrails within an agent execution**: Pydantic models can also be used within the logic of an agent to enforce constraints during execution with the guardrails feature. A step within an agent workflow may require data validation or a guardrail before proceeding to the next decision, and using Pydantic here helps catch any errors (through the use of guardrail triggers).

The following code snippet demonstrates how to define a structured Pydantic model and use it as input to an OpenAI tool, enabling automatic validation and schema clarity:

```
from pydantic import BaseModel, Field
from openai import OpenAI
from openai.agent import tool


# Step 1: Define the structured input using Pydantic
class PersonInput(BaseModel):
    name: str = Field(..., description="The full name of the person")
```

```
    age: int = Field(..., ge=0, le=150, description="The age of the person
in years")
    email: str = Field(..., description="The email address of the person")

# Step 2: Create the tool using the @function_tool decorator
@function_tool
def process_person(input: PersonInput) -> str:
    """Processes a person's information and returns a summary."""
    return f"{input.name} is {input.age} years old. Contact: {input.
email}"
```

Knowledge of Pydantic is useful for understanding how the SDK ensures data reliability. While technically it's not necessary to be a Pydantic expert to use the Agents SDK, being able to recognize when to use a Pydantic model instead of regular type hints can be helpful. In cases where complex agents exchange structured data, Pydantic models may be used to define these structures.

Developing your first AI Agent

Now that our environment is configured and we understand the core Python development concepts, it's time for the most exciting part: building and executing our first AI agent. We will first run our agent and then go through it step by step, examining the output and the internal stages that the agent went through. After that, we will add more complexity to our agent (e.g., integrating a tool, using multiple agents, etc.) to make it more sophisticated. Here is how the structure looks:

Figure 3.4: Agent components

A simple customer service agent

Suppose we are building a customer service agent, one that can be used by our company to facilitate customer requests. Create a new Python file under the Chapter3 folder called customer_service_agent.py, and write the code needed to define the agent, provide input, and then run the agent.

The following code snippet demonstrates how to create and execute a basic customer service agent using OpenAI Agents SDK:

```python
# Required imports
import os
from dotenv import load_dotenv
from agents import Agent, Runner


# Load environment variables from the .env file
load_dotenv()


# Access the API key
api_key = os.getenv("OPENAI_API_KEY")


# Define an agent
agent = Agent(name="Customer service agent",
              instructions="You are an AI Agent that helps respond to
customer queries for a local paper company",
              model="gpt-4o")


# Run the Control Logic Framework
result = Runner.run_sync(agent, "How do I cancel my order?")


# Print the result
print(result.final_output)
```

After activating our environment and running this file, you get the following output:

```
To cancel your order, please contact our customer service team directly.
You can reach us by phone at [Your Phone Number] or email us at [Your
Email Address]. Be sure to have your order number handy so we can assist
you quickly.
```

Note

In this particular example, the agent is trying to respond best to the customer's inquiry, and because of the probabilistic nature of LLMs, the response that you see may be different.

Let's break this down step by step:

1. We first loaded in all the required libraries and environment variables needed to build and run agents in Python; this is like what we had previously in the chapter.

2. We then instantiated a new Agent class called agent and defined its three arguments: name, instructions, and model. These form part of the **system prompt** of the agent, which we already defined earlier in the book as the prompt that tells the model of the agent how to act and drives its underlying behavior. In this case, it's meant to instruct the agent to act as a customer support agent that responds to customer queries for a local paper company.

3. We then call the Runner.run_sync function, passing the newly created agent object as well as input_context, which, in this case, is a question that a customer may ask. Under the hood, this Runner class is responsible for the control logic framework that we had described earlier in *Chapter 1*. This calls the LLM (as defined in agent) with the current input_context, receives the response from the LLM, and then starts a loop/lifecycle:

   • If the LLM returns what it believes to be the final output given the agent's instructions and the initial prompt, it returns the result and ends the loop

   • If the LLM returns a desired action to be made, whether it's calling a tool (or calling several tools) or performing a handoff, the Runner class runs those tool calls/performs the handoff, appends the outputs, and reruns the agent loop. This process continues until the desired objective is achieved (or until it exceeds a specified maximum number of loop turns).

4. Then, Runner.run_sync returns a RunResult object, which can be parsed. The final_output parameter of the object is then displayed to the user.

   In this case, the agent's sophistication is very simple. It is simply calling the LLM GPT-4o with the system prompt and input prompt, and then returning the response. So, in our first use case, the loop just ran once:

   • The LLM was called with the system prompt of You are an AI Agent that helps respond to customer queries for a local paper company, and an input prompt of How do I cancel my order?

   • The LLM returned a final_output (which is an object and hence did not want to perform a handoff or call a tool)

   • The loop ended as it was a final output, and the results were displayed to the user

It's important to understand this loop before we add more complexity. Remember that no matter how complex the agent gets, Runner is continuously reasoning through this loop, driven by the LLM's outputs, at each step. The benefit of the SDK is that it abstracts much of this process for us.

Now, let's progressively add features to make the system more agentic, starting with tools.

Adding a tool

We will first add a tool that enables the agent to see the order delivery status based on order IDs. This would typically be done with a database lookup, but we will hardcode the logic for simplicity. The underlying complexity of the function or tool is not relevant; what the SDK accomplishes for us is providing the agent with the decision-making of whether to call the tool, creating the inputs of the tool, running the tool, and then interpreting the outputs of the tool.

We must first make an additional import from the agents class:

```
from agents import Agent, Runner, function_tool
```

Let's add the following code snippet right above our agent definition:

```
# Create a tool
@function_tool
def get_order_status(orderID: int) -> str:
    """
    Returns the order status given an order ID
    """
    if orderID in (100, 101):
        return "Delivered"
    elif orderID in (200, 201):
        return "Delayed"
    elif orderID in (300, 301):
        return "Cancelled"
```

Then, let's modify our agent definition by adding another argument for tools:

```
# Define an agent
agent = Agent(name="Customer service agent",
              instructions="You are an AI Agent that helps respond to
customer queries for a local paper company",
              model="gpt-4o",
              tools=[get_order_status])
```

Finally, let's edit input_context to make the prompt relevant to the tool we just added:

```
result = Runner.run_sync(agent, "What's the status of my order? My Order
ID is 200")
```

After running our new Python program, here is the output:

```
Your order with ID 200 is currently delayed. If you have any further
questions or need assistance, feel free to let me know!
```

In this example, we added a tool called get_order_status to our customer service agent. We needed to do two things to add the tool to the agent:

1. We added a @function_tool decorator to the custom Python function. This decorator informs the SDK of the tool's name, its arguments, its purpose, and its return type, all done via the function's type hints and docstrings. This is important: any Python function can become a tool that is called by the agent once it's decorated with the @function_tool class.

2. We added the name of the function to a list, which we then passed in the tools argument when we instantiated the agent object.

After doing this, the agent can decide to use the tool based on its overall objectives and the input task it has been given. In our case, the user asked explicitly about the status of an order and provided an order ID.

During the control logic framework loop, the LLM did not return a final_output (object) Instead, it was provided with the tool called get_order_status (and its metadata), and decided that the tool must be executed next in its loop, providing the orderID input argument as 200. The Runner class then executed the function with the input and then added the function output (Delayed) to the agent's input_context (object), starting another loop iteration. At this point, the LLM is given not only the original user input (i.e., What's the status of my order 200?) but also the output of the function (i.e., The order is delayed). The LLM then constructs a final_output message, which is then displayed back to the user.

The series of steps here may be confusing, but they can be visualized. In fact, OpenAI maintains a very good log of each and every agent run, which displays every LLM call, tool execution, and handoff that is made – this is called a **trace**. To find the trace for our most recent agent call, follow these steps:

1. Go to https://platform.openai.com/ and log in with the same account you logged in with previously (where you had generated the API key).

2. Select **Dashboard** from the top-right menu and then select **Traces** from the left menu.

3.   Select the trace with the most recent **Created** time. You should see a trace that looks like the following:

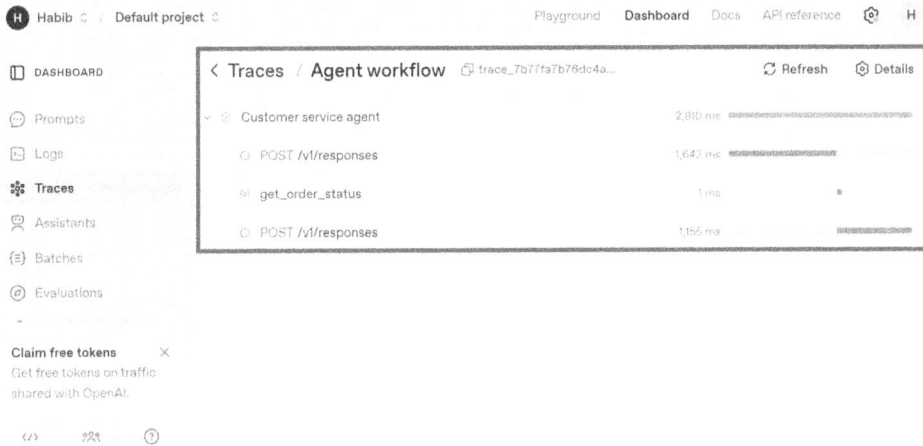

Figure 3.5: Tracing example in the OpenAI UI, showing different steps

This trace tells you everything you need to know about your agent run, and you can click each individual step within a trace to get more details. In my case, I see that the Runner class first called the LLM with the system prompt and input prompt we had described before. The result of that LLM call was to execute a function call, with "orderID": 200 as the input argument.

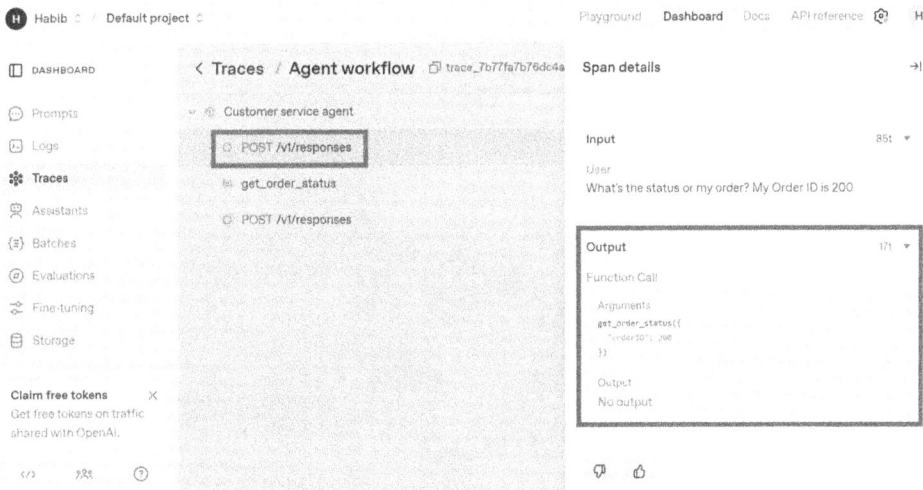

Figure 3.6: Tracing example in the OpenAI UI, showing details of the first step

4. Then, the get_order_status tool was called, with the string Delayed was returned by that tool.

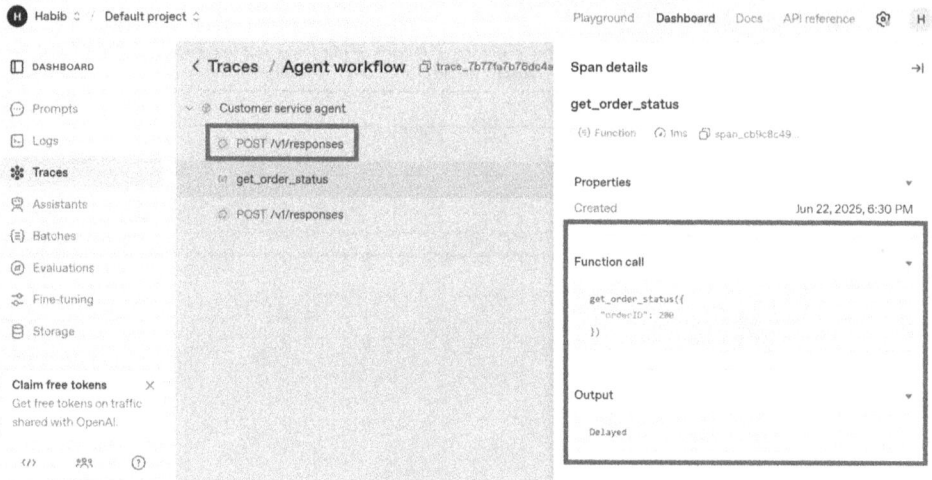

Figure 3.7: Tracing example in the OpenAI UI, showing details of the second step

5. Finally, one last LLM call was made with the input (What's the status or my order? My Order ID is 200, and Function call get_order_status("orderID": 200) returned Delayed). The LLM returned Your order with ID 200 is currently delayed. If you have any further questions or need assistance, feel free to let me know!, which is exactly what we saw before.

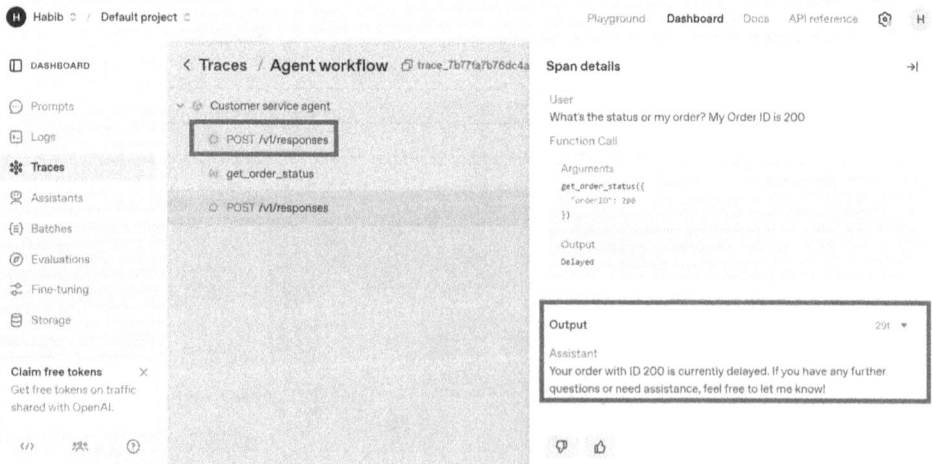

Figure 3.8: Tracing example in the OpenAI UI, showing details of the third step

Note that we will cover tracing in much greater detail in subsequent chapters, but it's useful to see behind the scenes on the "thinking" that is happening within the control logic framework.

> **Note**
>
> It is worth knowing that just because a tool is accessible to the agent does not mean that the agent will use it. In fact, this is one of the most important aspects of agentic AI: tool choice and other decisions are not deterministic. Instead, decision-making is made based on the context of the user's request. If the user instead asked How do I change my password?, then it would not need to call the get_order_status tool.

Adding a handoff

A useful feature of OpenAI Agents SDK is the ability for an agent to **hand off** a task to another agent. This is useful if you want to have multi-agent orchestration or agent specialization. For example, you may want to break a problem into sub-tasks handled by different agents specialized in their field. In our example, if the customer wants to cancel their order with us, we may want our agent to hand off to another agent that is uniquely specialized in customer retention (it may be instructed to utilize retention strategies or may be able to call tools that offer discounts to the customer). Agent handoffs are especially useful if you want agents that specialize in different knowledge domains.

Let's create a new agent that specializes in customer retention and add it as a potential handoff to our existing agent structure.

First, create a new agent that specializes in handling customer retention problems:

```python
# Define the customer retention agent
customer_retention_agent = Agent(
    name="Customer Retention Agent",
    instructions="You are an AI agent that responds to customers that want
to close their accounts and retains their business. Be very courteous,
relatable, and kind. Offer discounts up to 10% if it helps",
    model="gpt-4.1"
)
```

Then, add a new list argument called `handoffs` to our original agent, and add the newly created agent to it:

```
# Define an agent
agent = Agent(name="Customer service agent",
              instructions="You are an AI Agent that helps respond to
customer queries for a local paper company",
              model="gpt-4o",
              tools=[get_order_status],
              handoffs=[customer_retention_agent])
```

Finally, let's edit `input_context` to make the prompt relevant to the tool we just added:

```
result = Runner.run_sync(agent, "I want to cancel my order and account.
You delayed by order for the 3rd time!")
```

After running our new Python program, here is the output:

```
I sincerely apologize for the repeated delays with your order. I
understand how frustrating and disappointing this experience has been, and
I want to make things right.

While I know you're considering canceling, I'd love the opportunity to
make it up to you. As a thank you for your patience, I can offer you a 10%
discount on your order, and I will personally monitor your order to ensure
there are no further issues.

If you still prefer to cancel, I will completely respect your decision and
assist with that right away. Please let me know how you'd like to proceed—
your satisfaction is very important to us!
```

In this case, we have created two agents: the agent that we had before that acts as a customer service manager, and another called `customer_retention_agent` that specializes in customer retention. The customer service manager agent fields any requests from the customer, and then either responds to the inquiry, calls the `get_order_status` tool, or hands off the task to the customer retention agent.

In this example, during the control logic framework loop, the LLM again did not return a `final_output`. Instead, it decided to hand off the task and input context to another agent. The `Runner` class in the SDK sees that and switches context to the other agent (with the same user question). Then, that agent is now "in charge," processes the user request, and produces the final answer.

This series of steps can also be seen in the tracing for this workflow:

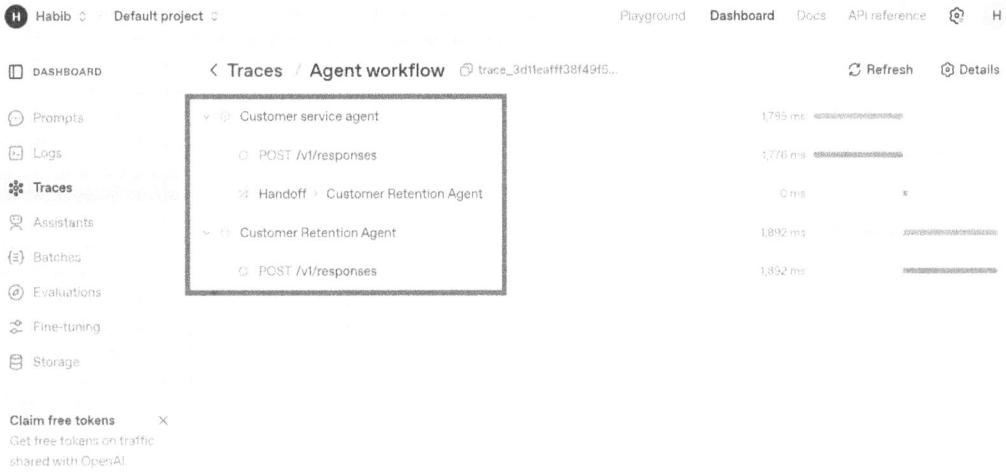

Figure 3.9: Tracing example in the OpenAI UI, showing all the steps

This multi-agent setup can be expanded to many agents and complex routing logic. The power here is that each agent can have its own persona and capabilities, and you let the model decide which agent is appropriate via the handoff mechanism. The SDK's role is to seamlessly pass control (including conversation history if any) from one agent to another as directed by the model's output.

Summary

In this chapter, we set up the development environment required to use OpenAI Agents SDK. We installed the SDK in an isolated Python environment, configured our OpenAI API key, and verified our setup by running a minimal agent.

We also covered key Python constructs that the SDK leans on heavily. We discussed how type hints and docstrings provide metadata that the LLM uses to interpret your tools and how decorators mark functions as callable tools. We then learned about asynchronous execution in Python and why that is relevant for agents. Finally, we saw how Pydantic models validate structured inputs and outputs.

We then built our first real agent, which was a simple customer service assistant, and then extended its capabilities by adding a tool and handoff. We added a new tool that the agent could execute when the customer wanted the status of an order. We did this by creating a custom Python function (get_order_status) that was well-typed and documented, and then added the @function_tool decorator to it.

We then introduced how multi-agent orchestrations can work by creating multiple agents and enabling them to hand off to one another. In our example, we created a customer agent that was specialized in retention and to which our main agent could hand off if needed.

In each enhancement, we discussed how the SDK's control logic framework handles reasoning, tool execution, and agent switching behind the scenes, letting you build complex, adaptive systems with minimal code.

We have only scratched the surface of AI agents and the SDK. In the next chapter, we'll deep dive into building and integrating AI agent tools.

Unlock this book's exclusive benefits now

Scan this QR code or go to packtpub.com/ unlock, then search this book by name.

Note: Keep your purchase invoice ready before you start.

Part 2

OpenAI Agents SDK

Part 2 is the technical core of the book. Here we move from "agent as an idea" to "agent as an engineered system," using OpenAI Agents SDK as our primary vehicle. Each chapter deepens one specific capability and the primitives set of OpenAI Agents SDK. For each component, we discuss the theory and then apply it to examples and demos as we build practical AI agents and agentic systems.

Specifically, you will extend your agent with tools (from simple functions to hosted tools and agents-as-tools), add memory and knowledge retrieval, and compose multi-agent systems with deliberate handoffs. You will learn how to tune models and context, how to structure multi-agent systems, and how to deploy and monitor them with guardrails and policies.

This part contains the following chapters:

- *Chapter 4, Agent Tools and MCPs*
- *Chapter 5, Memory and Knowledge*
- *Chapter 6, Multi-Agent Systems and Handoffs*
- *Chapter 7, Model and Context Management*
- *Chapter 8, Agent System Management*

4

Agent Tools and MCPs

Now that we've built our first working AI agent, it's time to give it some real capabilities. In this chapter, we'll go beyond the basics and dive deep into one of the most important elements of OpenAI Agents SDK: tools. **Tools** are what enable agents to interact with the outside world, such as querying databases, calling APIs, performing calculations, generating content, and even calling other agents.

Here is what you will learn as part of this chapter:

- **Custom tools**: Learn how to define Python functions and register them as tools using the @function_tool decorator. We'll explore how to configure tool metadata, validate inputs using Pydantic, and control how tools are described to the agent.
- **Agent-tool behavior**: Understand how to influence when and how an agent uses a tool by leveraging parameters such as tool_choice and tool_use_behavior.
- **OpenAI-hosted tools**: Use OpenAI's pre-built tools, such as WebSearchTool, FileSearchTool, and CodeInterpreterTool, to extend agent capabilities.
- **Agents as tools**: Learn how to turn an entire agent into a callable tool, enabling modular orchestration and hierarchical workflows.
- **MCPs**: Connect to external MCP servers to retrieve tools rather than building your own.

By the end of this chapter, you will be able to equip your agents with powerful capabilities, from simple arithmetic to real-time API access, from generating images to querying vector databases, and connecting to external MCP servers. You will also be able to control how agents use tools. Let's get right into it.

Technical requirements

Please follow the detailed steps in *Chapter 3* to set up your environment.

Throughout this book, practical examples and complete code from each chapter will be made available via the accompanying GitHub repository: `https://github.com/PacktPublishing/ Building-Agents-with-OpenAI-Agents-SDK`.

You are encouraged to clone the repository, reuse and adapt the provided code samples, and refer to it as needed while progressing through the chapters.

Using custom tools with Python functions

In this section, let's explore how to define and configure custom tools using Python functions within OpenAI Agents SDK. As a reminder, tools are a core part of the agent's capabilities as they enable the agent to go beyond its internal knowledge and perform tasks such as fetching data, processing user requests, or triggering actions. We'll begin with simple tool definitions using the `@function_tool` decorator and then progress to more advanced capabilities, such as overriding tool parameters and using `Pydantic` models for complex input validation.

Defining a new tool

As we discussed in the previous chapter, OpenAI Agents SDK provides a `@function_tool` decorator that turns any Python function into a tool that can be called by an agent. For example, we will bring back the code that we wrote in the previous chapter that creates a simple tool and calls an agent with that tool:

```python
# Required imports
import os
from dotenv import load_dotenv
from agents import Agent, Runner, function_tool

# Load environment variables from the .env file
load_dotenv()

# Access the API key
api_key = os.getenv("OPENAI_API_KEY")

# Create a tool
@function_tool
```

```
def get_order_status(orderID: int) -> str:
    """

    Returns the order status given an order ID
    Args:
        orderID (int) - Order ID of the customer's order
    Returns:
        string - Status message of the customer's order
    """

    if orderID in (100, 101):
        return "Delivered"
    elif orderID in (200, 201):
        return "Delayed"
    elif orderID in (300, 301):
        return "Cancelled"


# Define an agent
agent = Agent(name="Customer service agent",
              instructions="You are an AI Agent that helps respond to
customer queries for a local paper company",
              model="gpt-4o",
              tools=[get_order_status])


# Run the Control Logic Framework
result = Runner.run_sync(agent, "What's the status of my order? My Order
ID is 200")


# Print the result
print(result.final_output)
```

By decorating any Python function, the SDK infers the tool name, purpose, and input arguments from the function's name (get_order_status), description (*Returns the order status given an order ID*), and its input schema (orderID: int), respectively. A clear, human-readable name and docstring are very important as the agent will see this description when deciding whether to use the tool. It should explain what the tool does and what inputs it expects (including units or formats). In this case, we did not have to manually write a JSON schema; the SDK generated it from the function signature.

These tool parameters, however, can also be explicitly defined, if needed, by overriding the default characteristics of the function. Here's an example:

```python
# Create a tool
@function_tool(
        name_override="Get Status of Current Order",
        description_override="Returns the status of an order given the
customer's Order ID",
        docstring_style="Args: Order ID in Integer format"
)
def get_order_status(orderID: int) -> str:
    """

    Returns the order status given an order ID
    Args:
        orderID (int) - Order ID of the customer's order
    Returns:
        string - Status message of the customer's order
    """

    if orderID in (100, 101):
        return "Delivered"
    elif orderID in (200, 201):
        return "Delayed"
    elif orderID in (300, 301):
        return "Cancelled"
```

Typically, this is done to give developers more control over how the tool is represented and interpreted by the agent. For example, the name_override parameter lets you define a more descriptive or user-friendly name than what's derived from the function itself. This is particularly useful when the function name is too generic or not expressive enough for the agent to infer its purpose accurately.

This level of explicit control can be really valuable when tool behavior is ambiguous, when localization or formatting standards need to be enforced, or when multiple tools share similar structures but differ in subtle ways that the agent must distinguish.

Note

The @function_tool decorator works with both synchronous and asynchronous functions. If your function uses async def, the SDK will handle it correctly and the agent will be able to await its result automatically. This flexibility is useful when your tool interacts with external APIs, databases, or other async workflows.

Agent and tool behavior

The agent autonomously decides when to call a tool and what tool to call. We have already discussed previously that this decision is governed by the LLM in the control logic framework, a decision tree loop that is managed by the Runner class. On each cycle of the loop, the following happens:

1. The Runner class sends the current list of messages to the LLM.

2. The LLM responds either with a "final answer" or a "tool call" (for simplicity, let's assume these are the only two options for now).

3. If "tool call" is the response, the Runner class executes the corresponding Python functions and appends their string-based outputs to the message history, and the cycle repeats until a final answer is produced.

By default, the model will decide if and when to use a tool. However, we can ultimately influence the tool decision step, and for certain use cases, we may need to do this. The SDK gives developers control via several settings.

Tool choice

One such setting is called the ModelSettings.tool_choice parameter, which gives us the ability to control the model's approach to tool usage in the following way:

- auto: The model decides itself whether to call a tool and which one (default option)
- required: Forces the model to use a tool
- none: Prevents the model from using any tools

Modifying this setting is useful when you want to purposely control the agent's behavior. For example, if you are creating an agent that must always retrieve data from a database/internal knowledge base and never rely on the model's internal knowledge, you can set tool_choice to required, which ensures that the agent calls the tool every time.

In the following example, we explicitly set tool_choice to required to ensure the model does not attempt to respond without using the get_order_status tool. This guarantees that the agent's answer comes from the trusted source, regardless of how obvious or simple the answer might seem to the LLM.

```
from agents import Agent, Runner, function_tool, ModelSettings

@function_tool
def get_order_status(orderID: int) -> str:
    if orderID in (100, 101):
        return "Delivered"
    elif orderID in (200, 201):
        return "Delayed"
    elif orderID in (300, 301):
        return "Cancelled"

agent = Agent(
    name="Strict customer service agent",
    instructions="You are a customer service agent that must always use
the backend system to check order status. Do not guess.",
    model="gpt-4o",
    tools=[get_order_status],
    model_settings=ModelSettings(tool_choice="required")
)

result = Runner.run_sync(agent, "Can you check the status of Order ID 101?")
print(result.final_output)
```

This example demonstrates how setting tool_choice="required" ensures the model must invoke the get_order_status tool and cannot rely on its internal knowledge. This guarantees that all responses are based on the backend system, reinforcing accuracy and trust in the agent's behavior.

Note

If none of the available tools are appropriate for the task, and tool usage is required (tool_choice="required"), the model will raise an error or refuse to answer, since it is not permitted to respond without using a tool. This ensures that all outputs are grounded in trusted, explicitly defined logic.

This setting can also be used to mandate tool usage for compliance or auditability purposes, typically required for legal or finance use cases. We can also use this setting to restrict tool access in sensitive situations or isolate the LLM in a sandboxed environment during testing.

> **Note**
>
> The SDK also allows you to specify a particular tool name, such as `tool_choice="get_weather"`. This forces the model to call that specific tool and no others. It's a useful option when validating or testing individual tools in isolation, or when you want to bypass the model's tool selection logic entirely for consistency or control.

Tool use behavior

Another critical setting in agent and tool behavior is the aptly named `Agent.tool_use_behavior`, which controls what happens *after* a tool is called and its output is returned. The options for this setting are as follows:

- `run_llm_again`: After the tool executes, the agent returns the output to the LLM as part of the control logic framework, and the LLM then decides whether a "final output" has been reached to return the final answer. This enables the model to interpret the output of the tool and create a response in context with the user's question. This is the default option.

- `stop_on_first_tool`: The first tool output is treated as the "final response" and no further model calls are made.

- `agent.StopAtTools.stop_at_tool_names`: A list of strings that represent the list of tools for which we want the agent to stop running and simply respond with the output of the tool.

These options allow you to craft agents that behave more deterministically or with more flexibility, depending on the task. For example, the `stop_on_first_tool` option is especially useful when the tool's output is the answer (e.g., such as a database response, a computation, etc.) – anywhere where it does not make sense to process the output back to the LLM.

The last option is useful if you have a list of tools that, when triggered, should immediately terminate the agent's execution and return the tool's output as is. This could be either cases that match the preceding description, or perhaps "trigger points" where we would want the agent to stop executing (i.e., if the user asks to speak to a manager).

The following is an example use case of the agent.StopAtTools.stop_at_tool_names option. This is where our customer service agent has a tool that performs a sensitive operation, such as generating an invoice, where it is preferable to display the tool's output directly to preserve accuracy, formatting, or legal wording:

```python
from agents import Agent, Runner, function_tool, StopAtTools

@function_tool
def create_invoice(orderID: int) -> str:
    return f"Invoice for Order {orderID}: $123.45 (Generated on 2025-07-
05)"

agent = Agent(
    name="Invoice generator agent",
    instructions="Generate and return an invoice when requested.",
    model="gpt-4o",
    tools=[create_invoice],
    stop=StopAtTools.stop_at_tool_names(["create_invoice"])
)

result = Runner.run_sync(agent, "Please create an invoice for Order 300")
print(result.final_output)
```

In this example, the agent calls the create_invoice tool and returns the raw output string directly, without any additional LLM processing. This preserves the original content from the tool output.

Complex tool inputs with Pydantic

We discussed in the previous chapter that the SDK supports **Pydantic** for complex tool inputs and talked about its benefits, namely, in data validation. As a reminder, instead of using simple type hints such as str or int in your input arguments, you can define a Pydantic BaseModel object to represent hierarchical or detailed input structures. When used as a function argument, the SDK treats the entire model as a single parameter, automatically generating a corresponding nested JSON schema. This makes it easier for the LLM to understand and call tools with the right input schema for complex inputs.

Let's put this to the test and go through a concrete example. Following our customer service theme, suppose we want to create a tool that can process customer refunds. The problem? Processing a refund requires complex input: the order ID, the customer's email, the reason, and so on. To add to the complexity, the tool should be able to process multiple refunds at once. In this case, In this case, let's define a class of BaseModel, called RefundRequest:

```python
from pydantic import BaseModel, List


class RefundRequest(BaseModel):
    order_id: str
    customer_email: str
    reason: str


    requests: List[RefundRequest]
```

Now that we have done this, we can pass in `RefundRequest` as the input argument to our custom function.

```python
@function_tool
def process_refund(request: RefundRequest) -> str:
    """Process a refund request and return confirmation."""
    # Logic to interface with internal refund systems would go here
    return (f"Refund request for order {request.order_id} has been
submitted. "
            f"A confirmation will be sent to {request.customer_email}.")
```

When the agent decides to use `process_refund`, it knows from the schema that the request is a list of `RefundRequest` objects, each requiring three fields. The model's structure is made visible to the LLM.

Using Pydantic for structured tool input is especially powerful when dealing with real-world workflows that involve multiple fields, optional parameters, or repeated objects.

Also, it has a bonus of *non-LLM input validation*. If the LLM "hallucinates" and passes on incorrectly formatted data, the SDK will catch the problem by raising an error. You can then catch this error, making your application much more resilient. This is especially useful in agent-LLM interactions, which by definition are not deterministic.

For example, suppose the model mistakenly omits a required field or provides the wrong type for a value, perhaps due to a hallucination or misunderstanding of the tool schema. Let's say it submits the following JSON instead:

```
{
  "order_id": 12345,
  "customer_email": "customer@example.com"
}
```

This payload is missing the required reason field and also incorrectly types order_id as an integer instead of a string. When the SDK attempts to instantiate the RefundRequest model from this data, it will automatically raise a ValidationError object from Pydantic.

Examples of custom tools

Now that we have discussed how to define a new tool and configure its agent-calling behavior, let's put that into practical use and fully build a few concrete examples. Each example will be a standalone script that you can run (assuming that you have set up your environment successfully).

Arithmetic computation tool

The first agent with a custom tool that we will create will be one that performs arithmetic computation, something that LLMs are notorious for hallucinating. In fact, mathematical operations should never be performed by an LLM. As a result, we will build an agent that calls a tool that performs the mathematical operation instead.

In this case, we will build an agent that calculates the mortgage payment for a loan. Create a new Python script called mortgage_agent.py, with the following code:

```python
# Required imports
from dotenv import load_dotenv
from agents import Agent, Runner, function_tool

# Load environment variables from the .env file
load_dotenv()

@function_tool
def calculate_mortgage(
    principal_amount: float, annualized_rate: float, number_of_years: int
) -> str:
    """
```

```
    This function calculates the mortgage payment.

    Args:
        principal_amount: The mortgage amount.
        annual_rate: The annualized interest rate in percent form.
        years: The loan term in years.
    Returns:
        A message stating the monthly payment amount.
    """
    monthly_rate = (annualized_rate / 100) / 12
    months = number_of_years * 12
    payment = principal_amount * (monthly_rate) / (1 - (1 + monthly_rate)
** -months)
    print(payment)
    return f"${payment:,.2f}."


# Define an agent that uses the mortgage calculator tool
mortgage_agent = Agent(
    name="MortgageAdvisor",
    instructions=("You are a mortgage assistant"),
    tools=[calculate_mortgage]
)


# Run the agent with an example question
result = Runner.run_sync(mortgage_agent, "What is my monthly payments if I
borrow $800,000 at 6% interest for 30 years?")
print(result.final_output)
```

In this script, calculate_mortgage is decorated as a custom tool. It takes three inputs and returns a formatted string with the mortgage payment amount.

When running this script, the agent should recognize that the user's question is about calculating the mortgage payment and should call the calculate_mortgage tool with the appropriate arguments. The tool will compute the payment (about $4,796.84 per month) and then send the outputs to the LLM. The LLM will then output a completed message as the final answer.

In my case, the final answer was the following:

```
The monthly payment for your mortgage would be approximately $4,796.84.
```

However, note that since the LLM is non-deterministic, you may see slightly different outputs (but the payment amount should be the same, as it is computed using the tool).

Now, let's adjust the code to always force the agent to call the tool and to return the output from the tool instead of calling the LLM again. We will add two parameters: `tool_use_behavior="stop_on_first_tool"` and `ModelSettings.tool_choice="required"`. Here is the updated agent instantiation:

```python
# Add import
from agents import Agent, Runner, function_tool

# Define an agent that uses the mortgage calculator tool
mortgage_agent = Agent(
    name="MortgageAdvisor",
    instructions=("You are a mortgage assistant"),
    tools=[calculate_mortgage],
    tool_use_behavior="stop_on_first_tool",
    model_settings=ModelSettings(
        tool_choice="required"
    )
)
```

Running this will bypass any further reasoning or rewriting by the LLM. Instead, the agent will directly return the result produced by the tool as the final output. We may want to do this to guarantee deterministic and auditable responses, especially in scenarios where accuracy is critical, such as a mortgage application. It also improves performance by reducing the number of LLM calls in the loop.

This example shows a clear benefit of having tools: the calculation is precise and the agent does not have to rely on its trained knowledge (which may make – and is, in fact, infamous for making – arithmetic mistakes).

External API call tool

The next custom tool we will make uses an external API call. APIs are connectors to different programs and resources. The Gmail API enables you to read your emails, send an email, and view calendar invites. The Airbnb API enables you to find Airbnb listings, make a listing, or send a message. APIs are also used to access real-time data, such as customer records, weather information, or cryptocurrency prices.

In this example, we will create a tool that will fetch the current price of Bitcoin in USD. Create a new Python script called `crypto_pricing_agent.py`, with the following code:

```
import requests
from agents import Agent, Runner, function_tool


# Create the tool
@function_tool
def get_price_of_bitcoin() -> str:
    """Get the price of Bitcoin."""
    url = "https://api.coingecko.com/api/v3/simple/price?ids=bitcoin&vs_
currencies=usd"
    response = requests.get(url)
    price = response.json()["bitcoin"]["usd"]
    return f"${price:,.2f} USD."


# Create the agent
crypto_agent = Agent(
    name="CryptoTracker",
    instructions="You are a crypto assistant. Use tools to get real-time
data.",
    tools=[get_price_of_bitcoin]
)


# Run the agent with an example prompt
result = Runner.run_sync(crypto_agent, "What's the price of Bitcoin?")
print(result.final_output)
```

In this example, we have created a Python function, get_price_of_bitcoin, that calls the *CoinGecko API* (a free public API for cryptocurrency prices) via the requests library. When the agent calls the tool, the tool calls the API, and the information received from the API is then passed back to the agent.

Running this agent will always give us the most recent price of Bitcoin, no matter the recency of the LLM's training data. At the time of writing this book, the agent's output was as follows:

```
The current price of Bitcoin is $108,538.00 USD.
```

This showcases how agents can be extended with tools that can call APIs. This is important because it means agents are not bound to the LLM's own training data or Python capabilities. Tools can act as live extensions to the model's knowledge and capabilities, allowing it to interface with external systems, services, and data sources.

Now, let's extend our tool so that it can return any cryptocurrency price, and can return the prices of more than one cryptocurrency within one call. To achieve this, we must remember that tools can take in as input Pydantic base models. Let's define the following Pydantic base model:

```python
from pydantic import BaseModel
from typing import List


class Crypto(BaseModel):
    """
    coin_ids: full name string to represent the cryptocurrency
    """
    coin_ids: List[str]
```

Next, we must update our tool to add the Pydantic base model as an input argument and make modifications to the logic to accept a list of strings as an input:

```python
# Create the tool
@function_tool
def get_crypto_prices(crypto: Crypto) -> str:
    """Get the current prices of a list of cryptocurrencies.
    Args:
        Crypto: an object with list of coin_ids (e.g., bitcoinm ethereum,
    litecoin, etc.)
    """

    ids = ",".join(crypto.coin_ids)
```

```
    url = f"https://api.coingecko.com/api/v3/simple/price?ids={ids}&vs_
currencies=usd"
    response = requests.get(url)
    data = response.json()
    return data


# Create the agent
crypto_agent = Agent(
    name="CryptoTracker",
    instructions="You are a crypto assistant. Use tools to get real-time
data. When getting cryptocurrency prices, call the tool only once for all
requests.",
    tools=[get_crypto_prices]
)
```

With this structure in place, the LLM sees a clear schema: a single object with a required field, coin_ids, which must be a list of strings. The SDK will automatically validate that the data passed matches this structure. For example, if we run the script now after modifying the prompt to be *"What's the price of Bitcoin and Ethereum?"*, it responds with the following:

```
"The current price of Bitcoin is $108,575, and the price of Ethereum is
$2,534.56"
```

This is because it is able to pass a list of cryptocurrency strings as input into the Python function.

Note

We included an additional sentence in the agent instructions: "When getting cryptocurrency prices, call the tool only once for all requests." We did this to guide the LLM to batch multiple coin price queries into a single tool call. Without this prompt engineering, the agent may try to call the tool separately for each coin, resulting in redundant API calls.

We can also look at the **Traces** window to confirm this:

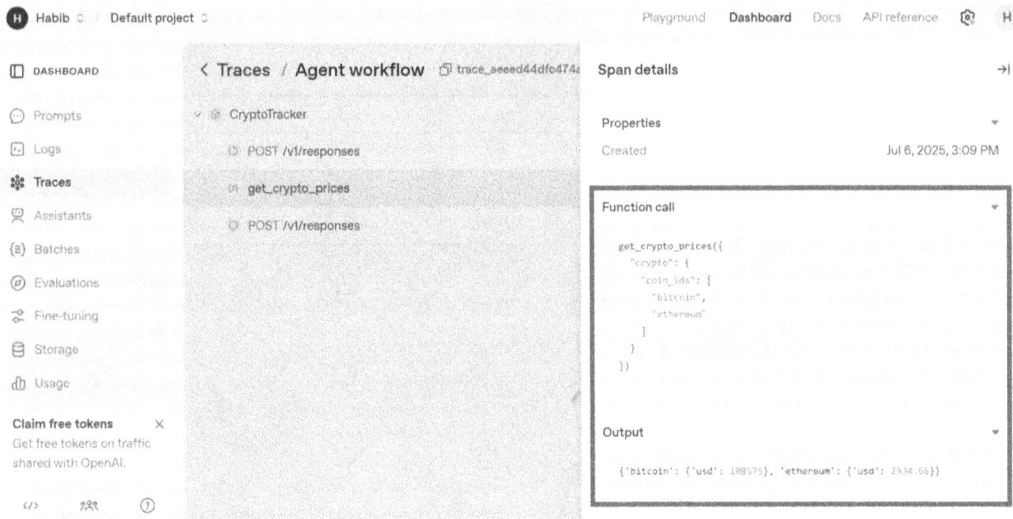

Figure 4.1: Function call within Traces

By using tools such as these, the agent can access real-time information that falls outside the model's training data. This effectively extends the model's capabilities, giving it dynamic awareness of the live environment.

Database query tool

In the previous examples, we demonstrated how tools can handle precise computation and real-time API access. Another powerful use case is enabling agents to query structured internal data sources (such as databases) without hardcoding queries or relying on the model to write raw SQL. Instead, we can encapsulate the logic in a tool that connects with a database. This is similar to an API call.

Let's build a simple agent that queries a customer support database to retrieve recent support tickets. To do this, we will simulate a database with a Python dictionary to avoid requiring a real database connection, but the same structure would apply when connecting to a live database.

Create a new script called `database_query.py` and run the following code:

```
from agents import Agent, Runner, function_tool
from pydantic import BaseModel
from typing import List

# create a simulated database
```

```python
TICKETS_DB = {
    "henry@gmail.com": [
        {"id": "TCKT-001", "issue": "Login not working",
            "status": "resolved"},
        {"id": "TCKT-002", "issue": "Password reset failed",
            "status": "open"},
    ],
    "tom@gmail.com": [
        {"id": "TCKT-003", "issue": "Billing error",
            "status": "in progress"},
    ]
}


# define Pydantic model
class CustomerQuery(BaseModel):
    email: str


# define the tool that does a database query
@function_tool
def get_customer_tickets(query: CustomerQuery) -> str:
    """Retrieve recent support tickets for a customer based on email."""
    tickets = TICKETS_DB.get(query.email.lower())
    if not tickets:
        return f"No tickets found for {query.email}."
    response = "\n".join(
        [f"ID: {t['id']}, Issue: {t['issue']}, Status: {t['status']}"
            for t in tickets]
    )
    return f"Tickets for {query.email}:\n{response}"


# create the agent
support_agent = Agent(
    name="SupportHelper",
    instructions="You are a customer support agent. Use tools to fetch
user support history when asked about their tickets.",
    tools=[get_customer_tickets]
)


# Run the agent
```

```
result = Runner.run_sync(support_agent, "Can you show me the ticket
history for henry@gmail.com?")
print(result.final_output)
```

In this example, we defined a `CustomerQuery` Pydantic model that enforces the expected input structure. The `get_customer_tickets` function uses this input to look up tickets in a mocked dictionary that simulates a support database.

When the agent receives a prompt such as *"Can you show me the ticket history for henry@gmail. com?"*, it correctly extracts the email, passes it to the tool, and returns a well-formatted summary of tickets:

```
Here is the ticket history for henry@gmail.com:

1. **ID:** TCKT-001
   - **Issue:** Login not working
   - **Status:** Resolved

2. **ID:** TCKT-002
   - **Issue:** Password reset failed
   - **Status:** Open
```

This pattern is applicable for many enterprise use cases, such as looking up customer data, querying inventory databases, and so on.

Chained tool calls

The LLM behind the agent can not only determine whether to use a tool and when, but also the order in which to call tools if needed. This is especially useful in cases where the agent has to perform a multi-step operation and use the outputs of the first tool call as an input to the second tool call. The agent can also call the same tool several times, if needed.

For example, following our customer service theme, we have a tool called `get_customer_orders` (which retrieves all orders for a specific customer ID) and another tool called `get_order_information` (which retrieves the status of an order ID). Create a new Python script called `tool_chaining.py`, with the following code:

```python
# Required imports
from typing import List
from pydantic import BaseModel
from agents import Agent, Runner, function_tool
```

```python
# Define the first tool to get all orders for a given customer
@function_tool
def get_customer_orders(customer_id: str) -> str:
    """

    Retrieve all order IDs associated with a given customer ID.
    Args:
        customer_id: the customer ID
    """

    # Dummy implementation
    if customer_id == "CUST123":
        return ["ORD001", "ORD002", "ORD003"]


# Define the second tool to get status of a specific order
@function_tool
def get_order_information(order_id: str) -> str:
    """

    Fetch detailed information about a specific order.
    """

    # Dummy implementation
    status_map = {
        "ORD001": "Shipped",
        "ORD002": "Processing",
        "ORD003": "Delivered"
    }
    return f"Order {order_id} is currently {status_map.get(order_id,
'Unknown')}."


# Define the agent
customer_service_agent = Agent(
    name="CustomerSupportAgent",
    instructions="You are a customer service assistant.",
    tools=[get_customer_orders, get_order_information]
)


# Run the agent
result = Runner.run_sync(customer_service_agent, "Please check the status
of my orders? My customer ID is CUST123.")
print(result.final_output)
```

In this example, the agent is capable of chaining multiple tool calls. When asked for the status of a customer's orders, it first calls get_customer_orders with the provided customer ID, receives a list of order IDs, and then sequentially calls get_order_information for each of those IDs. This multi-step reasoning is entirely driven by the LLM's control logic framework, and it dynamically determines the chaining sequence based on the intermediate tool outputs. We can even verify this series of operations with the **Traces** module:

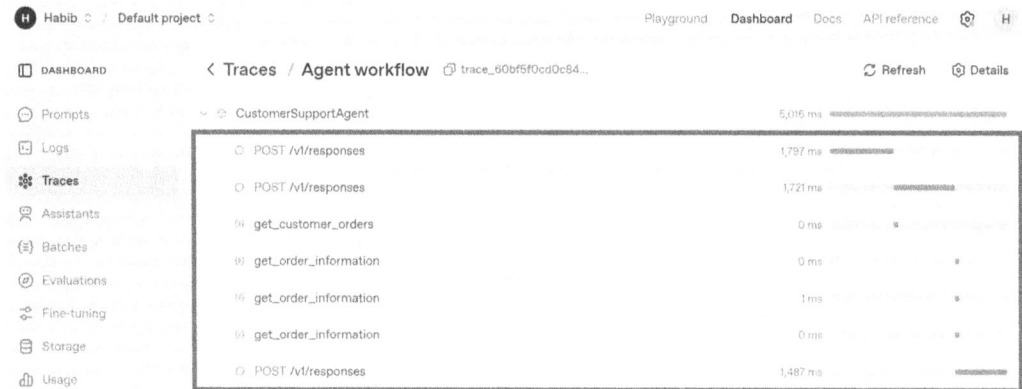

Figure 4.2: List of traces within the Traces module

This demonstrates the agent's ability for multi-step reasoning across tools and chaining them into subsequent calls. You don't have to hardcode the workflow; the SDK orchestrates it for you.

OpenAI hosted tools

The benefit of using the SDK that is built by OpenAI is that it comes with easy access to a set of powerful and pre-built tools. These tools require minimal setup; they are fully managed and hosted on OpenAI's servers (similar to how the LLM is also hosted on OpenAI's servers). They are also constantly updated, which means you can leverage the latest and greatest technology when calling these tools.

> **Note**
>
> OpenAI-hosted tools incur token costs, just like model LLM calls. When a model calls one of these tools, the tool call and any data passed between the model and tool are billed as tokens.

Hosted tools are included as part of OpenAI's *Responses API* framework. When you specify hosted tools via the Agents SDK, the model is aware of those tools and can call them as functions in the same way as custom Python functions. The hosted tools that are available are summarized in the following table:

Hosted tool	What it does
WebSearchTool	Performs real-time searches on the web for up-to-date information
FileSearchTool	Performs file information search and retrieval through vector stores
ImageGenerationTool	Generates images
CodeInterpreterTool	Runs code in a sandboxed Python execution environment
ComputerTool	Opens a computer/browser instance and performs tasks
LocalShellTool	Executes shell commands on your local machine

Table 4.1: OpenAI-hosted tools and their usages

Note

Hosted tools require models from OpenAI (e.g., GPT-4 or later). These models are aware of the tools and so can call them. Unfortunately, you cannot use your own models with these OpenAI-hosted tools.

On a general note, it rarely makes sense to create a custom tool for a use case that is already covered in the OpenAI-hosted tool. For example, WebSearchTool performs excellently to search and query web pages, so it would not make sense to "re-create the wheel" and create our own Python function to do that. Using these tools is as simple as importing a class, instantiating it, defining a set of inputs, and passing it to the agent.

We will go through each OpenAI-hosted tool and discuss its use case, its parameters, and create an agent that leverages the tool.

WebSearchTool

WebSearchTool enables the agent to perform web searches. It is one of the easiest tools to implement. In fact, most of my enterprise agents have this tool in case the user asks for information that the agent has not been trained on. This tool is best used when dealing with queries about recent developments, time-sensitive facts, or anything requiring real-time data.

The tool takes two optional inputs:

- user_location: Returns search results for a specific location. You can specify a location in the UserLocation format, which is just a dictionary with the type, country, city, and region keys. This is useful if you have queries where the answer changes based on location, such as, "Where's the best place to get bubble tea?".

- search_context_size: Specifies how much information to retrieve per website (and how many websites to search). You can either specify "low," "medium," or "high." The default option is "medium."

Let's go ahead and start using this tool. We will create an agent that performs simple web search queries for us. Start by creating a new Python file called web_search_tool.py and copy in the following code:

```python
from agents import Agent, Runner, WebSearchTool

# Instantiate the tool
websearchtool = WebSearchTool()

# Create an agent
agent = Agent(
    name="WebTool",
    instructions="You are an AI agent that answers web questions. Answer
in one sentence.",
    tools=[websearchtool]
)

result = Runner.run_sync(agent, "Who won the 2025 Stanley Cup?")
print(result.final_output)
```

Running this gives us the following output:

```
The Florida Panthers won the 2025 Stanley Cup, defeating the Edmonton
Oilers in six games to secure their second consecutive championship.
([reuters.com](https://www.reuters.com/sports/florida-panthers-beat-
edmonton-oilers-game-6-win-second-straight-stanley-cup-2025-06-18/?utm_
source=openai))
```

In this example, the agent has access to a tool that can search the internet for answers. When the tool is called, OpenAI will perform a web search for that query, read the results (possibly news articles or even Wikipedia pages), and return a text snippet with relevant info. The agent then takes that and formulates an answer to the user.

If we run the same agent without WebSearchTool, it's not able to provide an answer, as this piece of information is not in its training data: *I'm unable to provide real-time information or details about events occurring in 2025.*

Next, we will add a location parameter to the WebSearchTool class. Let's adjust our agent to search for information, assuming they are in Toronto, Canada, and ask for the top three Italian restaurants:

```python
from agents import Agent, Runner, WebSearchTool

# Instantiate the tool
websearchtool = WebSearchTool(user_location={
            "type": "approximate",
            "country": "CA",
            "city": "Toronto",
            "region": "Ontario",
        })

# Create an agent
agent = Agent(
    name="WebTool",
    instructions="You are an AI agent that answers web questions. Answer
in one sentence.",
    tools=[websearchtool]
)

result = Runner.run_sync(agent, "What are the top 3 Italian restaurants?")
print(result.final_output)
```

Here's the output:

```
## Output
Based on recent accolades and reviews, the top three Italian restaurants
in Toronto are:

1. **Don Alfonso 1890**: Located on the 38th floor of The Westin Harbour
Castle, this restaurant has retained its Michelin star since 2022 and was
named the Best Italian Restaurant in the World (outside of Italy) by 50
Top Italy in 2022. ([en.wikipedia.org](https://en.wikipedia.org/wiki/Don_
Alfonso_1890?utm_source=openai))
```

```
2. **Osteria Giulia**: Situated in Yorkville, Osteria Giulia has held a
Michelin star since 2022 and was ranked number 17 in Canada's 100 Best
Restaurants list in 2024. ([en.wikipedia.org](https://en.wikipedia.org/
wiki/Osteria_Giulia?utm_source=openai))

3. **DaNico**: Also Michelin-starred, DaNico was ranked 59th in Canada's
100 Best Restaurants list in 2025. ([en.wikipedia.org](https://
en.wikipedia.org/wiki/DaNico?utm_source=openai))
```

In this way, we have created a sophisticated internet-based agent in fewer than 15 lines of code. There is no other SDK where you can get so much for so little.

FileSearchTool

`FileSearchTool` enables an agent to query a vector store of documents for relevant information. This is effectively OpenAI's hosted solution for **retrieval-augmented generation (RAG)**. In this chapter, we will only demonstrate how to use the tool, but will deep dive much further into RAG and agent knowledge management in future chapters.

The most common use case for this tool is to query internal knowledge bases or a large corpus of text. This tool enables you to quickly spin up an agent that can answer questions from a set of documents. It can even reference the exact documents/chunks it used to derive the answer.

To use this tool, you must first upload your files to the OpenAI platform and create a vector store. A **vector store** is a special type of database that stores semantic embeddings of your documents. **Semantic embeddings** are numerical representations of text that capture its meaning, rather than just its exact words.

This enables the LLM to retrieve the most relevant pieces of text based on the meaning of a user's query, rather than relying on exact keyword matches. Once your files are uploaded, OpenAI automatically handles the embedding behind the scenes, enabling fast and accurate retrieval through RAG. This process happens outside the SDK itself, typically through the platform UI manually or through the regular OpenAI API spec.

Follow these steps to create a vector store:

1. Go to the OpenAI platform at `https://platform.openai.com/` and log in. Ensure you log in using the same account you used when generating the API key.

2. Select **Dashboard** from the top-right, then select **Storage**, and then toggle to **Vector stores**.

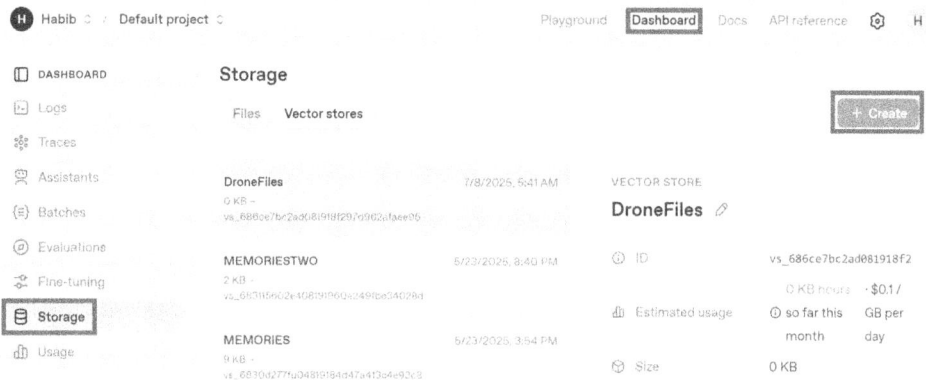

Figure 4.3: Storage page within OpenAI dashboard

3. Select **Create** to create a new vector store. Type in a vector store name such as `DroneFiles`.

4. Scroll down and add a file to the vector store by selecting **+ Add files**.

5. Upload the `XdroneManual.pdf` file (which can be found in the repository under *Chapter 4*). Give it the name `DroneManual.pdf` and select `user_data` for **Purpose**. Then, select **Attach**.

6. The PDF we uploaded has now been successfully added to our new vector store, and all the related operations to enable RAG (such as producing embeddings, etc.) are complete. Again, the subsequent chapter will cover this in much more detail.

7. Copy and save the vector store ID for the new vector store that you just created.

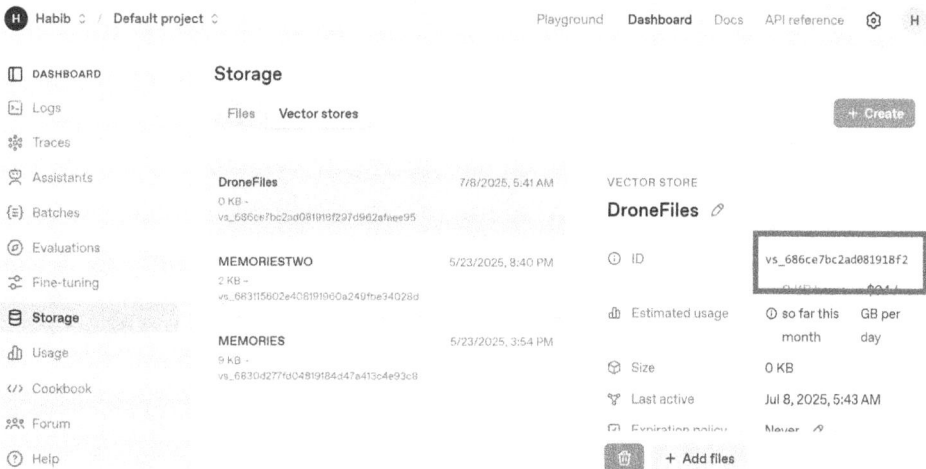

Figure 4.4: Vector store ID within OpenAI dashboard

Now that we have a vector store ID, we can use it as an input to the `FileSearchTool` class. In fact, the tool takes in the following key inputs:

- `vector_store_ids`: This is a required input that represents the list of vector store IDs to search through when calling this tool. Note that the OpenAI API key that you have provided to the Agents SDK must point to the same account that has access to the vector store (otherwise, you will run into permission errors).

- `max_num_results`: An integer that represents the number of search results to return.

- `include_search_results`: A boolean that determines whether to include the full text of the search results in the tool output.

We will create an agent that leverages the new vector store we have just created. Let's start by creating a new Python file called `file_search_tool.py` and copy in the following code:

```python
from agents import Agent, Runner, FileSearchTool

# Instantiate the tool
filesearchtool = FileSearchTool(
    vector_store_ids=['vs_686ce7bc2ad081918f297d962afaee95']
) # replace with your own vector store ID

# Create an agent
agent = Agent(
    name="WebTool",
    instructions="You are an AI agent that answers questions from the
listed vector stores. Answer in one sentence.",
    tools=[filesearchtool]
)

result = Runner.run_sync(agent, "How high can you fly this drone?")
print(result.final_output)
```

Running this script will give us the following answer, which the agent was able to pull from the manual that we uploaded:

```
## Output
The drone can be flown up to a maximum altitude of 60 feet (20 meters).
```

2.2 Flight Safety

> • Maximum Altitude: Do not fly the drone above 60 feet (20 meters) to avoid potential conflicts with manned aircraft.

In this way, `FileSearchTool` enables an agent to ground its responses in written material that it's been provided. Rather than relying solely on the LLM's prior training, the agent is able to fetch relevant information from your own internal documents.

ImageGenerationTool

`ImageGenerationTool` enables the agent to create images based on text prompts. This typically hooks into OpenAI's image generation service. After integrating this tool, the agent can respond to prompts such as "Generate an image of an elephant." Typically, the most common use case is generating visuals (product mockups, demos, designs, etc.).

In terms of inputs, the `ImageGenerationTool` class takes an `ImageGeneration` object as a `tool_config` argument, where you can specify size, quality, format, compression, and the background of your image. You must specify the type, which at this point is always equal to `image_generation`.

Let's build an agent that can generate images. Create a new Python file called `image_generation_tool.py` and copy in the following code:

```python
from agents import Agent, Runner, ImageGenerationTool
from agents.tool import ImageGeneration

# Instantiate the tool
tool_config = ImageGeneration(
    type="image_generation",
)
imagetool = ImageGenerationTool(tool_config=tool_config)

# Create an agent
agent = Agent(
    name="ImageTool",
    instructions="You are an AI agent that generates images.",
    tools=[imagetool]
)
```

```
result = Runner.run_sync(agent, "Generate an image of an elephant.")
print(result.final_output)
```

Running this script gives a URL to the following image:

Figure 4.5: Output generated after running the preceding code

> **Note**
>
> You may encounter a `PermissionDeniedError` object. If this occurs, follow the instructions to verify your organization within the OpenAI platform settings.

In this tool, OpenAI's servers will generate an image for that prompt and return a URL of where the image is hosted. You can then have a workflow that takes that image, saves it somewhere, or sends it to someone. This tool is great for creative or visual tasks. For instance, an agent could dynamically create data visualizations (by generating a chart image from a description) or just illustrate responses.

> **Note**
>
> Image generation is prone to hallucinations, much more than text output. The images generated may not be accurate or even logically consistent with the input prompt.

CodeInterpreterTool

CodeInterpreterTool enables the agent to write and execute Python code in a sandboxed environment. The tool is extremely useful for any data analysis or computation task. We've discussed before how mathematical computations should be performed by tools (not LLMs due to the risk of hallucinations), and we previously did that by building a custom Python function that computed monthly mortgage payments. CodeInterpreterTool takes this one step further: instead of needing to define the actual formula for mortgage payments, this tool can derive its own given a simple prompt, and then can execute that code.

This tool executes code in a sandboxed environment. As a result, the tool requires a container object to be initialized prior to use. It can either be created automatically (where the tool creates its own container at runtime) or explicitly (where you create a container using the OpenAI endpoint and then pass the container ID). In this case, for simplicity, we will choose the auto option.

Let's jump right into an example. Create a new file called code_interpreter_tool.py and run the following code:

```
from agents import Agent, Runner, CodeInterpreterTool
from agents.tool import CodeInterpreter

# Instantiate the tool
tool_config = CodeInterpreter(
    container={"type":"auto"},
    type="code_interpreter"
)
codetool = CodeInterpreterTool(tool_config=tool_config)

# Create an agent
agent = Agent(
    name="CodeTool",
    instructions="You are an AI agent that writes and runs Python code to
answer questions.",
```

```
    tools=[codetool]
)


result = Runner.run_sync(agent, "What is my monthly payment for a $800,000
mortgage at 6% for 30 years?")
print(result.final_output)
```

Running this code gives the following output:

```
The monthly payment for an $800,000 mortgage at 6% interest over 30 years
is approximately $4,796.40.
```

To derive the answer, the agent called `CodeInterpreterTool` and wrote the Python code to calculate the monthly mortgage payment given the inputs we provided. It then ran the code in a container environment, calculated the answer, and then passed the answer back to the LLM to produce a final output.

In fact, we can verify this by looking at the **Traces** module:

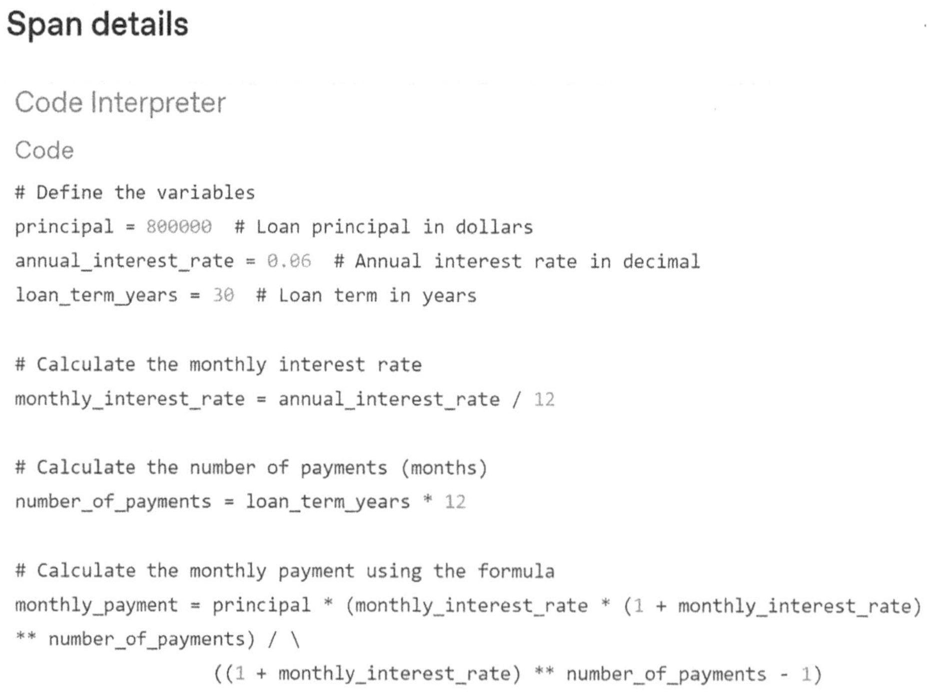

Span details

Code Interpreter

Code

```
# Define the variables
principal = 800000  # Loan principal in dollars
annual_interest_rate = 0.06  # Annual interest rate in decimal
loan_term_years = 30  # Loan term in years


# Calculate the monthly interest rate
monthly_interest_rate = annual_interest_rate / 12


# Calculate the number of payments (months)
number_of_payments = loan_term_years * 12


# Calculate the monthly payment using the formula
monthly_payment = principal * (monthly_interest_rate * (1 + monthly_interest_rate)
** number_of_payments) / \
                  ((1 + monthly_interest_rate) ** number_of_payments - 1)
```

Figure 4.6: Code Interpreter output within the Traces module

Note

There are inherent restrictions to what code can be executed in the container, such as quotas on processing, which Python libraries can be installed, and so on. To see a full list, go to `https://platform.openai.com/docs/guides/tools-code-interpreter`.

`CodeInterpreterTool` enables the agent to handle tasks that involve calculation, data crunching, or producing outputs such as charts, which pure LLMs might struggle with or be slow at. It's like giving the agent a smart junior data analyst.

With these predefined hosted tools, you can build sophisticated agents that can browse the web, search through files, generate images, and run code with just a few lines of code. There's nothing stopping you from adding multiple tools to one agent.

In this section, we explored the suite of OpenAI-hosted tools available through the Agents SDK, including `WebSearchTool`, `FileSearchTool`, `ImageGenerationTool`, and `CodeInterpreterTool`. These tools dramatically extend the capabilities of your agents, enabling them to access real-time information, retrieve knowledge from documents, generate images, and perform advanced computations – and all of that with minimal setup. Understanding how to integrate and configure these hosted tools is essential for building powerful, production-ready agents. In the next section, we'll shift our focus to agent-as-tools, where you will learn how to define agents as tools.

Agents as tools

One of the most powerful architectural patterns in the Agents SDK is the ability to use an *entire agent as a tool for another agent*. This is known as the **agent-as-tool pattern**, and it enables agents to work together in a hierarchical organization fashion. Typically, you have one agent that controls the workflow (often called the **orchestrator**) and a set of agents that are called to fulfill certain tasks (often called the **workers**).

Worker agents function as modular components, each with its own system prompts, reasoning process, and even tools. From the orchestrator's perspective, they are invoked like any other traditional tool. It would be the same if the orchestrator is calling a Python custom tool, an OpenAI-hosted tool, or an agent.

Handoff versus agent-as-tool patterns

Note that the agent-as-tool pattern is fundamentally different from **handoffs**, which we will cover in detail in a later chapter. In the handoff pattern, one agent fully delegates control to another agent, as shown in *Figure 4.7*. Once the handoff occurs, the second agent takes over the task or conversation completely until the task is complete or it chooses to hand control back:

Figure 4.7: Agent-as-tool pattern

In the agent-as-tool pattern, the orchestrating agent retains full control of the overall workflow and simply calls another agent to handle a specific subtask, as shown in *Figure 4.8*:

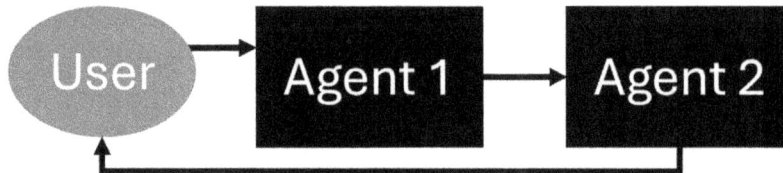

Figure 4.8: Handoff pattern

A good example is when you call a customer service line. The customer service manager can either transfer you to another department to continue the conversation (this would be the handoff pattern) or put you on hold while they ask for/gather necessary information from their coworkers, and then get back on the phone with you when they are done (this would be the agent-as-tool pattern).

Both orchestration patterns are fully supported in the SDK and can be combined for more complex workflows. The key trade-off that we need to consider is control: handoff offers modular autonomy, while agent-as-tool favors a more centralized coordination.

Typically, you choose the handoff pattern in the following situations:

- It fits well into another agent's domain
- The worker agent should own the entire user interaction for that segment
- Tight oversight of the intermediate steps is not needed

By contrast, you should choose the agent-as-tool pattern in the following situations:

- Maintaining central control of the logic and conversation is important
- Input from multiple workers needs to be synthesized into one answer
- Maximum visibility/oversight is needed

Both approaches have their own strengths and drawbacks, and choosing the right one depends on how much control, modularity, and visibility your agent workflow requires.

Functionality

The SDK enables you to convert any agent into a tool using the as_tool() function, which returns a FunctionTool object that can be added to an existing agent's tool argument. When calling as_tool(), you need to specify the name and description, similar to earlier in this chapter when we were building custom tool functions. The name and description are used by the orchestrator agent to determine whether that tool should be called (and so, making the name and description descriptive is very important).

Let's go through an example. Create a new Python script called agents_as_tool.py and run the following code:

```python
from agents import Agent, Runner, WebSearchTool, CodeInterpreterTool
from agents.tool import CodeInterpreter

# Instantiate the tool
websearchtool = WebSearchTool()

# Create a worker agent
location_agent = Agent(
    name="LocationAgent",
    instructions="You are an AI agent that searches the web and gets
latitude and longitude numbers for a particular city.",
    tools=[websearchtool]
)

# Instantiate the tool
tool_config = CodeInterpreter(
    container={"type":"auto"},
    type="code_interpreter"
)
```

```
codetool = CodeInterpreterTool(tool_config=tool_config)

# Create another worker agent
distance_calculator_agent = Agent(
    name="DistanceCalculatorAgent",
    instructions="You are an AI agent that writes and runs Python code to
calculate the distance in KM between two latitude/longitude points.",
    tools=[codetool]
)

# Create the orchestrator agent
agent = Agent(
    name="Agent",
    instructions="You are an AI agent that calculates the distance between
two locations. Use the Location Agent to get the latitude / longitude. Use
the Distance Calculator agent to calculate the distance.",
    tools=[
        location_agent.as_tool(
            tool_name="LocationAgent",
            tool_description="Returns the latitude and longitude for a
particular location"
        ),
        distance_calculator_agent.as_tool(
            tool_name="DistanceCalculatorAgent",
            tool_description="Calculates the distance between two
latitude/longitude points"
        )]
)

result = Runner.run_sync(agent, "What's the straight-line distance between
Toronto and Vancouver?")
print(result.final_output)
```

Let's walk through this code step by step.

We first create two agents:

- LocationAgent, whose sole purpose is to retrieve latitude and longitude values for a given city, using WebSearchTool

- DistanceCalculatorAgent, which is equipped with CodeInterpreterTool, allowing it to write and execute Python code to compute distances between two coordinate pairs

The important part comes when we call .as_tool() on each of these agents. This wraps each agent as a callable tool, assigning it a tool_name argument and tool_description argument so that the orchestrator agent can reason about when and how to call it. These names and descriptions play a key role in the LLM's ability to select the right worker agent for a given task, so they should be specific and informative.

Finally, we create an orchestrator agent. Its instructions guide it to use the worker agent (now wrapped as tools) to complete a larger goal: calculating the distance between two cities. When we run this agent with the input query, *What's the straight-line distance between Toronto and Vancouver?*, the system chains the tool calls behind the scenes. First, LocationAgent is invoked twice to fetch coordinates for each city. Then, DistanceCalculatorAgent processes those coordinates to compute the final result.

This final_output object contains the correct answer:

```
The straight-line distance between Toronto and Vancouver is approximately
3363.64 kilometers.
```

We can also see in the **Traces** module that it was derived by using the location agent as a tool twice (once for Toronto and once for Vancouver), and then using the distance calculator agent:

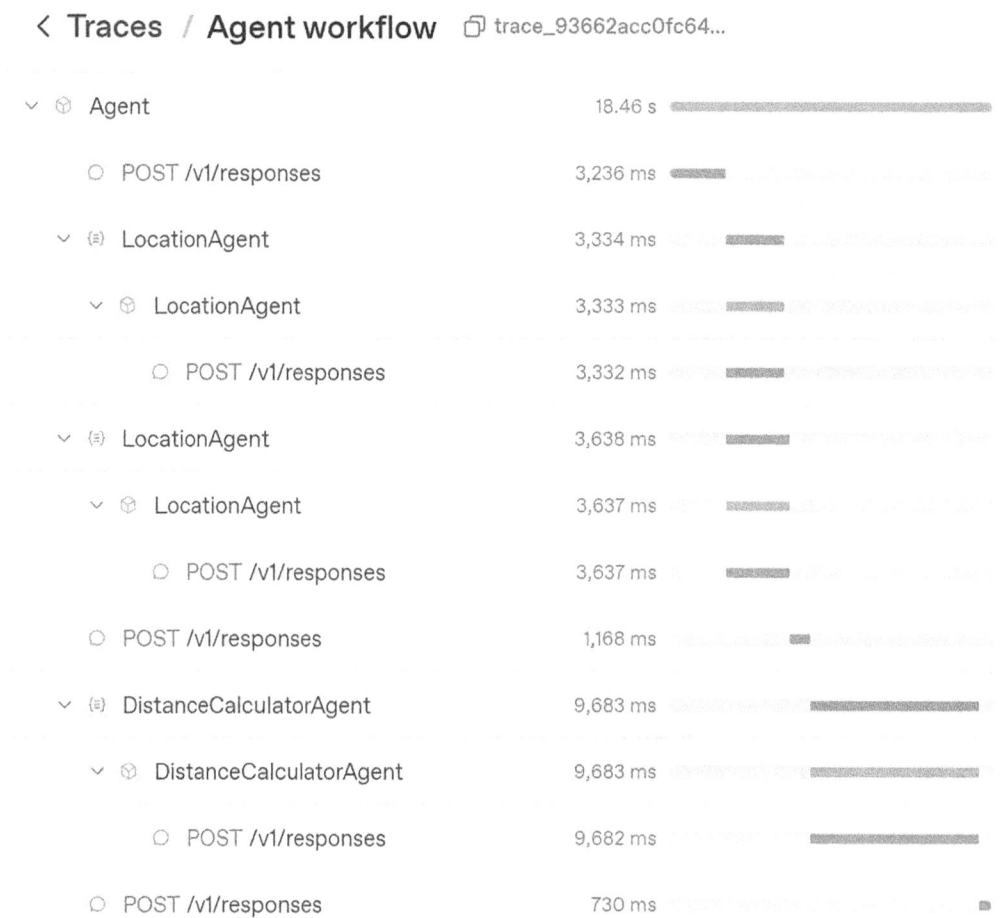

< Traces / **Agent workflow**   ⬚ trace_93662acc0fc64...

⌄ ⬡ Agent	18.46 s	
○ POST /v1/responses	3,236 ms	
⌄ ⊟ LocationAgent	3,334 ms	
⌄ ⬡ LocationAgent	3,333 ms	
○ POST /v1/responses	3,332 ms	
⌄ ⊟ LocationAgent	3,638 ms	
⌄ ⬡ LocationAgent	3,637 ms	
○ POST /v1/responses	3,637 ms	
○ POST /v1/responses	1,168 ms	
⌄ ⊟ DistanceCalculatorAgent	9,683 ms	
⌄ ⬡ DistanceCalculatorAgent	9,683 ms	
○ POST /v1/responses	9,682 ms	
○ POST /v1/responses	730 ms	

Figure 4.9: Workflow trace in the Traces module

In conclusion, the agent-as-tool pattern enables you to build composable, hierarchical systems where specialized agents tackle distinct subtasks, all coordinated by a central orchestrator. This model encourages modularity, reusability, and better oversight over complex workflows.

Now that we've explored how to compose agents using the "agent-as-tool" pattern, let's shift focus to a broader interoperability challenge: how agents and tools can communicate across frameworks using a shared standard. This is where the **Model Context Protocol (MCP)** comes into play.

MCP

Agentic AI development is still new but is significantly gaining in popularity. As developers started to build more agents and tools, there was no standardized way to connect tools to agents; every SDK did it differently. We are already familiar with how the Agents SDK connects tools to agents, but this differs significantly from other frameworks such as LangGraph or CrewAI. This was difficult – if you built an amazing tool in the Agents SDK, it was difficult to port it to other frameworks. Additionally, it did not make sense to develop a tool that did X, if someone else had already created a tool that did X for another framework.

As a result, a standard protocol was needed to define the connection between tools and agents that could apply to all SDKs, and MCP was born.

What is MCP?

MCP is a standardized protocol that defines how an AI agent can discover and call tools hosted locally or on external servers. Think of MCP as a universal adapter or a USB-C port for AI agents and their tools. Following this standard enables a tool provider to develop an MCP server that can plug into any MCP-compatible host (such as an agent built with the Agents SDK), ensuring interoperability across different models and frameworks.

MCP's main strength lies in fostering a plug-and-play ecosystem for tools. A developer can implement an MCP server for their database once, and it becomes instantly compatible with agents from OpenAI, Anthropic, or any other provider that supports the protocol. No additional integration is required.

> **Note**
>
> MCP is an expansive topic. A whole book could be written on just MCP. While we will show how to connect to an MCP server using the Agents SDK, we won't be covering the full protocol in depth. That is beyond the scope of this book.

Adding an MCP server as a tool

The Agents SDK makes it easy to consume tools from an MCP server. You simply instantiate a connection to the server and pass it to your agent as a tool. The Agents SDK will automatically handle the connection, query the server for its available tools, and make them available to the agent.

Note

When working with external MCP servers, it's important to consider the security and privacy implications. Authentication should be enforced to ensure that only authorized agents can access the tools provided, and rate limiting can help protect both your system and the MCP server from misuse or accidental overload. You should also be mindful of data exposure (i.e., sending sensitive inputs or receiving unfiltered outputs from external MCP tools can introduce risks if proper safeguards aren't in place).

Let's go through an example. Create a new Python script called mcp_tool.py and run the following code:

```python
from agents import Agent, Runner, HostedMCPTool
from agents.tool import Mcp

# Create the tool
tool_config = Mcp(
        server_label="CryptocurrencyPriceFetcher",
        server_url="https://mcp.api.coingecko.com/sse",
        type="mcp",
        require_approval="never"
    )
mcp_tool = HostedMCPTool(tool_config=tool_config)

# Create the agent
agent = Agent(
    name="Crypto Agent",
    instructions="You are an AI agent that returns crypto prices.",
    tools=[mcp_tool]
)

result = Runner.run_sync(agent, "What's the price of bitcoin?")
print(result.final_output)
```

In the code, instead of creating our own tool that makes an API call and returns the latest Bitcoin price, we are instead leveraging the MCP server built by Coin Gecko that contains all the tools that we would ever need. We don't need to create a custom function; instead, we just leverage the one that Coin Gecko has already created.

Let's break it down. The `Mcp` configuration specifies the label for the tool, the server's URL, the tool type ("mcp"), and a `require_approval` setting that tells the agent whether to prompt for human approval before using the tool. In this example, we've set `require_approval` to "never", meaning the agent can call the tool autonomously. The `server_url` argument is the endpoint of the MCP server for Coin Gecko, which you can find on their website. This URL should point to a valid MCP-compliant endpoint that serves tool definitions in real time.

When we define an agent, we add the MCP tool to its list of tool arguments. Since the MCP server may contain multiple tools technically (e.g., one for Bitcoin prices, another for Ethereum, etc.), the agent can reason over the available options and select the right tool for the task.

When we run the agent, behind the scenes, the agent sends the user's message to the LLM, and the LLM evaluates the message and decides to call the tool from the MCP server. The SDK handles calling the tool with the right arguments and passing the result back to the LLM, which then returns a final answer.

> **Note**
>
> The actual tool logic is not executed on your local machine. The request is sent to the MCP server, which hosts and runs the tool remotely. No processing happens on your machine, similar to when you make an API call.

In short, integrating MCP with the Agents SDK unlocks powerful new capabilities by enabling agents to seamlessly access a standardized ecosystem of external tools and services.

Summary

In this chapter, we gave agents the ability to perform real work by connecting them to tools (custom, hosted, agents, and external servers). We started with custom Python tools using @ `function_tool`, showing how to register and describe tools so the agent can understand and use them. We explored how we can impact tool decision logic through the `tool_choice` and `tool_use_behavior` parameters.

We then built several real-world tools and agents, using four different paradigms: custom tools via Python functions, hosted tools via OpenAI modules, agents as tools, and external server tools via MCP.

With these patterns in place, you now have everything you need to build agents that not only understand and reason, but also take action, connect to live systems, and integrate seamlessly with external services.

In the next chapter, we'll explore how to manage agent knowledge and memory.

Subscribe for a free eBook

New frameworks, evolving architectures, research drops, production breakdowns—*AI_Distilled* filters the noise into a weekly briefing for engineers and researchers working hands-on with LLMs and GenAI systems. Subscribe now and receive a free eBook, along with weekly insights that help you stay focused and informed.

Subscribe at `https://packt.link/80z6Y` or scan the QR code below.

5

Memory and Knowledge

Now that our agents can take action using tools, it's time to make them more intelligent in a more human-like way by giving them **memory and knowledge**. In this chapter, we will explore how to move beyond stateless interactions and give agents the ability to remember past messages, retain important facts, and reference external information sources when generating responses. This is a major leap forward in making agents more conversational, helpful, and context-aware.

Here is what you will learn as part of this chapter:

- **Short-term memory**: Learn how to track conversation history using message lists, loops, and the `Sessions` class to build multi-turn agents that remember what was said earlier in the session
- **Long-term memory**: Persist memory across sessions using `SQLiteSession`, and go further with structured memory using function tools that store and recall key facts
- **Training knowledge**: Understand what knowledge the model already has from pretraining and how fine-tuning modifies it
- **Retrieved knowledge**: Learn how to pull in dynamic, real-time information using tools for both structured (database queries and API calls) and unstructured data (embeddings and semantic search), through a process called retrieval-augmented generation

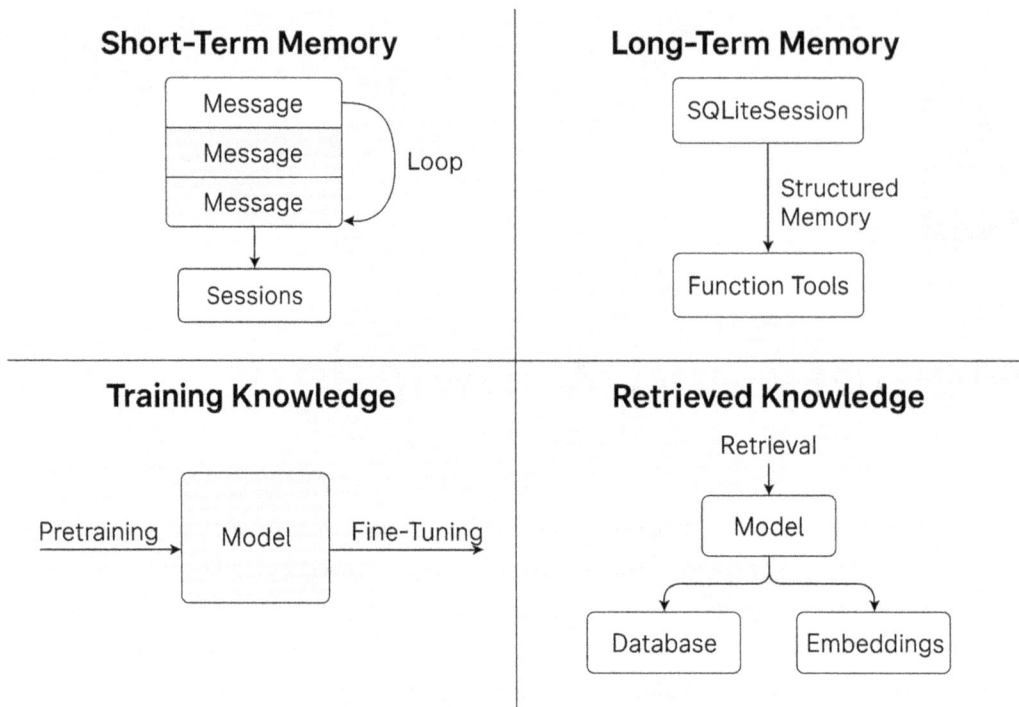

Short-Term Memory

Message
Message — Loop
Message

Sessions

Long-Term Memory

SQLiteSession

Structured Memory

Function Tools

Training Knowledge

Pretraining → Model → Fine-Tuning

Retrieved Knowledge

Retrieval

Model

Database   Embeddings

Figure 5.1: Memory and knowledge patterns

By the end of this chapter, you'll know how to make your agents smarter and be able to carry on meaningful conversations, remember preferences, and access external data sources when needed. Let's get right into it.

Technical requirements

Please follow the detailed steps in *Chapter 3* to set up your environment.

Throughout this book, practical examples and complete code from each chapter will be made available via the accompanying GitHub repository at `https://github.com/PacktPublishing/Building-Agents-with-OpenAI-Agents-SDK`.

You are encouraged to clone the repository, reuse and adapt the provided code samples, and refer to it as needed while progressing through the chapters.

Working memory

As discussed previously, **working memory** (also called **short-term memory**) is the information stored in the interaction history in the current session of the AI agent. The example we gave previously is that working memory is what enables you to ask first, *"How hot is the sun?"* and then *"How big is it?"*, and the agent can determine that *"it"* in the second request refers to the sun.

So far, all the AI agents have not passed this test; they do not have any concept of memory. In fact, all AI agents so far have been **stateless**, meaning that they do not retain any information from previous interactions. Each agent is treated as a completely new system, without any recollection of what happened before. Stateless systems are common in most computer systems. For example, most APIs serve as an independent and isolated transaction (it does not remember what you have previously asked and use that to determine their next output). **Stateful** systems are the opposite; they maintain information about previous interactions and use it to produce future output. For example, your Netflix page is stateful: it remembers what you've previously watched and recommends similar movies. Memory makes AI agents go from stateless systems to stateful systems.

How do you choose between a stateless and stateful AI agent? It depends on its purpose. AI agents that are conversational (i.e., chatbots) require multi-step input or require context within answers, and must be stateful systems. For example, a chatbot without memory would be very frustrating for the user. On the other hand, if the AI agent's purpose is simple, routine, one-shot, repetitive, and non-learning, then a stateless system is fine. Note that there is a cost to making a stateful AI agent: the overhead of managing memory, to which half of this chapter is dedicated.

Managing inputs and responses

The most fundamental way to give an agent memory is to do it manually. Recall that an agent is executed via the Runner class, which takes an input argument:

```
Runner.run_sync(agent, "How hot is the sun?")
```

The input argument can either be a string (which is what we have done so far) or it can be a list of ResponseInputItem objects. A ResponseInputItem object is a standard OpenAI specification that tracks a message. Each message has a "role" and a "content" field. If you have worked with the OpenAI API before, then this should be familiar to you. The following is an example of a ResponseInputItem object:

```
{"role": "user", "content": "How hot is the sun?"}
```

The "role" field can take three possible values:

- "system": Message that acts as the overall instruction set for the LLM
- "user": Messages that the user has submitted, which have a lower priority than the system message
- "assistant": Messages generated by the LLM

In order to provide an agent memory, we can simply add ResponseInputItem objects to a running list and pass that list to the Runner class whenever an agent is invoked. Let's put this to the test. Create a new file called memory_tracking_messages_simple.py and run the following code:

```python
from agents import Agent, Runner

# Create the agent
agent = Agent(
    name="QuestionAnswer",
    instructions="You are an AI agent that answers questions.",
)

# Create empty list (this will contain messages)
messages = []

# Initial message,
messages.append({"role": "user", "content": "How hot is the sun?"})

# Call agent
result = Runner.run_sync(agent, messages)
print(result.final_output)

# Add response to message
messages.append({"role": "assistant", "content": result.final_output})

# Add second question to message
messages.append({"role": "user", "content": "How big is it?"})

# Call agent
result = Runner.run_sync(agent, messages)
print(result.final_output)
```

💡 **Quick tip**: Enhance your coding experience with the **AI Code Explainer** and **Quick Copy** features. Open this book in the next-gen Packt Reader. Click the **Copy** button (**1**) to quickly copy code into your coding environment, or click the **Explain** button (**2**) to get the AI assistant to explain a block of code to you.

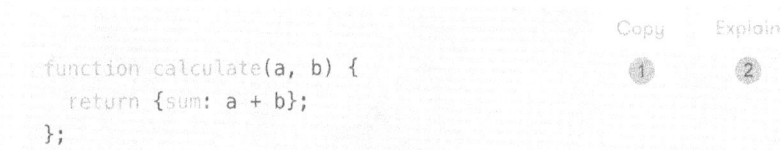

```
                                                          Copy      Explain
function calculate(a, b) {
    return {sum: a + b};                                   1          2
};
```

💡 📖 **The next-gen Packt Reader** is included for free with the purchase of this book. Scan the QR code OR visit `https://packtpub.com/unlock`, then use the search bar to find this book by name. Double-check the edition shown to make sure you get the right one.

Let's walk through this code snippet and see how the agent can remember what the user's first message is when the second message is being processed. We first created an empty list called `messages`, which will hold the full history of the interaction. We then append the first message from the user asking, "`How hot is the sun?`". This message is passed to the `Runner.run_sync()` function, and the model responds with a temperature-related answer. That answer is stored in the `result.final_output` variable, which we then add back into the message history, but this time, tagged with the "`assistant`" role, since it is the model's output.

Next, we append the user's follow-up question: "`How big is it?`". At this point, the message history has three items:

- The original user question (`How hot is the sun?`)
- The model's response (`The sun is ...`)
- The user's second question (`How big is it?`)

By passing this full list of messages into the `Runner.run_sync()` method again, the model has access to the previous conversation and can correctly determine that *it* in the second question refers to *the sun* from the initial message. Our response looks something like this:

```
## First response
The Sun's temperature varies in different regions:
1. **Core**: Around 15 million degrees Celsius (27 million degrees
Fahrenheit).
2. **Surface (photosphere)**: Approximately 5,500 degrees Celsius (9,932
degrees Fahrenheit).
3. **Corona**: Ranges from 1 to 3 million degrees Celsius (1.8 to 5.4
million degrees Fahrenheit).
The core is where nuclear fusion occurs, generating the Sun's energy,
while the corona is the outer atmosphere, surprisingly much hotter than
the surface.

## Second response
The Sun has a diameter of about 1.39 million kilometers (864,000 miles).
It is roughly 109 times the diameter of Earth and makes up over 99% of the
total mass of the solar system.
```

This pattern of maintaining and appending to a list of messages is the simplest way to create working memory for the agent. It actually mirrors how memory works in most chat interfaces and aligns directly with the message structure defined by the OpenAI API.

Chat conversations

We can actually make the preceding code snippet more dynamic so that the user messages are not hardcoded and the user is able to submit multiple messages, like an actual chat conversation.

To do this, we can use the native `input` and `while` loop functionalities from Python. Create a new file called `memory_tracking_messages_simple_loop.py` and run the following code:

```python
from agents import Agent, Runner

# Create the agent
agent = Agent(
    name="QuestionAnswer",
    instructions="You are an AI agent that answers questions.",
)
```

```
messages = []
while True:
    question = input("You: ")
    messages.append({"role": "user", "content": question})
    result = Runner.run_sync(agent, messages)
    print("Agent: ", result.final_output)
    messages.append({"role": "assistant", "content": result.final_output})
```

This program will ask you for a prompt, which you can type directly into the terminal where you're running the Python program. It will then give you the agent's response and ask you for a follow-up prompt, maintaining its message history. Now, we have converted our agent from a one-shot system to a multi-turn conversational system that can remember previous messages (assuming it's in the same session). We do this by adding a loop, where the following takes place in each iteration:

- The user is asked for a prompt
- The prompt is added as a ResponseInputItem object to a running list of ResponseInputItem objects, called messages
- The messages object is passed to the agent via the Runner class
- The model output is added as ResponseInputItem to messages

This loop continues on forever until an error is encountered or until the user force-exits the program (by clicking *Ctrl + C*). Here is an example conversation that proves that the agent has memory (as it remembered my name from the first conversation):

```
You: My name is Henry
Agent: Nice to meet you, Henry! How can I assist you today?
You: What's my name?
Agent: Your name is Henry.
```

Note

You might be wondering, what happens if the messages list keeps growing forever? Wouldn't that eventually become a problem? That's a great question, and yes, message history growth is something to keep in mind. Don't worry, we'll cover strategies for handling that later in this chapter.

The SDK also makes manual conversation management easier by providing a function that returns the list of messages from a `result` object. The `result.to_input_list()` function returns a list of `ResponseInputItem` objects to which you can then add additional `ResponseInputItem` objects. This makes the code a bit neater (but the functionality still works the same way), such as the following:

```python
from agents import Agent, Runner

# Create the agent
agent = Agent(
    name="QuestionAnswer",
    instructions="You are an AI agent that answers questions.",
)

messages = []
while True:
    question = input("You: ")
    messages.append({"role": "user", "content": question})
    result = Runner.run_sync(agent, messages)
    print("Agent: ", result.final_output)
    messages = result.to_input_list()
```

In practice, this technique forms the foundation of stateful conversational agents. From here, more advanced memory techniques can be layered on top to persist memory across sessions, extract structured data, adjust memory, and handle large conversations, but it all starts with tracking the conversation history.

Conversation management with Sessions

OpenAI Agents SDK provides a primitive for conversation management called `Sessions`. It acts as a class that enables you to automatically store, recall, and edit messages in a conversation. This means you don't have to manually call the `.to_input_list()` function or manage the conversation message manually; the SDK takes care of it. The `Sessions` class needs one input: a string that represents a unique identifier for the session called `session_id`.

Let's modify the previous script we had and add sessions to it. Create a new file called conversations_with_sessions.py and run the following code:

```
from agents import Agent, Runner, SQLiteSession

# Create the agent
agent = Agent(
    name="QuestionAnswer",
    instructions="You are an AI agent that answers questions.",
)

# Create a session
session = SQLiteSession("first_session")

while True:
    question = input("You: ")
    result = Runner.run_sync(agent, question, session=session)
    print("Agent: ", result.final_output)
```

After running this code (as you can see, it's a lot simpler), let's try our test case again:

```
You: My name is Henry
Agent: Nice to meet you, Henry! How can I assist you today?
You: What's my name?
Agent: Your name is Henry.
```

In this case, the conversation history is managed with the Sessions class. Instead of manually appending messages or calling .to_input_list(), the session object keeps track of the entire interaction history behind the scenes.

Sessions can be especially useful when managing multiple users or conversations. By using a unique session_id value for each interaction thread, agents can maintain separate memory contexts. For example, you might generate a session_id value based on a username and a conversation ID, ensuring that each user or conversation has its own isolated history.

This lays the groundwork for building truly stateful agents that feel more natural, responsive, and intelligent in extended interactions.

Note that `SQLiteSession` by default is in-memory (not persistent across process restarts). We'll discuss how to persist sessions to disk in the *Long-term memory* section. But first, we must address the issue of managing large conversation threads, where even short-term memory has a finite capacity.

Managing large conversation threads

Why is managing large conversation threads a problem with agents? Agents are powered by LLMs. LLMs have a fundamental problem of **finite context windows** (i.e., LLMs can only receive and process a certain number of characters, or "tokens" at one time). If a conversation continues, simply appending every message will eventually hit this limit, at which point the prompt becomes too large to process, and our agent will fail.

However, managing large conversation threads is important even without this technical limitation. Long prompts and context windows can significantly slow down responses and increase cost. Therefore, it's important to manage the short-term memory by discarding or compressing old information that's less important.

In this section, we will discuss two patterns to address this: sliding message window and message summarization.

Sliding message window

The **sliding message window** is the simplest and most cost-effective memory strategy. It works by retaining only the most recent *N* messages from the message log, acting as a **First-In, First-Out (FIFO)** queue. Older messages are dropped as new ones arrive, ensuring that the prompt remains within the model's context limit.

This method is ideal for agents that only need short-term memory, such as customer service agents focused on resolving a single query thread, but it does risk forgetting important context introduced earlier in the session. For example, if a user shares key information (such as their name, goals, or constraints) early in the conversation, and the window size is too small, the agent may lose this information entirely once it gets pushed out of the window.

Message summarization

A more advanced strategy is **message summarization**, which means instead of forgetting older messages, this approach condenses them into a compact summary that persists throughout the session. This allows the agent to retain key facts, decisions, or user preferences over long conversations, actually bridging short-term and long-term memory.

Summarization typically involves the following:

- Keep monitoring the size of the message history, and if it exceeds a certain threshold, collect the oldest *N* messages.
- Pass the oldest *N* messages to an LLM, with a prompt that summarizes them.
- Replace the oldest *N* messages with the summarized response in the message log. Since the summarized output is smaller than the length of the oldest *N* messages, this effectively shortens the context window of the message log.

This method allows the agent to retain long-term context without exceeding token limits. Of course, the trade-off here is significant cost and latency as each summarization task requires an additional LLM call. In practice, many agents combine both patterns: using a sliding window to remove old messages and a summarization chain to retain older context in compressed form.

Short-term memory is all about making the agent context-aware within a single session. With OpenAI Agents SDK, enabling this is the most straightforward using the Sessions class. However, there are limitations, and making that memory scalable (not exceeding context limits) requires thoughtful strategies such as sliding windows or message summarization.

Here's an example of a sliding window pattern:

```python
from agents import Agent, Runner
from collections import deque

# Create the agent
agent = Agent(
    name="QuestionAnswer",
    instructions="You are an AI agent that answers questions."
)

# Sliding window size (keep only the most recent 5 messages)
WINDOW_SIZE = 5
messages = deque(maxlen=WINDOW_SIZE)

while True:
    question = input("You: ")
    messages.append({"role": "user", "content": question})

    # Run the agent with only the most recent N messages
```

```
result = Runner.run_sync(agent, list(messages))
print("Agent:", result.final_output)

messages.append({"role": "assistant", "content": result.final_output})
```

Next, we will explore long-term memory and see how an agent can retain information across sessions or over extended periods.

Long-term memory

Long-term memory is the ability for an agent to remember pertinent details across multiple sessions for a long period of time. This "superpower" is what enables agents to retain and recall information across multiple sessions. It is the foundation for creating truly stateful, personalized, and persistent AI experiences. This is sometimes dubbed the ultimate "hindrance" between an AI agent and a human agent, as a human agent can naturally remember important facts, preferences, or past conversations and assign them to every person, whereas an AI agent typically struggles with this.

We discussed the difference between stateless and stateful in the context of single sessions previously. It extends to multi-session interactions as well. An agent without long-term memory is essentially stateless between sessions. An AI agent without long-term memory cannot remember information such as a user's name, past preferences, or completed tasks, even after it has been shut down or restarted. For example, if a user tells a customer service agent, *"I prefer my orders be sent to the back door instead of the front,"* and then returns a week later, a long-term memory-enabled agent can proactively set the desired delivery method to *"back door."*

The crux of enabling agents to have long-term memory is **memory storage and recall**. This is the idea of storing an agent's memory in a persistent state to be recalled later. There are many different patterns that accomplish this, which is what we will cover in this section.

Persistent message logs

The easiest pattern to establish long-term memory is also the most intuitive: simply store the entire contents of the message log somewhere when the agent session ends, and then recall it when the agent restarts. The Agents SDK provides a mechanism for this using the Sessions class we discussed previously (SQLiteSession). This class can accept not only a session ID, but also a db_path argument, where you can input a file location on your computer, and it will automatically save and load message logs to a SQL database on your local machine.

Let's go through an example. Create a new Python file called `ltm_sessions.py` and run the following code:

```python
from agents import Agent, Runner, SQLiteSession

# Create the agent
agent = Agent(
    name="QuestionAnswer",
    instructions="You are an AI agent that answers questions.",
)

# Create a session
session = SQLiteSession("first_session", db_path="messages.db")

while True:
    question = input("You: ")
    result = Runner.run_sync(agent, question, session=session)
    print("Agent: ", result.final_output)
```

In this case, we had added a db_path argument to the session object, which tells the Agents SDK to store the conversation on our local machine and load the conversation again when the agent is re-instantiated. We can test that this works by running the program, passing information through it, exiting the program, running the program again, and seeing whether the agent remembers the information.

Let's run the program and provide the agent with our name:

```
You: Hello, I'm Henry
Agent: Hi Henry! What would you like to talk about today?
```

Next, let's quit the program by clicking *Ctrl + C*. After that, rerun the program and let's ask it for my name:

```
You: What's my name?
Agent:  You mentioned your name is Henry. How can I assist you further?
```

In this way, we have created an agent with long-term memory. It will also remember how you interacted with it because it is storing your message log on your local machine and loading it every time you start the program. You may also notice a `messages.db` file in the root folder of where you run your code; this is where your message log and conversation are saved.

The benefit of using the built-in session object for persistence is that it's seamless, or in other words, you do not have to implement your own file format or database schema for storing chats.

However, this pattern does have some obvious limitations, namely, that storing and loading full message logs can become inefficient as the number of sessions or the length of conversations grows. There's also the fact that, as we discussed before, the message log may bloat so much that the LLM can no longer process it due to context window limitations.

Additionally, storing all messages verbatim may not be the most intelligent form of long-term memory. Often, what we want to retain is not every message, but only the key facts, decisions, preferences, or outcomes. That's where more structured memory architectures come into play.

Structured memory recall

Structured memory recall leverages tool-calling to solve the agent-memory problem. Specifically, this pattern focuses on the following concepts:

- Instead of storing every single message, the agent has access to a tool that stores only the important information that the user shares
- Instead of loading every single message, the agent has access to a tool that retrieves and loads only the relevant piece of information needed

In this way, the agent's prompt and message log for a session stays clean, but if the model determines that it should consult the long-term memory (for example, the user asks about something mentioned "earlier" or in a past session), it can call that function to fetch that relevant information.

Let's go through an example. Create a new Python file called ltm_structured_memory_call.py. First, we will initialize the memory file. Here we check whether a JSON file already exists. If not, we create one with a default structure:

```
from agents import Agent, Runner, function_tool
import os
import json

# Create JSON file if it does not exist
FILENAME = 'memory.json'
memory_default = {
    "user_profile": [],
    "order_preferences": [],
    "other": []
}
```

```
if not os.path.exists(FILENAME):
    with open(FILENAME, 'w') as f:
        json.dump(memory_default, f, indent=4)
        print(f"Created '{FILENAME}' with default data.")
else:
    print(f"'{FILENAME}' already exists.")
```

Next, we will define the tool to save a memory piece. This function allows the agent to store important facts in the JSON file:

```
@function_tool
def save_memory(memory_type: str, memory: str) -> str:
    """

    Saves a memory to a memory store.

    Args:
        memory_type: the type of memory to store. Choose between user_
profile, order_preferences, or other.
        memory: the memory to save
    """

    with open(FILENAME, 'r') as f:
        data = json.load(f)
    data[memory_type].append(memory)

    with open(FILENAME, 'w') as f:
        json.dump(data, f, indent=4)

    print(f"Memory ({memory}) saved")
    return f"Memory ({memory}) saved"
```

We will also create a function to load memory. This function retrieves relevant facts from the JSON memory store:

```
@function_tool
def load_memory(memory_type: str) -> str:
    """

    Loads a set of memory from a memory store.

    Args:
        memory_type: the type of memory to load. Choose between user_
profile, order_preferences, or other.
```

```
    """
    with open(FILENAME, 'r') as f:
        data = json.load(f)
    return "|".join(data[memory_type])
```

Finally, we create the agent, give it access to the tools, and run an interactive loop:

```
# Create the agent
agent = Agent(
    name="QuestionAnswer",
    instructions="You are an AI agent that answers questions. You have
    access to two tools that enable you to save memories and load memories.
    Save memories when you learn an important fact. Load memories when
    something is asked for about the user.",
    tools=[save_memory, load_memory]
)

while True:
    question = input("You: ")
    result = Runner.run_sync(agent, question)
    print("Agent: ", result.final_output)
```

Let's break down what's happening in this code, starting with the two function tools that save and load memory.

The save_memory function allows the agent to store important facts under specific categories, such as user_profile or order_preferences. This function writes to a local memory.json file, appending the new piece of information to the relevant section. For instance, if the user says, *"I prefer front-door deliveries,"* the agent can call save_memory("user_profile", "Prefers deliveries through the front door"), and that fact will be added to the persistent storage. The persistent storage in this case is simply a local JSON file, but it could just as easily be a database.

On the other hand, the load_memory function is designed to retrieve previously stored facts. When the user references a preference or detail from an earlier conversation, perhaps asking, *"What are my delivery preferences?"*, the agent can call load_memory("order_preferences ") to fetch and summarize the relevant stored facts from that category.

These functions give the agent a structured and lightweight mechanism for handling long-term memory. Rather than storing full message transcripts, the agent only retains distilled insights that are important and reusable. This is much more scalable than keeping every single message log. It also works how a human thinks about memory. Imagine if you had a conversation with your friend and they told you *they like to eat sushi*. In that case, you don't simply remember the whole transcript of the conversation. Instead, you just "log" the important information that *they like sushi*, and "store" it in your memory.

Let's try it out with an example. After running the code, let's type in the following:

```
You: I like to have orders sent to the office
Memory (User prefers orders to be sent to the office.) saved
Agent: Got it! I'll remember that you prefer to have orders sent to the
office.
```

The agent, recognizing this as a useful preference, will call the save_memory tool. You can even see this if you open memory.json:

```
{
    "user_profile": [
    ],
    "order_preferences": [
        "User prefers orders to be sent to the office."
    ],
    "other": []
}
```

Now, let's quit the current session and open a new session by running the preceding Python program again, and then asking the agent for our preference:

```
You: Where do I like my orders sent?
Agent: You like your orders sent to the office.
```

In this case, the agent called the load_memory tool to retrieve all the memories under order_preferences. It finds the relevant information and then provides the correct response.

This structured approach to long-term memory is more scalable, semantically precise, and avoids the pitfalls of exceeding context window limitations. It also sets the foundation for more advanced memory systems, where facts can be embedded and indexed for semantic search, or tagged with metadata such as timestamps and source credibility.

Note

The structured memory pattern that we have implemented here is simple and effective for "lightweight" scenarios. However, as your agent begins to accumulate more facts over time (or if you need to support fuzzy, semantically rich memory retrieval), this basic key-value approach may become limiting. That's where vector databases and semantic embeddings come in.

Rather than storing facts as raw text entries in a JSON file, you can represent each memory as a vector embedding, which can be stored in a vector store and then semantically searched. We discuss how this concept works later in the chapter.

As you build more sophisticated agents, you'll likely want to combine these two long-term memory patterns (persistent message logs and structured memory recall), and OpenAI Agents SDK is flexible enough to support both at the same time.

Training knowledge

As discussed in *Chapter 1*, **training knowledge** refers to information that is inherently stored in the model through its training data. Every LLM begins with a vast repository of inherent knowledge derived from the massive datasets (typically, a large corpus of internet text) on which it was initially trained. The benefit of an LLM having internal knowledge is that the knowledge itself has the following advantages:

- **It is quickly retrievable**: Since the inherent knowledge is "baked" into the model weights, the model can retrieve the information very quickly and is typically limited only by the LLM's compute speed
- **It has a wide coverage**: Since the training data is vast (the corpus of the internet), the inherent knowledge can cover lots of topics in fairly great detail

The process of changing the model's inherent knowledge is called **fine-tuning**. Unlike prompting or retrieval-based techniques that guide a model's existing knowledge, fine-tuning directly reshapes the model by retraining it on a carefully selected dataset. This process updates the model's weights, allowing it to adopt new terminology, patterns, or behaviors that it couldn't previously handle well. The result is a version of the model that's more specialized and more accurate for a specific domain or task.

Let's take the medical field as an example. A general-purpose LLM such as GPT-4o may understand broad health-related topics, but will likely fall short when asked to interpret complex reports or suggest treatment protocols based on nuanced guidelines. By fine-tuning the model on a dataset of, for example, structured patient records and doctor notes, we can create a more tailored model that is able to answer more nuanced health-related questions.

Fine-tuning is most appropriate in fields such as medicine, where domain expertise is essential and where accuracy directly impacts outcomes. However, it has some severe limitations and disadvantages:

- **Computationally intensive (and expensive)**: Fine-tuning requires large-scale compute resources and GPU time, particularly when working with high-capacity models. There are some fine-tuning-as-a-service options out there, but even they can be prohibitively expensive (typically starting at $10,000 to train the model, and that does not include costs to host the model).

- **Inflexible**: Once a model is fine-tuned, it must be maintained separately from the "base" model. As new knowledge emerges or if a base model is updated, the whole fine-tuning process must start over

- **Knowledge-mixing**: When fine-tuning, the knowledge that is being added in may "mix" or counter other information that the model was originally trained on. As a result, the model may become confused and provide contradictory statements as it seeks to prioritize information in its training data. Technically, there is no guarantee that the LLM will prioritize the information that it was fine-tuned on.

As a result, for many practical applications, especially those that do not demand such tight domain control, it is often more efficient to use alternatives such as prompt engineering or retrieval-augmented generation, which we will discuss next.

Retrieved knowledge

As discussed previously, **retrieved knowledge** refers to information that is retrieved in real time from a knowledge store based on the user's request. Unlike training knowledge, which is static and fixed at the time the model was trained, retrieved knowledge is dynamic to the context of the conversation. The pattern is as follows:

1. User asks a question that requires external knowledge.
2. The agent system retrieves data relevant to that question from a knowledge source. This is achieved through a tool call, which could search a database, a piece of text, a vector store of embedded documents, a search engine API, etc.

3. The retrieved information is then fed into the LLM.

4. The LLM generates an answer that incorporates or is grounded in the retrieved information.

This incorporates external knowledge into an agent. In this context, "external" knowledge refers to any information that is not inherently stored in the model's training weights.

Recall that we have already created agents that leverage retrieved knowledge in *Chapter 4*. In many of the example agents that we created, we used tools that retrieve relevant information for the user. For example, here is an agent we created that retrieves the price of Bitcoin when asked:

```python
import requests
from agents import Agent, Runner, function_tool


# Create the tool
@function_tool
def get_price_of_bitcoin() -> str:
    """Get the price of Bitcoin."""
    url = "https://api.coingecko.com/api/v3/simple/price?ids=bitcoin&vs_currencies=usd"
    response = requests.get(url)
    price = response.json()["bitcoin"]["usd"]
    return f"${price:,.2f} USD."


# Create the agent
crypto_agent = Agent(
    name="CryptoTracker",
    instructions="You are a crypto assistant. Use tools to get real-time data.",
    tools=[get_price_of_bitcoin]
)


# Run the agent with an example prompt
result = Runner.run_sync(crypto_agent, "What's the price of Bitcoin?")
print(result.final_output)
```

Here is another example where we retrieved knowledge from a database:

```python
from agents import Agent, Runner, function_tool
from pydantic import BaseModel
from typing import List
```

```python
# create a simulated database
TICKETS_DB = {
    "henry@gmail.com": [
        {"id": "TCKT-001", "issue": "Login not working",
            "status": "resolved"},
        {"id": "TCKT-002", "issue": "Password reset failed",
            "status": "open"},
    ],
    "tom@gmail.com": [
        {"id": "TCKT-003", "issue": "Billing error",
            "status": "in progress"},
    ]
}


# define Pydantic model
class CustomerQuery(BaseModel):
    email: str


# define the tool that does a database query
@function_tool
def get_customer_tickets(query: CustomerQuery) -> str:
    """Retrieve recent support tickets for a customer based on email."""
    tickets = TICKETS_DB.get(query.email.lower())
    if not tickets:
        return f"No tickets found for {query.email}."
    response = "\n".join(
        [f"ID: {t['id']}, Issue: {t['issue']}, Status: {t['status']}"
            for t in tickets]
    )
    return f"Tickets for {query.email}:\n{response}"


# create the agent
support_agent = Agent(
    name="SupportHelper",
    instructions="You are a customer support agent. Use tools to fetch
user support history when asked about their tickets.",
    tools=[get_customer_tickets]
```

```
)

# Run the agent
result = Runner.run_sync(support_agent, "Can you show me the ticket
history for henry@gmail.com?")
print(result.final_output)
```

Both examples follow the pattern we laid out previously, as follows:

1. **User initiates a request and agent retrieves information**: In both examples, the user poses a question that requires information beyond what the model was trained on. This includes real-time data (e.g., Bitcoin price) or user-specific information (e.g., support ticket history). The agent detects that it cannot answer the question with built-in knowledge alone. It invokes a retrieval tool:

    - In the CryptoTracker example, the agent uses an HTTP call to the CoinGecko API
    - In the SupportHelper example, the agent performs a simulated database lookup based on the user's email address

2. **External knowledge is retrieved**: The tool retrieves the relevant information in a structured format (e.g., a JSON response from an API, or a list of ticket records from the database), and the retrieved data is passed back into the model.

3. **LLM integrates the information**: The LLM then uses this input to formulate a natural language response that reflects the external knowledge.

This is the fundamental cycle of **retrieval-augmented generation** (**RAG**), a term that you may be familiar with. As the name suggests, there are three steps in this process: **retrieve** (the system retrieves relevant information based on the user's request), **augment** (the system adds the retrieved information to the LLM's prompt), and **generate** (the LLM produces a response with the added retrieved information). In fact, if you look at the previous pattern steps, it perfectly corresponds to the three-step process within RAG.

Unlike static knowledge embedded in model weights, retrieved knowledge can be updated independently of the model's training, tailored to the user or situation, and is grounded in real-world referenceable sources.

The most interesting step under RAG is the *retrieve* step. The method to retrieve data in the preceding examples, using API calls or database queries, works well for structured information, such as cryptocurrency prices or customer profile information. However, how do we solve the *retrieve* problem when data is unstructured text, such as a set of documents on a SharePoint team site? This is where embeddings, semantic searches, and vector stores enter the chat.

Unstructured data

Note

Before we proceed, note that we will go through a simplified overview of this topic instead of discussing the deep and complex math concepts that sit behind it. To read more about how embeddings work from a more detailed point of view, refer to this book: https://www.packtpub.com/en-mx/product/vector-search-for-practitioners-with-elastic-9781805121022/chapter/chapter-1-introduction-to-vectors-and-embeddings-2/section/chapter-1-introduction-to-vectors-and-embeddings-ch02lv1lsec02?srsltid=AfmB OoqKY6Vgqv9_MDNW5p4mDEXQBdQXQWFt9fRFM63RMebJWEWx8ide.

First, let's define our terminology.

Embeddings are numerical representations of text. Think of it as a secret language whose syntax is a list of numbers and that only machines can understand. These embeddings capture the essence of words, sentences, and even entire documents. For example, the embeddings of the following sentences are listed alongside (this is purely illustrative):

Sentence	Embedding
I like apples	[3432, 75, 32, ..., 76, 980]
I like bananas	[85, 1, 4, ..., 695, 47]
This is very difficult	[5, 596, 1254, ..., 7, 1]
This is like fitting a square peg into a round hole	[5, 4, 365, ..., 748, 9]

Table 5.1: Example embeddings

Since embeddings capture the "meaning" or "essence" of text, two pieces of text that are about the same topic or have similar meaning will produce vectors that are very similar. For example, the embedding of *I like apples* will be more similar to the embedding of *I like bananas* than to something random, such as *All legislative Powers herein granted shall be vested in a Congress of the United States, which shall consist of a Senate and House of Representatives*. This is where semantic search comes in.

Semantic search is the process of comparing two pieces of text by using their semantic meaning (or, in other words, comparing their embeddings) rather than comparing keywords. We compare two embeddings by calculating the distance between them in vector space, which is called the cosine similarity. **Cosine similarity** measures the cosine of the angle between two vectors, resulting in a number between 0 and 1.

The math does not matter here; the implication is that the higher the cosine similarity, the more closely the two texts are semantically related:

- **Cosine similarity close to 1**: The texts are very similar or have similar context or meaning
- **Cosine similarity close to 0**: The texts are unrelated

Here is the cosine similarity between the embeddings of different pieces of text:

Test	Base text	Comparison text	Cosine similarity of embeddings
1	I like apples	I like bananas	`0.90`
		All legislative Powers herein granted shall be vested in a Congress of the United States, which shall consist of a Senate and House of Representatives	`0.71`
2	This is very difficult	I'm fitting a square peg into a round hole	`0.88`
		All legislative Powers herein granted shall be vested in a Congress of the United States, which shall consist of a Senate and House of Representatives	`0.64`

Table 5.2: Table of cosine similarities between embeddings of different pieces of text

In this table, you can see that with cosine similarity, the text *I like apples* is more semantically similar to the text *I like bananas* than to the excerpt from the US Constitution. This is also the case with *This is very difficult* and *I'm fitting a square peg into a round hole*. In this example, these two pieces of text share no keywords, but they are semantically similar and, as a result, have very high cosine similarity scores.

Finally, we have **vector stores**, which are simply a database that is optimized to hold pieces of text and their embeddings. A simple database may hold a tabular-like structure of data, whereas a vector store holds these large embedding vectors. Vector stores also have another special property: When a new document is added to a vector store, the database automatically **chunks** the text into smaller segments, generates embeddings for each chunk, and **indexes** them (i.e., stores them with a dictionary that supports fast retrieval) for fast similarity search. This *chunk and index step* is needed to enable semantic search. Each chunk typically contains a few hundred tokens of text and is embedded using a dedicated model.

Now that we understand the terminology, let's discuss how this all comes together when performing a RAG model on unstructured data: document ingestion and retrieval.

Document ingestion

Before we can retrieve anything, we first need to prepare our knowledge base. This involves transforming raw text documents into a format suitable for semantic search using a vector store. The ingestion process typically looks like the following:

1. **Chunking**: The raw document is split into smaller segments (or "chunks"). This ensures that each chunk is small enough to be embedded and later injected into the prompt if retrieved.

2. **Generate embeddings**: Each chunk is passed through an embedding model to produce its corresponding vector.

3. **Store in a vector store**: These embeddings, along with the associated chunk text, are stored in a vector store, which is indexed.

At this point, the vector store holds all embeddings of our unstructured documents. Note that this step only needs to occur once for each new set of documents.

Retrieval

Once the documents are ingested, we have what we need to perform the *retrieve* step for unstructured data in RAG. The process of dynamically retrieving data based on the user's query works like the following:

1. **Embed the query**: When a user submits a question to the agent, the system first converts the query into an embedding using the same embedding model used during ingestion

2. **Perform a semantic search**: The vector store performs a semantic similarity search, comparing the query embedding to the embeddings of the chunks of text, using cosine similarity. This step typically returns the top-N most semantically relevant chunks, based on cosine similarity scores.

After that, the *augment* and *generate* steps take over, as described before. The only difference is that in the *retrieve* step, the output is semantically similar chunks of text rather than a cryptocurrency price from an API call or an order status from a database query.

Using vector stores and FileSearchTool in the Agents SDK

Thankfully, OpenAI Agents SDK automates the RAG process for unstructured text, for both the document ingestion and retrieval parts, so that you do not need to do it manually. Let's go through an example, first by creating a vector store:

1. Go to the OpenAI platform at https://platform.openai.com/ and log in. Ensure you log in using the same account you used when generating the API key.

2. Select **Dashboard** from the top right, then select **Storage**, and then toggle to **Vector stores**.

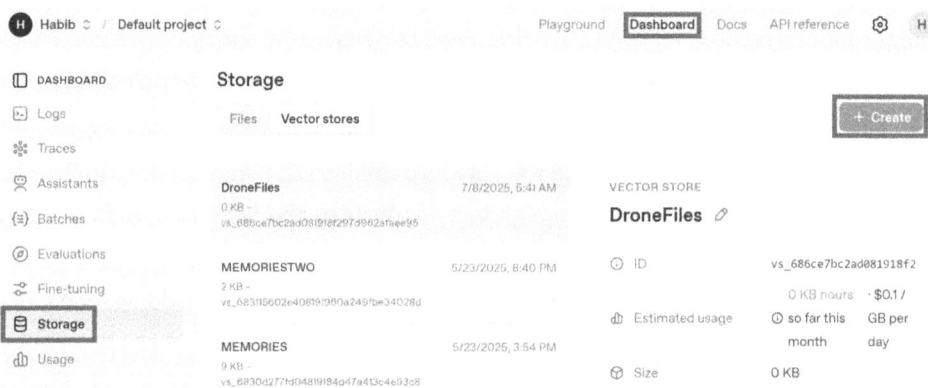

Figure 5.2: Storage menu in OpenAI Dashboard

3. Select **Create** to create a new vector store. Type in a vector store name such as USConstitution.

4. Scroll down and add a file to the vector store by selecting **+ Add files**.

5. Upload the USConstitution.txt file (which can be found in the repository under Chapter 5). Give it the name USConstitution.txt and select **user_data** for **Purpose**. Then, select **Attach**.

6. The TXT we uploaded has now been successfully added to our new vector store, and all the related operations to enable RAG (such as producing embeddings, indexing, etc.) are complete.

7. Copy and save the vector store ID for the new vector store that you just created.

Now that we have created a vector store, let's use the Agents SDK for retrieval through FileSearchTool, which we covered in detail in the previous chapter. As a reminder, the class takes, as input, a list of vector store IDs that it automatically searches and retrieves the correct chunk, and then passes it to the LLM for augmentation. Using the vector store we built in the previous section, we can build an agent that answers questions by referencing the USConstitution file.

Create a new Python file called us_constitution_agent.py and run the following code:

```python
from agents import Agent, Runner, FileSearchTool, SQLiteSession

# Instantiate the tool
filesearchtool = FileSearchTool(
    vector_store_ids=['vs_687ed4bb479c81919b530ab152f373d8']
) # replace with your own vector store ID

# Create an agent
agent = Agent(
    name="USConstitutionTool",
    instructions="You are an AI agent that answers questions from the
listed vector store, which has the US Constitution. Answer in one
sentence.",
    tools=[filesearchtool]
)

# Create a session
session = SQLiteSession("first_session")

while True:
    question = input("You: ")
    result = Runner.run_sync(agent, question, session=session)
    print("Agent: ", result.final_output)
```

After running this program, you can ask any question, and the agent will perform RAG on the vector store it has been given to answer the question, as in this example:

```
You: How old do senators need to be?
Agent:  Senators must be at least 30 years old.
```

In fact, you can see all the chunks that the RAG search has returned by going to the **Traces** module for this agent run:

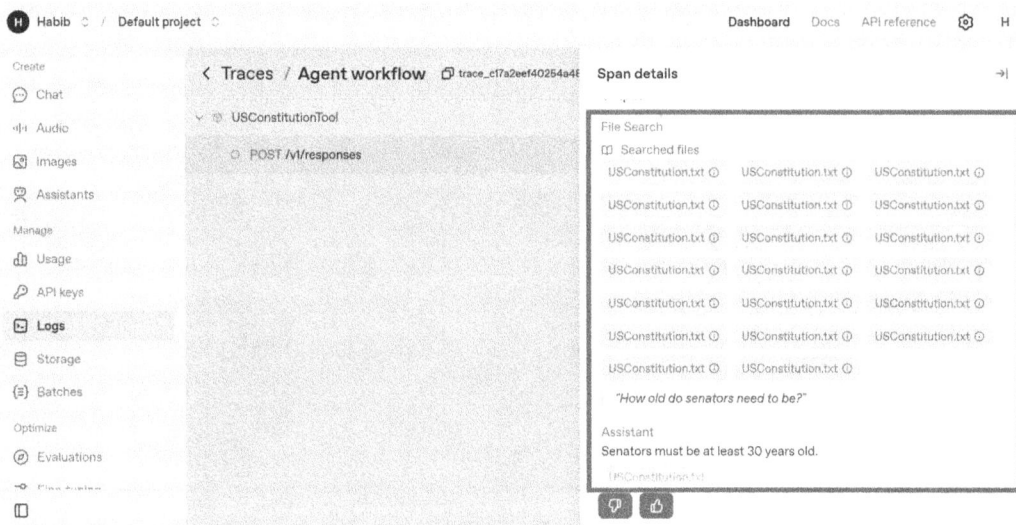

Figure 5.3: OpenAI Dashboard logs

In this way, the Agents SDK automates the document ingestion and retrieval process, enabling you to add retrieved knowledge capabilities to your agent with a few lines of code. However, it's still useful to know what is happening behind the scenes so that you can understand the process and its limitations.

Limitations

Adding retrieved knowledge to your agent has certain limitations and pitfalls, especially when unstructured data is used. Here are three of the most common ones that may occur with unstructured data:

- **Ambiguous questions**: If a user asks, *"What is your return policy?"*, are they asking about online orders, in-store returns, or a specific product? This can lead the agent to produce incorrect answers.

- **No relevant information found**: Sometimes, the knowledge base doesn't have the answer. The agent may, instead, hallucinate and make something up.

- **Conflicting or multiple sources**: If the information from the *retrieval* step is inconsistent (e.g., two docs say different return windows), the agent may ignore one of them.

Overall, building any knowledge-based agent means paying attention to the preceding pitfalls and understanding that even the best AI agents can succumb to them. As with any system that relies on real-world information, occasional gaps, contradictions, or misinterpretations may occur. However, with both memory and knowledge in place, we now have an agent that is far more capable: it remembers context and can pull in outside facts, making it a powerful agent.

Summary

In this chapter, we equipped agents with two useful skill sets to make them more intelligent: memory and knowledge.

We started by implementing short-term memory, manually tracking message history, and using the Sessions class to support multi-turn conversations. We addressed the challenge of growing context windows by introducing the sliding message window and message summarization techniques.

Next, we explored long-term memory. We made agent memory persistent across sessions using SQLiteSession with a file-backed database, and introduced structured memory recall through tool-calling. This approach enabled agents to store only the most relevant facts, reducing memory bloat while increasing recall precision.

We then looked at two distinct types of model knowledge:

- Training knowledge, which is the static information "baked into" the model during its initial training.
- Retrieved knowledge, which is the dynamic, context-specific data fetched at runtime via tool calls. We explored the RAG pattern, where agents pull external data from APIs, databases, or knowledge stores, and feed it into the LLM to produce informed responses.

With these patterns, your agents can now hold memory, retain user-specific context, and pull in relevant knowledge as needed, bringing them one step closer to true usefulness in real-world applications.

In the next chapter, we'll shift focus to multi-agent systems, where multiple specialized agents can collaborate to complete more complex tasks.

Unlock this book's exclusive benefits now

Scan this QR code or go to https://packtpub.com/unlock,
then search for this book by name.

Note: Keep your purchase invoice ready before you start.

6

Multi-Agent Systems and Handoffs

There are certain tasks that an individual human cannot complete themselves. Instead, an organization of humans (i.e., a team) is needed. Think about any large company. The reason why these big enterprises can complete their objectives is because of an organization of different specialized human beings working together. In the same way, a one-agent system can only go so far. A multi-agent system, however, can do anything.

While a single agent can be highly capable, it has natural limitations. A lone agent often struggles when problems span multiple domains, require diverse expertise, or need parallel processing. For example, a customer support agent might handle simple inquiries well, but it may fall short when the task also involves financial analysis, legal reasoning, or technical troubleshooting. By distributing responsibilities across multiple specialized agents, you can achieve higher accuracy, scalability, and resilience than any single agent could provide.

In this chapter, we'll explore how to build **multi-agent systems**, which are systems that coordinate multiple agents working together. Whether you're building a simple router or a complex organizational hierarchy, understanding how agents can interact, delegate, and collaborate is key to unlocking the full potential of agents. OpenAI Agents SDK contains a key primitive to enable multi-agent systems: the handoff.

Here is what you will learn as part of this chapter:

- **Orchestration types**: We'll begin by comparing two multi-agent orchestration strategies—deterministic (hardcoded) and dynamic (system-driven)—and walk through examples of each
- **Handoffs**: You'll learn how to use the handoffs feature in the Agents SDK to transfer control from one agent to another, allowing agents to delegate tasks while maintaining context
- **Multi-agent patterns**: Finally, we'll explore architectural patterns for multi-agent systems (centralized, decentralized, hierarchical, and swarm) and show how to implement each using the SDK

By the end of this chapter, you'll have learned how to design and implement multi-agent systems that mirror real-world teams.

Technical requirements

Follow the detailed steps in *Chapter 3* to set up your environment.

Throughout this book, practical examples and complete code from each chapter will be made available via the accompanying GitHub repository: `https://github.com/PacktPublishing/Building-Agents-with-OpenAI-Agents-SDK`.

You are encouraged to clone the repository, reuse and adapt the provided code samples, and refer to them as needed while progressing through the chapters.

Multi-agent orchestrations

When building systems that use multiple agents, one of the key decisions is figuring out how to manage the flow of information and tasks between those agents. Broadly, there are two strategies you can take:

- **Deterministic orchestration**: This is where you write out the logic yourself and explicitly control how agents interact; see *Figure 6.1*:

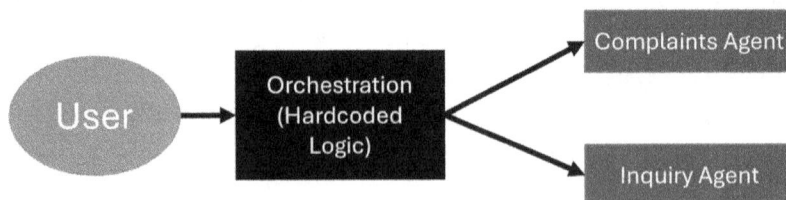

Figure 6.1: Deterministic orchestration

- **Dynamic orchestration**: This is where you delegate the flow decisions to another system (such as an LLM), enabling the system to adjust its behavior on the fly; refer to *Figure 6.2*:

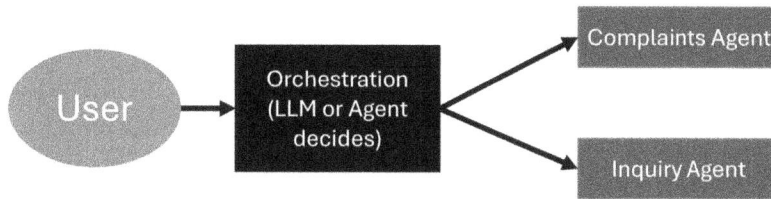

Figure 6.2: Dynamic orchestration

In this section, we will discuss both approaches and the benefits/drawbacks of each one. It is worth noting that many orchestrations actually involve a combination of both approaches. In an agentic system, you may want some parts of it to be explicitly deterministic to have greater control and autonomy, whereas you may want other areas to be more dynamic and to handle ambiguity better.

Deterministic orchestration

Deterministic orchestration is where the interaction flow between different agents is hardcoded (or deterministic). This approach is all about keeping control over how and when your agents run. In this setup, you can define the exact workflow ahead of time, coding in the order and the rules that govern which agents handle which tasks. A good analogy is a well-choreographed dance, with every step planned in advance. There is no improvising, and the agent flow does not deviate from the script you've given them.

The primary strength of deterministic orchestration is predictability. The agent flow will always unfold the same way for the same input, making it easy to test, audit, and debug. It is also straightforward to measure costs and runtime since you know exactly how many agent calls your workflow will make. Deterministic patterns are especially useful in systems where stable, repeatable results are a must, and where you need confidence that nothing unexpected happens.

The main drawback, as with all deterministic systems, is flexibility. We discussed this in *Chapter 1*, but deterministic orchestration patterns are not able to adapt to requests or situations that are not explicitly defined in the agent control logic. If you discover the need for a new step or want to handle a new kind of request, you'll need to change and redeploy your agent logic. As your workflow grows more complex, maintaining all those branches and pathways can become a burden.

Let's go through an example of a deterministic approach. In this example, we'll walk through a deterministic orchestration pattern, where requests are routed between two customer service agents using hardcoded logic. This will show you how predictable, rule-based delegation works, and why it can be both powerful and limiting. Create a new Python file called `deterministic_approach.py` and run the following code:

```python
from agents import Agent, Runner

# Create two agents
complaints_agent = Agent(
    name="Complaints Agent",
    instructions="Handle any customer complaints with empathy and clear
next steps."
)
inquiry_agent = Agent(
    name="General Inquiry Agent",
    instructions="Answer general questions about our services promptly."
)

# Create orchestration
def orchestrate(user_message: str):
    # Deterministically delegates requests to the right customer service
agent.
    if ("complaint" in user_message.lower()
        or "problem" in user_message.lower()):
        print('Redirecting you to the Complaints agent')
        chosen_agent = complaints_agent
    else:
        print('Redirecting you to the Inquiry agent')
        chosen_agent = inquiry_agent
    result = Runner.run_sync(chosen_agent, user_message)
    return result.final_output

while True:
    question = input("You: ")
    result = orchestrate(question)
    print("Agent: ", result)
```

💡 **Quick tip**: Enhance your coding experience with the **AI Code Explainer** and **Quick Copy** features. Open this book in the next-gen Packt Reader. Click the **Copy** button

(1) to quickly copy code into your coding environment, or click the **Explain** button

(2) to get the AI assistant to explain a block of code to you.

```
                                                           Copy      Explain
function calculate(a, b) {
    return {sum: a + b};                                    1          2
};
```

📖 **The next-gen Packt Reader** is included for free with the purchase of this book. Scan the QR code OR go to `packtpub.com/unlock`, then use the search bar to find this book by name. Double-check the edition shown to make sure you get the right one.

In this code, here are the key takeaways:

- Deterministic orchestration gives you full control over agent flow, making it predictable and easy to test
- The downside is a lack of flexibility; if a user phrases something differently than expected, the system may misroute the request

The choice of what agent to call is managed by the `orchestrate` function, which contains hardcoded logic on which agent to call based on the contents of the user's question. This is deterministic as this system always redirects to `complaints_agent` if the user's question contains the word *complaint* or *problem*.

Here's an example interaction:

```
You: I have a complaint, my meal was too hot
Redirecting you to the Complaints agent
Agent:  I'm really sorry to hear that your meal was too hot. I can
understand how that could be uncomfortable. To make it right, I'd like
to offer you a replacement meal at no extra charge. Additionally, please
let us know how you'd like your meal temperature adjusted in the future,
and we'll make sure it meets your preference. Let me know how else I can
assist you!
```

From this, it is obvious to see the weakness of this system. A user may have a complaint, but may not actually use the word *complaint* or *problem* in their message. In that case, the user will be redirected to the wrong agent. The following is an example of that:

```
You: my meal is too hot
Redirecting you to the Inquiry agent
Agent: Try eating in smaller bites.
```

Dynamic orchestration

Dynamic orchestration is where the interaction flow between different agents is dynamic and is controlled autonomously by an external system (typically a human, but in this case an LLM). This offers a more flexible orchestration pattern as the responsibility of the agent selection and flow is given to another LLM-powered agent. In fact, in almost all cases in this book so far, the systems we have created have used dynamic orchestration as an agent has been controlling how to address the user's response (whether it's a tool call, which tool to call, etc.).

Typically, in dynamic orchestration, you have an agent that accepts incoming queries and redirects them as appropriate. This agent reasons about each incoming request in real time, choosing which tools, functions, or specialist agents to route to at each step. Going back to the dance analogy, think of this as more of an *improv show*, where the system is able to improvise based on unheard prompts from the audience.

The benefits and drawbacks of dynamic orchestration are the drawbacks and benefits of deterministic orchestration, respectively. Flexibility is the main advantage. A dynamic system can handle a much wider variety of conversational inputs without needing hardcoded logic for every possible scenario. Agents instructed appropriately can tackle unfamiliar problems and plot out new solutions, making this approach a good fit for customer support, sales triage, and other open-ended tasks. However, the trade-off is predictability; you won't always know in advance which path the conversation will take, which may mean unpredictable answers, costs, and runtime.

Let's return to the previous example and make it into a dynamic orchestration. The first step is to create a triage agent that can choose which agent to call based on the user's query. Create a new Python file called dynamic_approach.py and run the following code:

```
from agents import Agent, Runner

# Create two agents
complaints_agent = Agent(
    name="Complaints Agent",
    instructions="Handle any customer complaints with empathy and clear
next steps."
)
inquiry_agent = Agent(
    name="General Inquiry Agent",
    instructions="Answer general questions about our services promptly."
)
triage_agent = Agent(
    name="Triage Agent",
    instructions="Triage the user's request and call the appropriate
agent",
    tools=[
        complaints_agent.as_tool(
            tool_name="ComplaintsAgent",
            tool_description="Introduce yourself as the Complaints agent.
Handle any customer complaints with empathy and clear next steps."
        ),
        inquiry_agent.as_tool(
            tool_name="GeneralInquiryAgent",
            tool_description="Introduce yourself as the General Inquiry
agent. Answer general questions about our services promptly."
        )]
)

while True:
    question = input("You: ")
    result = Runner.run_sync(triage_agent, question)
    print("Agent: ", result.final_output)
```

In this case, let's try a prompt that the triage agent should interpret as being a complaint (without using the word complaint) and then send it to the `complaints_agent` accordingly:

```
You: My meal is too hot
Agent:  I'm sorry to hear about your meal. I understand how unexpected
that can be. Would you like us to replace your meal, or can I assist you
with a refund or credit? Please let me know how you'd like to proceed.
```

We can verify that it was sent to the correct agent by looking at the **Traces** module:

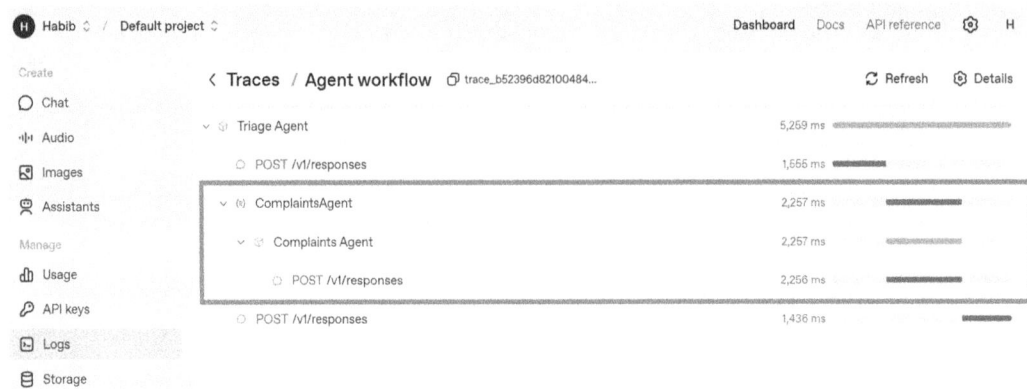

Figure 6.3: Trace of the previous example

In this way, we're able to delegate the decision-making process to the triage agent itself, rather than hardcoding the logic in advance. The agent interprets the intent behind the user's message (identifying a complaint) and dynamically decides to route the message to the right agent. This allows our system to respond to a wide range of inputs more naturally and efficiently, without needing a rigid *if-else* structure to handle each possible case.

Another benefit of this type of orchestration is that it can handle multiple requests. For example, if the user's request is, "My meal is too hot, and how do I get my receipt?" the triage agent will call both `complaints_agent` and `inquiry_agent` to answer that question in one go:

```
You: My meal is too hot, and how do I get my receipt?
Agent:  Here's how I can assist you:

**For the hot meal:**
- Allow the meal to cool for a few minutes while we offer a complimentary
drink to help balance things out.
- If it remains an issue, we can arrange for a replacement. Let me know
your preference!
```

```
**For the receipt:**
- Check your confirmation email for a copy.
- Log into your account on our website, where you can view and download it
from your order history.

If you need further help, please feel free to ask!
```

Here's what it looks like in the **Traces** module:

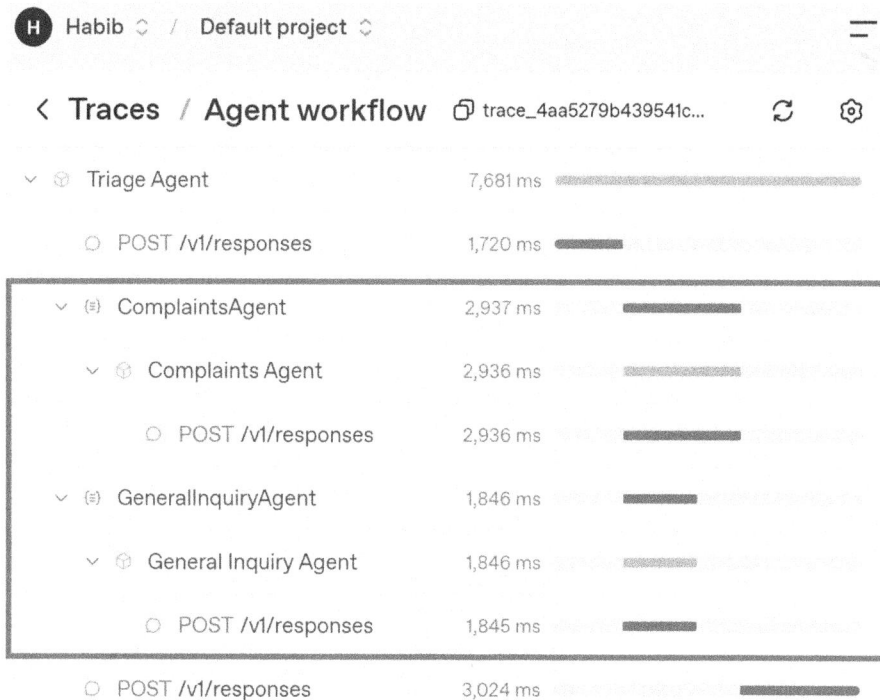

Figure 6.4: Traces example of an agent workflow

All of this happens dynamically in the agent's reasoning process rather than via fixed code branches. We only defined the agents and their capabilities; the triage agent's LLM did the decision-making.

Handoffs in OpenAI Agents SDK

Now that we understand the different orchestration methods with multi-agent systems, let's discuss the constructs that are available to us in OpenAI Agents SDK that make this possible. One of the most important primitives that the SDK provides is handoffs.

A **handoff** is the mechanism by which an agent can pass control to another agent. It's equivalent to an agent saying, "I'm going to hand over this task to you. You can answer it better than I. Here are all the details." Handoffs are required in multi-agent systems as it's the *layer* that connects different agents together.

> **Note**
>
> There are generally two ways for agents to interact with each other, one of which we have already covered in great detail within *Chapter 4*, called as_tool().
>
> The as_tool() function enables an agent to become a tool that can be added to another agent. Think of it as calling a helper function: the main agent remains in charge, temporarily consults a sub-agent for input or a decision, and then continues the conversation. This pattern is useful when the main agent needs specialized input without giving up the overall flow.
>
> Here, however, we will cover handoffs. A handoff, by contrast, is a complete transfer of control from one agent to another. Here, an agent passes the conversation to another agent, which then assumes full responsibility. The original agent no longer participates.

You can find a visual example of the two approaches in the following figure. In the agent-as-tool pattern, the orchestrating agent retains full control of the overall workflow and simply calls another agent to handle a specific subtask, as shown in *Figure 6.5*:

Figure 6.5: Agent-as-tool pattern

In the handoff pattern, one agent fully delegates control to another agent, as shown in *Figure 6.6*:

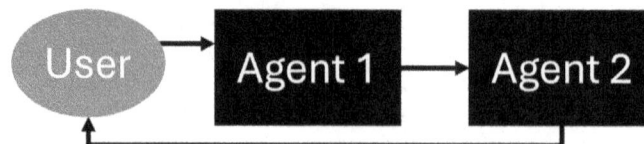

Figure 6.6: Handoff pattern

In this section, we'll cover how to set up handoffs, how to customize their behavior, what information gets passed during a handoff, how to filter or modify that information, and how to handle errors or multi-step handoffs. After that, we'll use handoffs to build different multi-agent systems.

Introduction to handoffs

Defining a handoff is very easy: when a new agent is instantiated, simply set a new argument called handoffs. This argument can accept a list of other agents that you have previously built. Each agent in the list can be a potential agent to which the starting agent can transfer control.

Let's dive right in and build a multi-agent system with a handoff. We will start with the previous example and simply change the tools argument to handoffs, and then remove the as_tool() function we had before. Create a new Python file called basic_handoff.py and type in the following code:

```python
from agents import Agent, Runner

# Create two agents
complaints_agent = Agent(
    name="Complaints Agent",
    instructions="Handle any customer complaints with empathy and clear
next steps."
)
inquiry_agent = Agent(
    name="General Inquiry Agent",
    instructions="Answer general questions about our services promptly."
)

# Create the triage agent with handoffs
triage_agent = Agent(
    name="Triage Agent",
    instructions="Triage the user's request and call the appropriate
agent",
    handoffs=[complaints_agent, inquiry_agent]
)

while True:
    question = input("You: ")
    result = Runner.run_sync(triage_agent, question)
    print("Agent: ", result.final_output)
```

In this program, triage_agent has two agents to which it can *hand off* the task: complaints_agent and inquiry_agent. An analogy is that we have created an office with three people: triage_agent answers the door and then walks the customer over to the appropriate person based on their question.

How does the triage agent know to which agent to hand off? Similar to the Tool primitive, the Handoff primitive exposes the name and instructions of the sub-agents to the triage agent, so it knows the roles of the two agents and can use that to determine whether it should hand off to them or not.

Let's try this out and verify that the agent is performing the handoff:

```
You: My meal is too hot
Agent:  Hi there, I'm sorry to hear that your meal is too hot. I
understand how this can be inconvenient. May I offer a few options to help
resolve this for you? We can provide a replacement meal, or if you prefer,
offer a partial refund. Let me know which option works best for you!
```

If we look at the **Traces** module, we can confirm that triage_agent is passing the task to complaints_agents:

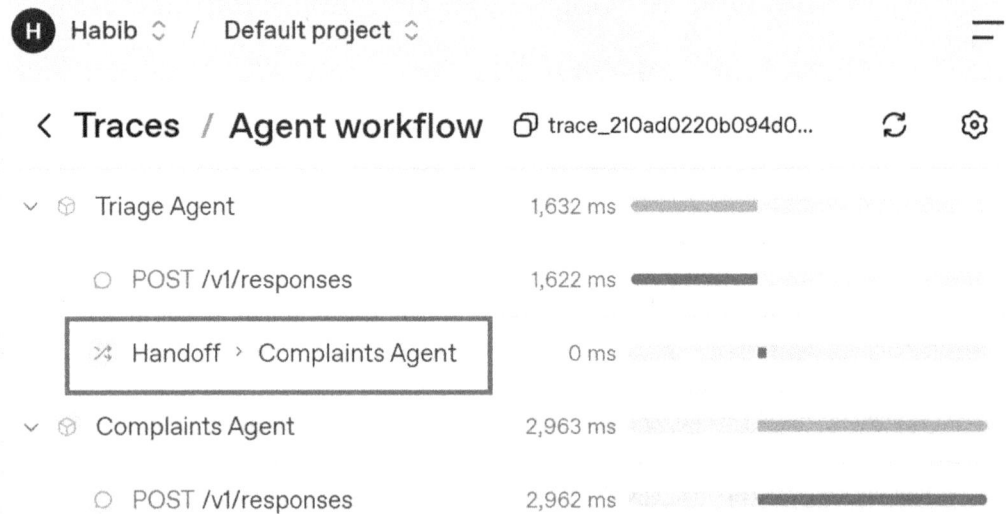

Figure 6.7: Handoff from one agent to another

The **Traces** module shows the transfer to complaints_agent, and complaints_agent fully takes over the task afterward.

Multi-agent switching

Note that complaints_agent is itself an agent, and so can have its own tools and handoffs. Currently, once complaints_agent gets control, it cannot transfer to any other agent. To fix this, let's go ahead and add handoffs to both complaints_agent and inquiry_agent, and allow Runner not to call the same triage_agent every time, but the last agent that responded to the user. This will enable us to see the power of a true dynamic multi-agent system that can easily switch between all agents. We are also going to amend the code so that we can have a multi-turn conversation with our agent.

Create a new Python file called multi_agent_switching.py and run the following code:

```python
from agents import Agent, Runner, SQLiteSession, trace

# Create two agents
complaints_agent = Agent(
    name="Complaints Agent",
    instructions="Introduce yourself as the complaints agent. Handle any
customer complaints with empathy and clear next steps."
)
sales_agent = Agent(
    name="Sales Agent",
    instructions="Introduce yourself as the sales agent. Answer general
questions about our services promptly."
)

# Create the triage agent with handoffs
triage_agent = Agent(
    name="Triage Agent",
    instructions="Answer general questions. Triage the user's request and
call the appropriate agent",
)

# Handoff all agents with each other
complaints_agent.handoffs = [sales_agent, triage_agent]
sales_agent.handoffs = [complaints_agent, triage_agent]
triage_agent.handoffs = [complaints_agent, sales_agent]
```

```
# Create a session
session = SQLiteSession("first_session")
last_agent = triage_agent

with trace("Multi-agent system"):
    while True:
        question = input("You: ")
        result = Runner.run_sync(last_agent, question, session=session)
        print("Agent: ", result.final_output)
        last_agent = result.last_agent
```

Let's examine what's happening in the code, especially with the sections that are highlighted.

We first establish our three agents. Next, we establish mutual handoffs between all three agents. This is key: previously, once control was passed to a secondary agent such as complaints_agent, the conversation was locked in with that agent for the remainder of the session. Now, by explicitly assigning .handoffs to each agent to include the others, any agent can delegate to any other, including back to triage_agent if needed. This sets the foundation for a fully dynamic multi-agent system.

We also introduce a persistent SQLiteSession to ensure that the conversation state is maintained across turns, which is what we learned in the previous chapter. This enables us to build on prior exchanges and lets agents remember where the conversation left off. Combined with the trace() context manager, which we will deep dive into in the next chapter, we can record all interactions for later debugging or inspection.

The last_agent variable tracks which agent was most recently active. Inside the loop, we continue the conversation by invoking Runner.run_sync(last_agent, question, session=session). This ensures that the agent currently handling the conversation receives the next user input, rather than always restarting with the triage agent. Once the response is processed, we update last_agent with result.last_agent, enabling seamless handoffs between agents as determined by the interaction flow.

For example, let's have the following conversation with the multi-agent system. Note that it seamlessly switches between multiple agents based on the messages in the conversation:

```
You: Hi, I'm Henry
Agent:  Hello Henry! How can I assist you today?
You: Transfer me to the complaints agent - My meal is too hot
```

```
Agent:  Hello Henry, I'm the complaints agent here to assist you. I
understand your meal was too hot, and I apologize for the inconvenience.
Could you tell me a bit more about the situation, so I can help resolve it
for you?
You: I have a general inquiry - how do I get my receipts?
Agent:  For receipt inquiries, you typically have a few options …
```

Here's what this example looks like on the **Traces** module:

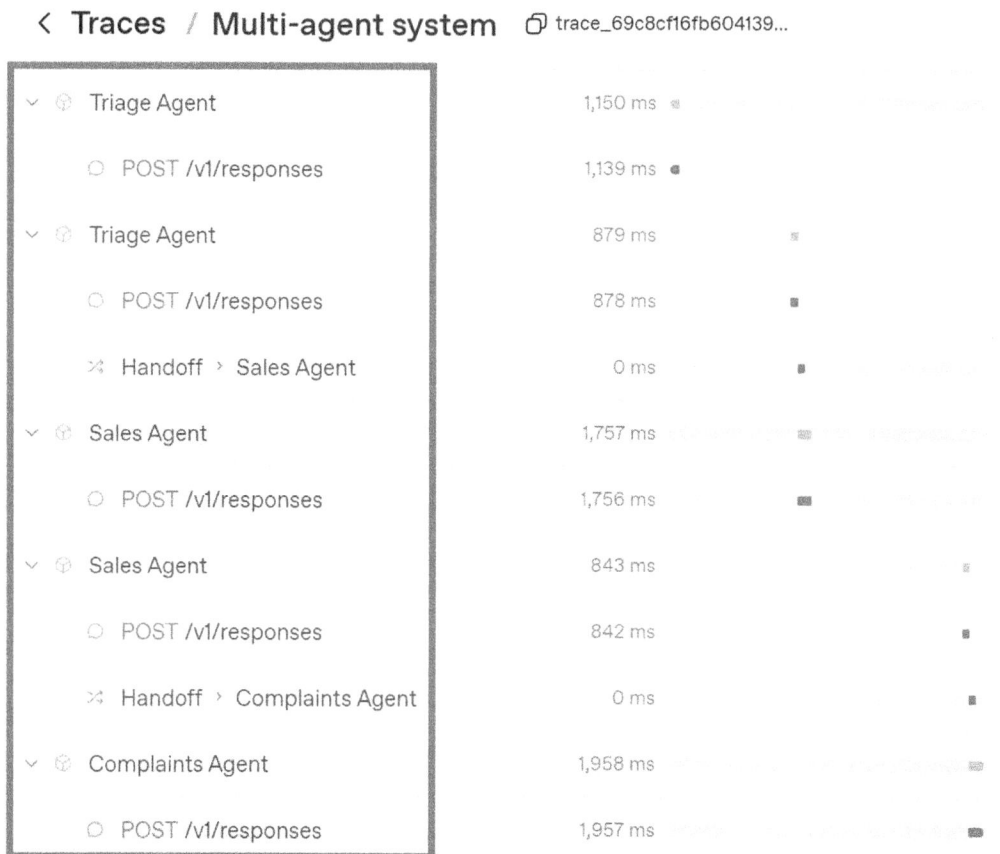

‹ Traces / Multi-agent system ⬡ trace_69c8cf16fb604139…

⌄ ⬡ Triage Agent	1,150 ms	
○ POST /v1/responses	1,139 ms	
⌄ ⬡ Triage Agent	879 ms	
○ POST /v1/responses	878 ms	
⤬ Handoff › Sales Agent	0 ms	
⌄ ⬡ Sales Agent	1,757 ms	
○ POST /v1/responses	1,756 ms	
⌄ ⬡ Sales Agent	843 ms	
○ POST /v1/responses	842 ms	
⤬ Handoff › Complaints Agent	0 ms	
⌄ ⬡ Complaints Agent	1,958 ms	
○ POST /v1/responses	1,957 ms	

Figure 6.8: Traces module in this example

This structure opens the door to truly dynamic multi-agent conversations where agents can not only take turns but also intelligently decide when to pass control to each other, depending on context. We have now created a flexible agent network that can assign the right agents for our tasks mid-conversation.

Customizing handoffs

OpenAI Agents SDK enables you to customize the properties of a handoff, which can be very useful under certain circumstances. The first thing to know is that the SDK contains a way to instantiate a handoff object with additional properties. These properties are as follows:

- agent: The agent to which the handoff will occur.

- `tool_name_override` and `tool_description_override`: Enable you to override what the description of the handoff is within the **Traces** module. As you've already seen, the default is "transfer to X."

- on_handoff: A function that will be triggered when the handoff is made. This is very useful for invoking functions if a handoff occurs (such as informing the user or even for logging purposes). The Agents SDK will also pass the conversation history to your callback function.

- `input_type` and `input_filter`: Enable you to refine the input expected by the handoff (you can, for example, instruct the LLM to pass a summarized view of the conversation so far, or trim the conversation history to the last five messages).

> **Note**
>
> A key consideration in handoffs is determining what context gets carried over to the new agent. By default, the SDK automatically transfers the full conversation history up to the handoff point. This includes all user inputs, system instructions, and the previous agent's messages and actions (essentially everything to which the original agent had access). From the user's point of view, there should be no need to repeat anything.

Let's go through an example of a handoff customization. We'll use a property that I most often use, which is the on_handoff property. We'll define a custom function that prints out when the system is handed off to a new agent. Create a new Python file called handoff_customization. py and run the following code:

```python
from agents import Agent, Runner, SQLiteSession, trace, handoff
from pydantic import BaseModel
import os

# Create two agents
complaints_agent = Agent(
    name="Complaints Agent",
```

```
    instructions="Introduce yourself as the complaints agent. Handle any
customer complaints with empathy and clear next steps."
)
sales_agent = Agent(
    name="Sales Agent",
    instructions="Introduce yourself as the sales agent. Answer general
questions about our services promptly."
)

# Create the triage agent with handoffs
triage_agent = Agent(
    name="Triage Agent",
    instructions="Answer general questions. Triage the user's request and
call the appropriate agent",
)
```

In this first section, we set up three agents: one for complaints, one for sales, and a triage agent that decides where to route a request. So far, this should feel familiar—it's the same setup you've seen earlier, but now we're preparing these agents for customized handoffs.

Next, let's define a model and logging function, and then create the handoff objects:

```
class NameOfAgentToBeHandedOff(BaseModel):
    name_of_agents_to_be_handed_off: str

# Create logging function
def log(ctx, name_of_agent):
    msg = f"The system has transferred you to another agent: {name_of_
agent.name_of_agents_to_be_handed_off}"
    print(msg)

# Create custom handoff
complaints_handoff = handoff(agent=complaints_agent, on_handoff=log,
input_type=NameOfAgentToBeHandedOff)
sales_handoff = handoff(agent=sales_agent, on_handoff=log, input_
type=NameOfAgentToBeHandedOff)
triage_handoff = handoff(agent=triage_agent, on_handoff=log, input_
type=NameOfAgentToBeHandedOff)
```

```
# Handoff all agents with each other
complaints_agent.handoffs = [sales_handoff, triage_handoff]
sales_agent.handoffs = [complaints_handoff, triage_handoff]
triage_agent.handoffs = [complaints_handoff, sales_handoff]

# Create a session
session = SQLiteSession("first_session")
last_agent = triage_agent

with trace("Multi-agent system"):
    while True:
        question = input("You: ")
        result = Runner.run_sync(last_agent, question, session=session)
        print("Agent: ", result.final_output)
        last_agent = result.last_agent
```

Let's walk through the changes we've made to this program from the previous section.

The first thing to notice is that instead of assigning agents directly to `.handoffs`, we now construct each handoff using the `handoff()` function from the SDK. This allows us to customize the behavior of the handoff in more advanced ways. In our case, we're attaching a logging function to each handoff using the on_handoff argument.

We define a simple `log()` function that prints out a message every time a handoff occurs. It receives the handoff context (`ctx`) and a model input (`name_of_agent`), and then prints a message indicating which agent the conversation is being transferred to. This gives us an effective way to track and debug agent transitions in real time.

To ensure our logging function receives structured input, we define a NameOfAgentToBeHandedOff class using Pydantic. This sets a clear expectation for the type of input data the handoff should use, and allows the SDK to validate and pass relevant fields into our `log()` function when the handoff occurs.

Each handoff is then initialized using this structure:

```
complaints_handoff = handoff(
    agent=complaints_agent, on_handoff=log,
    input_type=NameOfAgentToBeHandedOff)
```

This tells the SDK: "When handing off to `complaints_agent`, trigger the `log()` function and provide a structured input of type `NameOfAgentToBeHandedOff`." We repeat this for each agent, so that every handoff across the system is tracked.

Finally, instead of assigning bare agents to `.handoffs`, we now assign the corresponding handoff objects:

```
complaints_agent.handoffs = [sales_handoff, triage_handoff]
```

This gives us full control over how transitions happen and allows us to hook into those transitions with side effects such as logging, analytics, or even customized prompts. When we run the program and a handoff is performed, the following log is printed:

```
You: I want to make a complaint
The system has transferred you to another agent: Complaints Agent
Agent: Hello, I'm the Complaints Agent, and I'm here to help. Could you
please tell me what happened? Your feedback is important, and I want to
ensure we're addressing your concerns.
```

In short, this pattern adds a programmable hook to a simple delegation mechanic, so you can track agent behavior, enforce transition rules, or even edit the context dynamically. This is useful in real-world applications where logging and auditing are critical.

Handoff prompting

The ability for agents to hand off to other agents is just as good as the instructions that you provide to each agent. The agents involved in handoffs should have clear instructions about when and how to hand off, and what to do after a handoff. To do this, OpenAI Agents SDK actually provides you with a recommended prompt prefix to add to your agents:

```python
from agents import Agent, Runner
from agents.extensions.handoff_prompt import RECOMMENDED_PROMPT_PREFIX

print(RECOMMENDED_PROMPT_PREFIX)

# Create two agents
complaints_agent = Agent(
    name="Complaints Agent",
    instructions=f"{RECOMMENDED_PROMPT_PREFIX}. Introduce yourself as the
complaints agent. Handle any customer complaints with empathy and clear
next steps."
)
```

```python
inquiry_agent = Agent(
    name="General Inquiry Agent",
    instructions=f"{RECOMMENDED_PROMPT_PREFIX}. Introduce yourself as the
inquiry agent. Answer general questions about our services promptly."
)

# Create the triage agent with handoffs
triage_agent = Agent(
    name="Triage Agent",
    instructions=f"{RECOMMENDED_PROMPT_PREFIX}. Triage the user's request
and call the appropriate agent",
    handoffs=[complaints_agent, inquiry_agent]
)

while True:
    question = input("You: ")
    result = Runner.run_sync(triage_agent, question)
    print("Agent: ", result.final_output)
```

As you can see, `RECOMMENDED_PROMPT_PREFIX` is a string that represents a prompt prefix to add to all your agents:

```
# System context
You are part of a multi-agent system called the Agents SDK, designed
to make agent coordination and execution easy. Agents uses two primary
abstraction: **Agents** and **Handoffs**. An agent encompasses
instructions and tools and can hand off a conversation to another agent
when appropriate. Handoffs are achieved by calling a handoff function,
generally named `transfer_to_<agent_name>`. Transfers between agents are
handled seamlessly in the background; do not mention or draw attention to
these transfers in your conversation with the user.
```

This prefix contains system-level instructions that inform the agent that it's in a multi-agent environment and how to handle transfers (for example, it tells the agent that transfers are handled seamlessly and it shouldn't mention them to the user). It also updates dynamically; as you update the SDK, the underlying system prompt will also update. Placing this instruction at the beginning of an agent's system prompt (particularly for orchestrator or "triage" agents) guides the model to work in harmony with the handoff system. It informs the LLM that it has the ability to delegate tasks to other agents when appropriate, without openly disclosing that transition to the user.

There are other prompt-related tasks to make better multi-agent systems with handoffs:

- **Explicit handoff instructions**: Each agent's system prompt should specify the exact conditions under which a task should be delegated. For instance, "If the user asks a question related to sales, route it to the sales agent." The more explicit the instructions, the better the agent system will be.

- **Explicit agent instructions**: Each agent's instructions should clearly define its purpose and when it should be used. This helps the orchestrator or "triage" agent route to the appropriate agent.

Now that we know more about how to use handoffs within OpenAI Agents SDK, let's learn about the different multi-agent system patterns and how handoffs can be used to implement each one.

Multi-agent patterns

Describing how multiple agents are organized and structured refers to their architectural pattern. In this section, we are going to learn about the two main multi-agent architectural patterns, their benefits and drawbacks, and how we can use OpenAI Agents SDK to implement each one.

The two multi-agent architectural patterns are as follows:

- Centralized system
- Decentralized system

Let's go through each one.

Centralized system

The **centralized system** pattern is a multi-agent system where there is one central agent that then routes requests to other appropriate agents. This is the most common architectural pattern. The central agent is most often referred to as the "manager," "orchestrator," or "triage" agent, and the other agents are most often referred to as the "specialized" agents. The central agent is responsible for routing the user's requests, while the specialized agents are each experts in a particular function.

The benefits here are organization and a clear separation of responsibilities. The central agent specializes in routing requests; that is its only job. The specialized agents are "fine-tuned" (whether it's through prompting, choice of tools, model selection, or truly "fine-tuned" weights) for their specific purpose.

A structure where there are lots of specialized agents typically outperforms one agent doing everything; it's the same reason why, in a company, you have separate roles for each domain (HR, sales, engineering, etc.). Additional specialized agents can also be easily added to the system.

The biggest disadvantage with this approach is that the system is only as good as its central agent. If the central agent routes requests to agents incorrectly, the entire system fails. In this system, too, typically, specialized agents cannot communicate with each other. Instead, they are silo-ed. This is not optimal for specific tasks where interaction and teamwork between different domains are helpful.

This system is best for architectures that are naturally "top-down." An example is a customer support bot, where you typically describe your issue to a triaging agent that then hands off to the right agent for your query. Another example is a corporate internal assistant that helps employees navigate HR, IT, and facilities requests. The employee begins by describing their need to a central assistant, which then routes the query to the relevant specialized department agent. This mirrors how many real-world helpdesk ticketing systems work.

We are not going to go through an example here as all of the previous examples in this chapter have been done using a centralized system where there was a centralized triage agent that then routed the request to other specialized agents.

Hierarchical system

A subset of the centralized system is the hierarchical system. A **hierarchical system** is like a centralized system but with many tiers of hierarchy (picture a pyramid of multiple agents that become more and more specialized). This is typically how an organization works; you have the CEO (or the top orchestrator), and then you have a series of specialized agents below that, such as the CFO, COO, and CHRO, which then have a series of specialized agents underneath them. A hierarchical system has a set of intermediate agents that further divide tasks and provide context/instruction to their own subset of specialized agents.

This hierarchical pattern excels in handling complex tasks by breaking them down into manageable subcomponents, which are then broken down even further. It also promotes the reuse of common subtasks and helps keep each agent's scope focused. The downside is that this structure can introduce unnecessary overhead if the task does not warrant it. More layers mean more cost, more latency, more risk of failure, and more communication complexity. Poorly managed hierarchies can also distort or confuse information, and debugging becomes almost impossible.

As mentioned before, the best use case for these types of systems is handling large, complex queries, such as deep research.

Let's create an example of a hierarchical system to answer complex research questions. We will create a centralized triage agent, two manager agents (one that manages science questions and the other that manages history questions), and a subset of specialized agents (three for each manager, each one specializing in a sub-domain).

Create a new Python file called hierarchical.py and run the following code:

```python
from agents import Agent, Runner, SQLiteSession, trace


# Create our agents
# Specialized science agents
physics_agent = Agent(name="Physics Agent", instructions="Answer questions
about physics.")
chemistry_agent = Agent(name="Chemistry Agent", instructions="Answer
questions about chemistry.")
medical_agent = Agent(name="Medical Agent", instructions="Answer questions
about medical science.")


# Specialized history agents
politics_agent = Agent(name="Politics Agent", instructions="Answer
questions about political history.")
warfare_agent = Agent(name="Warfare Agent", instructions="Answer questions
about wars and military history.")
culture_agent = Agent(name="Culture Agent", instructions="Answer questions
about cultural history.")


# Manager agents with handoffs to their respective domains
science_manager = Agent(
    name="Science Manager",
    instructions="Manage science-related queries and route them to the
appropriate subdomain agent.",
    handoffs=[physics_agent, chemistry_agent, medical_agent]
)

history_manager = Agent(
    name="History Manager",
```

```
    instructions="Manage history-related queries and route them to the
appropriate subdomain agent.",
    handoffs=[politics_agent, warfare_agent, culture_agent]
)


# Top-level triage agent
triage_agent = Agent(
    name="Research Triage Agent",
    instructions="Triage the user's question and decide whether it's
science or history related, and route accordingly.",
    handoffs=[science_manager, history_manager]
)


# Create a session
session = SQLiteSession("hierarchy")
last_agent = triage_agent

with trace("Hierarchical system"):
    while True:
        question = input("You: ")
        result = Runner.run_sync(last_agent, question, session=session)
        print("Agent: ", result.final_output)
        last_agent = result.last_agent
```

Let's try this agent and look at the traces log:

```
You: Which war after the year 1600 led to the greatest death toll?
Agent:  The war after 1600 that led to the greatest death toll is World
War II. It is estimated to have caused the deaths of approximately 70 to
85 million people, including military personnel and civilians.
```

Now, let's see what this looks like in the **Traces** module.

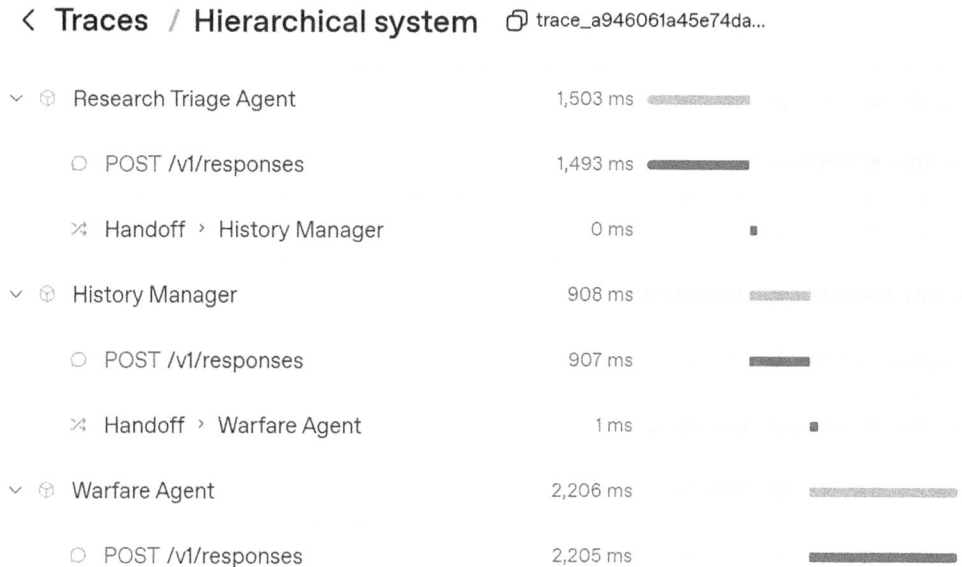

< **Traces** / **Hierarchical system**   ⬡ trace_a946061a45e74da...

⌄ ⬡ Research Triage Agent	1,503 ms	
○ POST /v1/responses	1,493 ms	
⤢ Handoff › History Manager	0 ms	
⌄ ⬡ History Manager	908 ms	
○ POST /v1/responses	907 ms	
⤢ Handoff › Warfare Agent	1 ms	
⌄ ⬡ Warfare Agent	2,206 ms	
○ POST /v1/responses	2,205 ms	

Figure 6.9: Traces module of the example

Let's walk through what's happening here.

When the user enters a question, it first reaches the top-level agent, the research triage agent. This agent's job is to determine whether the question is related to science or history. In this case, the question is clearly historical in nature, so the triage agent hands it off to **History Manager**. Once **History Manager** receives the query, it further inspects the topic and decides which of its specialized agents is best suited to answer it. Since the question is about wars and death tolls, **History Manager** routes the question to **Warfare Agent**.

Warfare Agent is a domain expert in military history, so it processes the question and generates a response. The answer is then returned up the chain to the user.

This layered delegation ensures that each agent operates within a well-bounded responsibility, mirroring how complex tasks are broken down in structured organizations. The user, however, only experiences a single seamless interaction.

We can see this clearly in the **Traces** module: the triage agent passes the task to **History Manager**, which then passes the task to the warfare agent. The user is now speaking to **Warfare Agent** directly as their question relates to war.

In a more realistic example, the specialized agents would probably contain their own subset of tools and knowledge relevant to their purpose. For instance, **Warfare Agent** could be equipped with a tool to query a historical conflict database or access long-form research documents on global conflicts. Similarly, **Chemistry Agent** might have access to a scientific paper summarizer or a periodic table calculator.

Decentralized system

A **decentralized system** is the exact opposite of a centralized system. Here, there is no single triage agent; instead, multiple agents collaborate directly to address the user's request. In this system, there are no silos; all agents can communicate with each other. A good analogy is a roundtable discussion where there is no leader and instead all agents weigh in to produce the final answer.

The benefit of this pattern is that it enables creativity, and so excels at brainstorming, ideation, or debate-type exercises. Decentralized agents can enhance solutions collaboratively through iterative dialogue or idea exchange, as seen in some research on agent self-play (see Google AlphaZero). The decentralized system enables agents to tackle problems from different angles.

A large downside here is the lack of coordination. Managing conversation flow in a decentralized system requires deterministic orchestration (recall that deterministic orchestration refers to hardcoded control logic and all the drawbacks that the system provides) since OpenAI Agents SDK does not support this.

Again, the best use case for these types of systems is where creativity and novel thinking are required: brainstorming, ideation, negotiation, debate, and so on.

Let's go through an example. We'll create two agents that are specialists in opposing viewpoints: one of them will act as a landlord and the other will act as a tenant. We will then force a conversation flow between the two agents on a particular controversial topic, such as "Should there be rent control?" After a few rounds of back and forth, we will pass the conversation history to another agent that will summarize the main arguments and return that back to us.

Create a new Python file called `decentralized.py` and run the following code:

```
from agents import Agent, Runner, SQLiteSession, trace

# Create our agents
```

```
landlord_agent = Agent(
    name="Landlord Agent",
    instructions="Argue against rent control from the perspective of a
landlord. Present strong economic and property-rights arguments."
)

tenant_agent = Agent(
    name="Tenant Agent",
    instructions="Argue in favor of rent control from the perspective of a
tenant. Emphasize affordability, housing rights, and tenant protections."
)

summarizer_agent = Agent(
    name="Summarizer Agent",
    instructions="Summarize the main arguments presented by both the
landlord and tenant agents in a neutral and concise way."
)

# Create a session
session = SQLiteSession("decentralized")
landlord_turn = True
conversation_history = []

with trace("Decentralized system"):
    print("Topic: Should there be rent control?")
    for _ in range(6):  # 6 rounds of back-and-forth
        if landlord_turn:
            agent = landlord_agent
        else:
            agent = tenant_agent
        prompt = "\n".join([f"{msg['role']}: {msg['content']}"
                            for msg in conversation_history])
        response = Runner.run_sync(agent,
            prompt or "Debate starting now.", session=session)
        print(f"{agent.name}: {response.final_output}")
        conversation_history.append({"role": agent.name,
            "content": response.final_output})
        landlord_turn = not landlord_turn
```

```
# After the debate, have the moderator summarize
summary_prompt = "\n".join([f"{msg['role']}: {msg['content']}"
                    for msg in conversation_history])
result = Runner.run_sync(summarizer_agent, summary_prompt,
    session=session)
print("\nSummary of the Debate:")
print(result.final_output)
```

In this file, we created two opposing agents (Landlord Agent and Tenant Agent), each with a specific viewpoint and set of instructions tailored to argue one side of a contentious issue. These agents are not orchestrated by a triage or manager agent; instead, they take alternating turns in a back-and-forth conversation, simulating a debate.

This illustrates how a decentralized system can foster dynamic multi-agent interaction without relying on a central decision-maker. Each agent is autonomous but still builds on the contributions of others. The result is a layered, collaborative conversation that evolves through emergent behavior rather than rigid orchestration.

If we run the program, we can see the entire negotiation in the conversation history and the following summarized version:

```
In the debate on rent control, the landlord agent argues that it
discourages investment in property maintenance due to capped revenue,
reduces housing supply by deterring new investment, creates market
distortions by not reflecting supply and demand, and decreases tenant
mobility by encouraging them to stay in units that may no longer suit
their needs. They also claim it infringes on property rights, often favors
long-term tenants unfairly, imposes administrative burdens, and undermines
fair compensation for landlords.

Conversely, the tenant agent supports rent control for stabilizing rents,
reducing economic anxiety, promoting housing security, and ensuring
equitable access. They emphasize tenant protections against exploitation
and the preservation of community ties. The tenant agent argues that rent
control encourages efficient use of housing and should be part of broader
policies addressing housing issues, promoting stability and fairness as
essential for community sustainability
```

We can also see the back-and-forth in the **Traces** module:

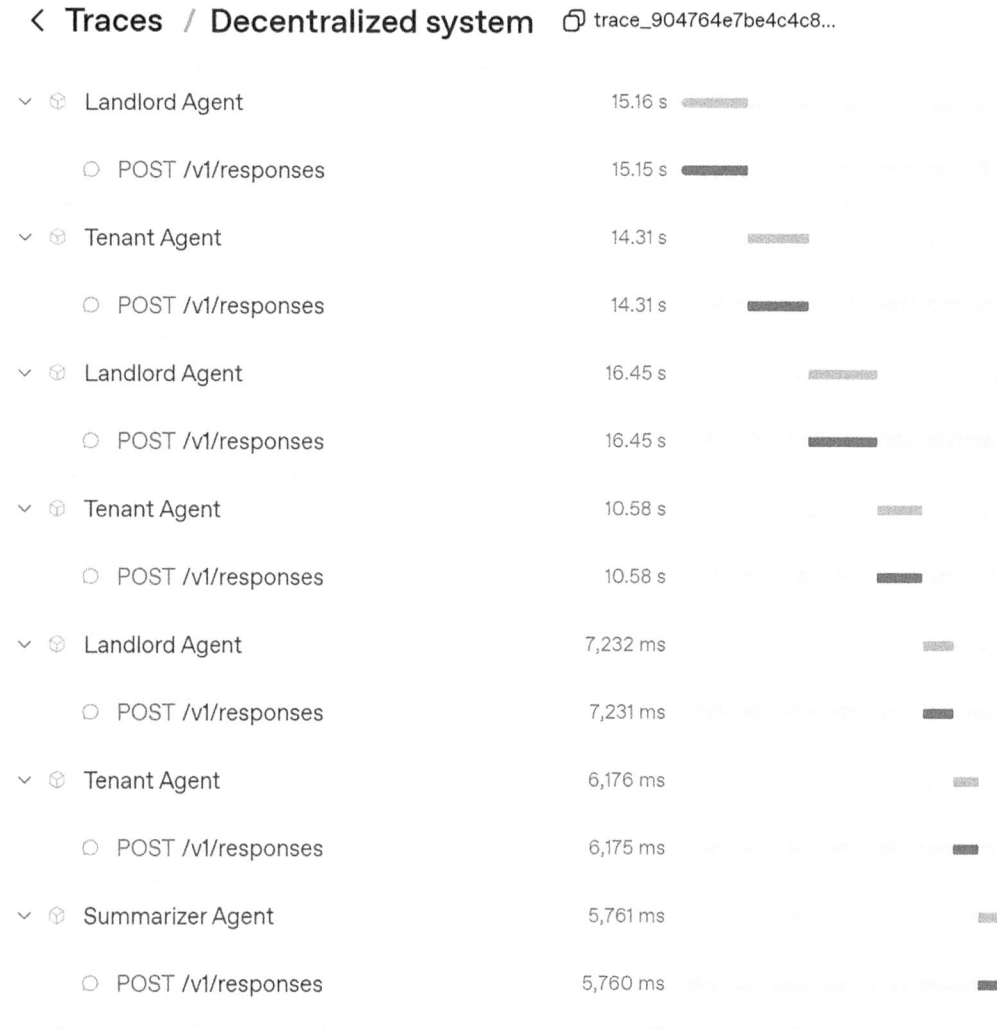

Figure 6.10: Traces module for this example

Again, this pattern is excellent for scenarios that depend on idea diversity and exchange.

Swarm system

A subset of a decentralized system is the **swarm system**, where there are many relatively simple agents that work together (typically in parallel) to produce an answer. This relies on a concept called **emergent properties**, where a global system can become intelligent and complex by relying on many unintelligent and simple smaller systems. A good analogy is cells in your body. Each cell by itself is not that intelligent and focuses on doing a small subset of tasks. Millions of different specialized cells, however, can come together to produce a human being, which is an intelligent system. Another example, which is more data science-related, is the random forest model. This model relies on hundreds of weak models that, when they come together, produce an intelligent prediction model.

Swarm systems can produce very creative and novel ideas, and can distribute tasks in parallel (so, they are ultimately very scalable). There's also no single failure point as multiple agents are deployed; if one fails, that's okay. The biggest downside of swarm systems is managing the overhead. With multiple (even thousands of) agents, cost is a big factor, and managing them all in a computerized way is difficult. Also, there's a risk that the swarm system does not show any emergent properties, which, in that case, is a complete waste of time and money.

Swarm patterns are especially useful for tasks that benefit from exploration, such as creative generation, optimization, or problem-solving with multiple potential approaches. One common use case is generating a variety of solution candidates and then refining or selecting among them.

Let's go through a very simple example. In this case, we'll create a program that spins up 10 agents in parallel that act as different roles within a city (a doctor, a mechanic, a chef, etc.). Each agent will answer the same question: "If you were to design your dream city from scratch, what would it have?" We will then pass these results to another agent that will consolidate all the points and return to us the final summary.

Create a new Python file called swarm.py and enter the following code:

```python
from agents import Agent, Runner, SQLiteSession, trace
import concurrent.futures

# Create our agents
roles = [
    "Urban Planner", "Artist", "Chef", "Engineer", "Teacher",
    "Doctor", "Mechanic", "Lawyer", "Historian", "Environmentalist"
]
```

```
city_agents = [
    Agent(
        name=f"{role} Agent",
        instructions=f"You are a {role.lower()}. Answer the question: 'If
you were to design your dream city from scratch, what would it have?' Be
creative and imaginative, but concise"
    ) for role in roles
]


# Define the summary agent
summary_agent = Agent(
    name="City Design Aggregator",
    instructions="You are a city designer. You've just received 10
creative responses from different citizens. Read all of their responses
and consolidate them into a cohesive, imaginative, and well-rounded city
plan."
)


# Create a session
session = SQLiteSession("swarm")
conversation_history = []

with trace("Swarm system"):
    prompt = "Design your dream city from scratch. What would it have?"

    # Collect individual responses one by one
    for agent in city_agents:
        result = Runner.run_sync(agent, prompt, session=session)
        print(f"{agent.name}: {result.final_output}\n")
        conversation_history.append(
            f"{agent.name}: {result.final_output}")

    # Combine responses into one prompt
    combined responses = "\n\n".join(conversation_history)
    final_result = Runner.run_sync(summary_agent, combined_responses,
        session=session)

    # Output the final city plan
    print("\nFinal City Design Summary:")
    print(final_result.final_output)
```

In this code, we defined a "swarm" of 10 agents, each with its own identity and creative perspective based on its role in a city. All agents receive the same prompt about designing a dream city, and they respond independently in parallel using a thread pool. Because each agent was instructed to lean into its domain expertise, the swarm approach allows us to explore the design space from 10 different vantage points.

Once all responses are gathered, we pass them to a summary_agent object, which synthesizes the collective input into a single, imaginative city plan. This final output represents the *emergent* result of many independent thinkers contributing their ideas.

The final city plan incorporates all the sub-agents' ideas:

```
Final City Design Summary:
Creating a dream city involves synthesizing ideas from various
perspectives to form a cohesive and innovative urban landscape. Here's a
consolidated plan:


### **Ecological Balance and Sustainability:**
1. **Green Infrastructure**: Expansive parks, urban forests, rooftop
gardens, and community gardens to promote biodiversity and provide
recreational spaces.
2. **Sustainable Architecture**: Buildings with solar panels, green roofs,
energy-efficient systems, and natural materials to minimize environmental
impact.


### **Transportation and Connectivity:**
3. **Integrated Public Transport**: A seamless network of trams, buses,
bike lanes, and pedestrian paths that reduces reliance on cars and
encourages eco-friendly commuting.
4. **Smart Technology**: IoT systems for efficient energy use, traffic
management, and public services, enhancing connectivity and convenience.


### **Cultural and Community Enrichment:**
5. **Cultural Hubs**: Dynamic districts with theaters, galleries, and
multicultural festivals celebrating global traditions and creativity.
6. **Mixed-Use Developments**: Blending residential, commercial, and
cultural spaces to create vibrant, walkable neighborhoods.
```

```
### **Energy and Resource Management:**
7. **Renewable Energy**: Wind turbines and solar farms providing clean
power supply, alongside innovative systems for recycling and conserving
water.
8. **Water Management**: Advanced recycling and conservation measures,
integrating natural waterways into urban planning.

### **Housing and Social Equity:**
9. **Inclusive Housing**: Affordable, diverse options ensuring
accessibility for all income levels, fostering social equity and
community.
10. **Community Spaces**: Libraries, cultural centers, sports facilities,
and community hubs to promote engagement and inclusivity.

### **Education, Innovation, and Safety:**
11. **Educational and Innovation Centers**: State-of-the-art schools
and research facilities supporting lifelong learning and creativity.12.
**Resilient Infrastructure**: Climate-adaptive designs and resilient
infrastructure to manage and mitigate environmental changes and
extreme weather.

### **Local and Sustainable Food Systems:**
13. **Local Food Networks**: Urban farms and farmers' markets promoting
fresh, local produce and food security.

By integrating these elements, the city would thrive on sustainability,
innovation, and inclusivity, setting a benchmark for future urban
developments.
```

To summarize, OpenAI Agents SDK provides the flexibility to implement all architectural patterns for multi-agent systems. As you've seen in this section, each pattern can be implemented as a stand-alone script using the SDK's agent creation, handoff, and memory management capabilities.

Summary

In this chapter, we explored how to coordinate multiple agents to solve complex tasks by introducing orchestration and handoff strategies in OpenAI Agents SDK.

We first distinguished between deterministic and dynamic orchestration. We then introduced the handoff mechanism, a core OpenAI Agents SDK primitive that enables one agent to pass control to another. We expanded this further with multi-agent switching, allowing agents to transfer control back and forth in longer conversations using persistent memory, and customizing handoffs through callback functions and prompts.

Finally, we explored the four different multi-agent system patterns: centralized, hierarchical (subset of centralized), decentralized, and swarm (subset of decentralized).

In the next chapter, we'll learn how to manage the underlying workhorse of agents: the LLM.

Subscribe for a free eBook

New frameworks, evolving architectures, research drops, production breakdowns—*AI_Distilled* filters the noise into a weekly briefing for engineers and researchers working hands-on with LLMs and GenAI systems. Subscribe now and receive a free eBook, along with weekly insights that help you stay focused and informed.

Subscribe at `https://packt.link/80z6Y` or scan the QR code below.

7

Model and Context Management

Up to this point, we've mostly relied on the default GPT-4o model when building agents with OpenAI Agents SDK. One of the most powerful features of OpenAI Agents SDK, however, is its **model-agnostic** design. In other words, you are not locked into a single model provider or configuration. This flexibility becomes especially valuable in complex workflows or multi-agent systems, where different stages of the process might benefit from different capabilities or cost/latency.

Consider a multi-agent system that begins with a triage agent, whose simple job is to ask simple questions to the user. Using GPT-4 for this task may not be appropriate. Instead, we may want a simpler model or a non-OpenAI open sourced model, such as LLaMA, which costs next to nothing. Meanwhile, a more demanding task, such as performing research or math operations, may require advanced Anthropic models. At the same time, a brainstorming agent may need the standard GPT-4o LLM, but with a much higher temperature.

OpenAI Agents SDK supports this architectural pattern. Each agent can use a different model and its own configuration settings.

Here is what you will learn as part of this chapter:

- **Model management**: We'll begin by learning how to adjust the model, model settings, and how to integrate third-party models into agents
- **Context management**: You'll learn how to leverage local context to pass information into tools without the LLM being privy to that information

By the end of this chapter, you'll learn how to manage models and contexts effectively in your agent solutions.

Technical requirements

Please follow the detailed steps in *Chapter 3* to set up your environment.

Throughout this book, practical examples and the complete code from each chapter will be made available via the accompanying GitHub repository at `https://github.com/PacktPublishing/Building-Agents-with-OpenAI-Agents-SDK`.

You are encouraged to clone the repository, reuse and adapt the provided code samples, and refer to it as needed while progressing through the chapters.

Model management

In OpenAI Agents SDK, each agent must be powered by an LLM. The LLM acts as the brain of the agent, being able to read information, call tools, and generate responses. So far, we have used the default configuration when instantiating an agent. This defaults the agent's model to *GPT-4o* with default model settings. In this section, we will go through how and when to modify this parameter.

Adjusting the underlying model

OpenAI Agents SDK enables you to explicitly select the underlying model you want to use. Each model has its own benefits and drawbacks, and it is advantageous to use the right model for the right type of agent that you are building. For example, GPT-4o can produce fast and accurate responses, whereas o3-pro can reason and address complex questions but is far slower.

To adjust the model, you can simply use the `model` parameter when instantiating an agent. This demo will show how to adjust the model that the agent uses:

```
agent = Agent(
    name="SampleAgent",
    instructions="You are an AI agent",
    model="gpt-4o"
)
```

This parameter can take any valid model name from OpenAI. To see a list of all model names, their benefits, and their cost, go to `https://platform.openai.com/docs/models`.

Let's go through an example of why it is so critical to choose the right model using this parameter. In this example, we will create two agents, each one with a different model parameter (GPT-4o versus o3-pro). We will then see how it answers the same question and see how long each one takes to answer.

Create a new Python file called `different_models.py` and type in the following code. This demo will show us how we can have agents that use different underlying models:

```
from agents import Agent, Runner
import time

# Create two agents
gpt4o_agent = Agent(
    name="GPT4o Agent",
    instructions="You are an AI Agent",
    model="gpt-4o"
)
o3pro_agent = Agent(
    name="o3-pro Agent",
    instructions="You are an AI Agent",
    model="o3-pro"
)

prompt = "How many integers from 1 to 10000 (inclusive) are divisible by 3
or by 5 but not by both? Do reasoning but only return only the answer."

print("gpt4o agent")
start_fast = time.time()
response = Runner.run_sync(gpt4o_agent, prompt)
print(response.final_output)
end_fast = time.time()
print(f"Time taken: {end_fast - start_fast:.2f} seconds")
print("---")

start_fast = time.time()
print("o3pro agent")
response = Runner.run_sync(o3pro_agent, prompt)
print(response.final_output)
```

```
end_fast = time.time()
print(f"Time taken: {end_fast - start_fast:.2f} seconds")
print("---")
```

Running this program gives the following output:

```
gpt4o agent
3334
Time taken: 1.18 seconds
---
o3pro agent
4001
Time taken: 8.41 seconds
---
```

In practice, the GPT-4o agent typically responds within a couple of seconds, but unfortunately, it produces the wrong answer to this complex math problem. The o3-pro agent, however, answers it correctly but takes almost eight times the amount of time (and can actually cost up to 10x more than the standard GPT-4o model).

So, there is an inherent trade-off between accuracy versus latency/cost, but OpenAI Agents SDK enables you to choose the right model for each agent.

Adjusting the model settings

Let's go beyond choosing which model to use. Often, you want to keep the same model for each agent, but instead, you may want to fine-tune how the model generates responses. For instance, you might want shorter answers or more creative phrasing. OpenAI's API (and most LLM APIs) provide model settings or parameters for this purpose. OpenAI Agents SDK exposes this as a ModelSettings object that can be passed into the model_settings argument when instantiating an object. We have discussed a few of these settings previously, but listed here are the most common settings that are used:

- temperature: This parameter controls randomness in the output. Lower values (e.g., 0.2) make the model more deterministic, while higher values (e.g., 0.8) generate more creative or diverse responses.
- max_tokens: This limits the maximum number of tokens (or words) the model can generate in its response. This is helpful for controlling how verbose the agent's response is.

You can find a full list of these settings in the OpenAI Agents SDK reference guide: `https://openai.github.io/openai-agents-python/ref/model_settings/#agents.model_settings.ModelSettings`

Let's go through an example of changing the model settings and then observing its impact on the generated response. Similar to the previous example, we will create two agents: one with a high temperature and a long `max_tokens` amount, and another with a low temperature and a short `max_tokens` amount.

Create a new Python file called `different_model_settings.py` and enter the following code:

```
from agents import Agent, Runner
from agents.model_settings import ModelSettings

# create agents
creative_agent = Agent(
    name="CreativeAgent",
    instructions="You are an AI agent that answers questions.",
    model="gpt-4o",
    model_settings=ModelSettings(
        temperature=1.0,
        max_tokens=300
    )
)

precise_agent = Agent(
    name="PreciseAgent",
    instructions="You are an AI agent that answers questions.",
    model="gpt-4o",
    model_settings=ModelSettings(
        temperature=0.2,
        max_tokens=50
    )
)

prompt = "Describe the future of AI in customer service."

print("Creative agent:")
response = Runner.run_sync(creative_agent, prompt)
```

```
print(response.final_output)
print("---")

print("Precise agent:")
response = Runner.run_sync(precise_agent, prompt)
print(response.final_output)
print("---")
```

Running this script yields two very different styles of output. The `creative_agent` object produces a longer and more imaginative response, sometimes including speculative or futuristic language. The `precise_agent` object, on the other hand, responds with a shorter and more cautious summary. In fact, because the `max_tokens` parameter is so small, the `precise_agent` object actually gets cut off. The following shows both outputs:

```
Creative agent:
The future of AI in customer service is set to be transformative,
continuing to enhance efficiency, personalization, and customer
satisfaction. Here are some key trends and developments:

1. **Advanced Chatbots and Virtual Assistants**: AI-powered chatbots will
become more sophisticated, handling complex queries, understanding context
better, and providing more human-like interactions. They will seamlessly
integrate across multiple communication channels.
...
6. **AI-Agent Collaboration**: Human agents will increasingly work
alongside AI, using AI-driven insights to enhance their own response
capabilities. AI will handle routine inquiries, freeing humans to focus on
complex issues.

7. **Self-Service Optimization**: AI will enhance self-service platforms,
making it easier and faster for customers to find solutions without direct
human intervention
---
Precise agent:
The future of AI in customer service is poised to be transformative,
offering enhanced efficiency, personalization, and scalability. Here are
some key trends and developments:

1. **24/7 Availability**: AI-powered chatbots and virtual assistants will
provide round-the
```

This simple example shows how tuning model settings such as temperature (which controls randomness) and max_tokens (which controls response length) can dramatically change an agent's tone and verbosity, without needing to change the underlying model. This enables you to adapt the same model to different types of agents, such as a customer service sales bot versus a research idea generator, simply by modifying the model settings.

Third-party models

As we mentioned at the beginning of this chapter, OpenAI Agents SDK is model-agnostic. It can run with any model, from any provider, provided that it follows certain characteristics. While GPT-4o and other OpenAI models are excellent defaults, there are many scenarios where using a different LLM might be preferable. For example, the Claude models from Anthropic might follow certain instructions better, or you may want to use Meta's LLaMA models for cost reasons.

OpenAI Agents SDK achieves being able to accommodate other models with LiteLLM. **LiteLLM** is a lightweight Python library that provides a unified API over many popular LLM providers (Anthropic, Google, etc.). Using LiteLLM makes integrating third-party models super straightforward. LiteLLM takes care of API key handling, request routing, and response formatting behind the scenes, so you can switch model providers without changing your agent code.

The first step is installing the LiteLLM library. To do this, open your terminal and enter the following command:

```
$ pip install "openai-agents[litellm]"
```

After that, we need the API key of a non-OpenAI model provider. For this example, we are going to choose Anthropic. To get an Anthropic API key, go to https://www.anthropic.com/, create an account, and go to your account dashboard. Under **API keys**, click **Create new key**, and then copy your API key. After that, go to your .env file that we set up in *Chapter 3* and add a new line with the following contents:

```
ANTHROPIC_API_KEY=sk-ant-api03-[your-remaining-api-key]-995
```

With LiteLLM installed and the required API key being provisioned, we can now build AI agents by using Anthropic's LLMs. To do this, you can simply set the model parameter (when instantiating the agent) to a LiteLLM string that specifies the model parameter and the model. Here are some example LiteLLM strings:

- litellm/gemini/gemini-pro
- litellm/anthropic/claude-opus-4-20250514
- litellm/meta_llama/Llama-3.3-70B-Instruct

Let's go through a simple example. Create a new file called `third_party_models.py` and enter the following code:

```python
from agents import Agent, Runner
import time

# Create an agent
agent = Agent(
    name="Claude Agent",
    instructions="You are an AI Agent",
    model="litellm/anthropic/claude-opus-4-20250514"
)

question = "How do I restart my computer? Answer in a few words."

response = Runner.run_sync(agent, question)
print(response.final_output)
```

Running this program creates and executes an agent just as before, but it uses the Anthropic Claude model to do it instead. Here's an example response.

```
**Windows:** Start menu → Power → Restart
**Mac:** Apple menu → Restart
**Or:** Press and hold power button, then turn back on
```

In this way, you can seamlessly swap out the underlying LLM behind your agent without needing to refactor your logic or pipeline. The agent behaves the same way, regardless of whether it's powered by GPT-4o, Claude, or LLaMA (so long as the model interface is handled within LiteLLM).

This abstraction is very useful when benchmarking different providers for your use case, or when deploying agents across environments with varying privacy, latency, or cost constraints. For example, you might want to prototype with GPT-4o during development and switch to Claude for better summarization in production.

Context management

The **context** refers to everything to which an agent has access. A good analogy is that the agent's LLM is its brain, whereas the agent's context is the information that is communicated to the brain to generate a response. We have already discussed several ways to expose important information to the agent, through system instructions, previous conversation history, prompt injections, and even through knowledge retrieval from tool calls.

In this section, we will narrow the context down to the **local context** (also called the run context). This refers to the information that is needed to instantiate the agent and acts as a dependency on tools and other hooks.

Local context

Local context enables your agent to access information (from when the agent was instantiated) without that data being explicitly part of the LLM's prompt. This is most useful for storing user-specific information (e.g., user ID, name, preferences) so that tools can fetch or compute answers based on it. This unlocks a powerful design pattern. It enables your agent to operate with privileged or application-specific data (such as user preferences, authentication tokens, or internal state) without ever embedding that data into the prompt sent to the model. This means your agent can make decisions or generate personalized outputs based on sensitive or proprietary information while keeping that information entirely outside the LLM's prompt.

In OpenAI Agents SDK, you implement local context by creating a context object and then passing it to the Runner call via the context argument. After you've instantiated the agent with that context object, any tool can use it, provided that it also contains a context parameter.

Let's illustrate this with a concrete example. Imagine our customer service agent can check the shipping status of an order based on a user's profile and their active order. We'll simulate that by providing an OrderContext object containing the user's name and order details, and a tool function that uses that information to provide a shipping update.

First, create a new Python file called local_context.py and type in the following code:

```python
from dataclasses import dataclass
from agents import Agent, Runner, RunContextWrapper, function_tool


@dataclass
class OrderContext:
    customer_name: str
    order_id: str
    shipping_status: str


order_context = OrderContext(
    customer_name="Henry Habib",
    order_id="123",
    shipping_status="Delayed"
)
```

```python
@function_tool
def get_shipping_status(wrapper: RunContextWrapper[OrderContext]) -> str:
    """Provide the shipping status for the current order."""
    ctx = wrapper.context
    return (
        f"Hi {ctx.customer_name}, your order {ctx.order_id} is currently:
"
        f"{ctx.shipping_status}."
    )


agent = Agent[OrderContext](
    name="Shipping Support Agent",
    instructions="You are a helpful support agent who can check the
shipping status of a user's order.",
    tools=[get_shipping_status]
)

question = "Where is my order?"
result = Runner.run_sync(agent, input=question, context=order_context)
print(result.final_output)
```

We start by defining a data class called OrderContext, which includes three fields: the customer's name, their order ID, and the current shipping status. This object represents the local context we want the agent to have access to (i.e., the information that will be readily available for tool functions to consume).

We then create an OrderContext object with a sample customer and order information. In a real-world application, this context might be generated dynamically for each user session, based on where this agent is "invoked."

Next, when we define a tool function called get_shipping_status, we have it consume a context object (RunContextWrapper[OrderContext]) as an argument. This tells the agent to pass the context object as an argument to the tool function. When we define an agent named "Shipping Support Agent", this agent is equipped with the get_shipping_status tool, but most importantly, the agent is parameterized with the same OrderContext type, so it knows what kind of context it will receive. This is very important. This is done when the agent is instantiated (agent = Agent[OrderContext]).

Because the agent has this additional parameter, a context object of that type must be defined when `Runner.run_sync()` is called. The SDK automatically routes the query to the tool, which generates a response using the context data.

Here is an example response, showing that the agent passed the context information to the tool function call:

```
Hi Henry Habib, your order (123) is currently delayed. If you have any
further questions or need assistance, please let me know!
```

This illustrates one of the key benefits of local context: the agent can generate accurate, personalized responses using sensitive information that never appears in the model's prompt. To summarize, local context objects give your agent a way to have an "internal memory" that isn't directly revealed to the user or the model's prompt. It's a form of injecting domain knowledge or user-specific data into the agent's tooling.

Summary

In this chapter, we covered how to select and configure the model behind each agent. We learned how to adjust the model and model settings for each agent. We learned how to integrate third-party models via LiteLLM, enabling easy switching between providers such as Claude, Gemini, and LLaMA. Finally, we introduced local context, a way to give agents access to sensitive or session-specific data without including it in the model prompt.

Together, these techniques give you full control over how your agents think and respond. In the next chapter, we'll shift focus to managing, administering, and securing your agents. You'll learn how to monitor agent activity, enforce guardrails, and apply best practices for governance in production environments.

8

Agent System Management

As your agentic systems grow in complexity, keeping them reliable and understandable becomes just as important as building their core logic. Multi-agent systems can quickly become difficult to reason about, with many agents, tools, and handoffs interacting in non-obvious ways. To manage this complexity, OpenAI Agents SDK provides powerful features for visualization, guardrails, observability, and testing.

Here is what you will learn as part of this chapter:

- **Agent visualization**: You'll learn how to generate graphical diagrams of multi-agent systems, showing agents, tools, and their interactions to improve clarity and debugging
- **Guardrails**: You'll see how to implement both input and output guardrails, ensuring that unsafe, irrelevant, or policy-violating content is intercepted before it enters or leaves your system
- **Logging, tracing, and observability**: You'll explore how the **Traces** module records model calls, tool calls, handoffs, and guardrail triggers, and how you can add your own custom traces and spans
- **Agent testing**: You'll learn approaches for both end-to-end and unit testing of agents, helping you validate system reliability even with non-deterministic behavior

By the end of this chapter, you'll know how to manage, monitor, and validate agentic systems.

Technical requirements

Please follow the detailed steps in *Chapter 3* to set up your environment.

Practical examples and complete code from each chapter are available via the accompanying GitHub repository at https://github.com/PacktPublishing/Building-Agents-with-OpenAI-Agents-SDK.

You are encouraged to clone the repository, reuse and adapt the provided code samples, and refer to them as needed while progressing through the chapters.

Agent visualization

As we have seen in previous chapters, agents can involve multiple complex components, especially in a multi-agent system. This can get overwhelming with the mix of agents, tools, handoffs, and MCP servers. Thankfully, OpenAI Agents SDK provides a visualization utility that can generate a graphical representation of your agent system, which depicts agents, tools, and their relationships.

Let's jump right in and create some visualization graphs of agent systems. To create the visualization graphs, we must first install the required dependencies. In your terminal, activate your environment, and then run the following command, which installs the dependency:

```
$ pip install "openai-agents[viz]"
```

After that, let's bring back a hierarchical agentic system that we had created in a previous chapter. We will also add a few tools to the agentic system to see how they are visualized in the graph. Create a new Python file called visualization.py and run the following code, starting with tool creation:

```python
from agents import Agent, Runner, SQLiteSession, trace, function_tool
from agents.extensions.visualization import draw_graph

# Create tools
@function_tool
def calculate_physics_equation(equation):
    pass

@function_tool
def perform_culture_survey(goal):
    pass
```

Here, we define two example tools: one for solving physics equations and one for running cultural surveys. These will later be attached to relevant agents.

Next, define the specialized domain agents:

```
# Create our agents
# Specialized science agents
physics_agent = Agent(name="Physics Agent", instructions="Answer questions
about physics.", tools=[calculate_physics_equation])
chemistry_agent = Agent(name="Chemistry Agent", instructions="Answer
questions about chemistry.")
medical_agent = Agent(name="Medical Agent", instructions="Answer questions
about medical science.")


# Specialized history agents
politics_agent = Agent(name="Politics Agent", instructions="Answer
questions about political history.")
warfare_agent = Agent(name="Warfare Agent", instructions="Answer questions
about wars and military history.")
culture_agent = Agent(name="Culture Agent", instructions="Answer questions
about cultural history.", tools=[perform_culture_survey])
```

This section creates both science and history sub-agents. Some of them have tools attached, while others rely only on instructions.

Now, create manager agents who orchestrate their respective domains:

```
# Manager agents with handoffs to their respective domains
science_manager = Agent(
    name="Science Manager",
    instructions="Manage science-related queries and route them to the
appropriate subdomain agent.",
    handoffs=[physics_agent, chemistry_agent, medical_agent]
)

history_manager = Agent(
    name="History Manager",
    instructions="Manage history-related queries and route them to the
appropriate subdomain agent.",
    handoffs=[politics_agent, warfare_agent, culture_agent]
)
```

The manager agents act as coordinators. They don't answer questions themselves but route tasks to the correct specialized agent.

Finally, define the top-level triage agent and visualize the graph:

```
# Top-level triage agent
triage_agent = Agent(
    name="Research Triage Agent",
    instructions="Triage the user's question and decide whether it's
science or history related, and route accordingly.",
    handoffs=[science_manager, history_manager]
)


# Draw agent graph
draw_graph(triage_agent, filename="graph_visualization")
```

This agent sits at the top, receives user questions, and decides which manager to forward the query to. The draw_graph function from the agents.extensions.visualization class takes as input any agent, draws the multi-agent system visualization, and saves it to your project's root folder as graph_visualization.png:

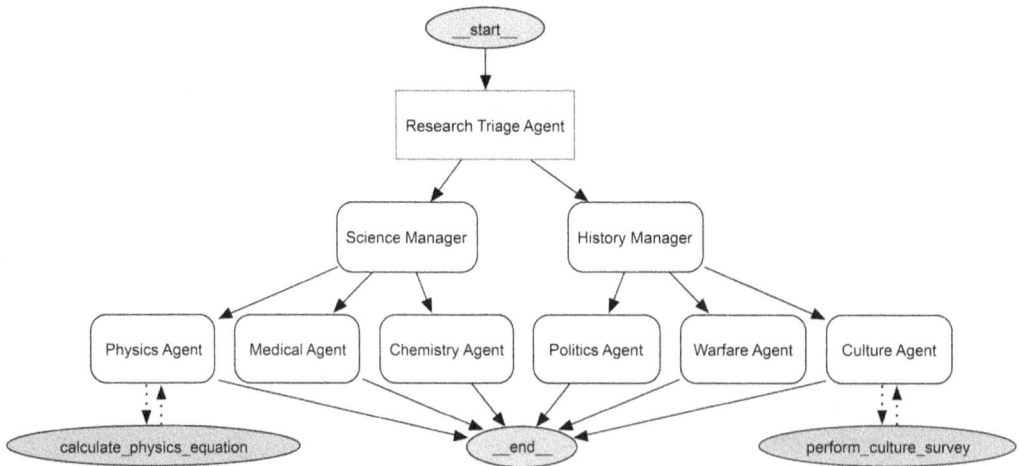

Figure 8.1: Example of a visualization graph

🔍**Quick tip:** Need to see a high-resolution version of this image? Open this book in the next-gen Packt Reader or view it in the PDF/ePub copy.

📖**The next-gen Packt Reader** is included for free with the purchase of this book. Scan the QR code OR go to `https://packtpub.com/unlock`, then use the search bar to find this book by name. Double-check the edition shown to make sure you get the right one.

In the visualization, agents are drawn as boxes (nodes) and tools as ellipses, and arrows indicate interactions (solid arrows for agent-to-agent handoffs and dotted arrows for agent-to-tool calls). There's also always one start node and one or multiple end nodes, dictating the possible path of an agent flow.

This tool (pun intended) is useful for management, clarity, and debugging of large, multi-agent systems. By examining this visualization, we can verify that our system is structured as intended. For instance, if we expected a tool to be connected or an agent to have a handoff that is not shown, the graph would quickly reveal any missing configuration. Also, it can serve as valuable documentation for collaborators, stakeholders, or future maintainers of the system, providing them with an at-a-glance overview of how agents interact.

Guardrails

Guardrails are another useful OpenAI Agents SDK primitive that helps support multi-agent systems by performing validation checks. These checks can either be performed on the user input as it's passed to the agent system, or on the output as the agent output is transferred to the user.

The benefit of having guardrails in your agentic system is that it makes it more resilient. They act as a protective layer, ensuring that invalid, unsafe, or undesirable inputs and outputs are intercepted before they can cause issues. This can help prevent harmful responses, enforce compliance rules, and maintain a consistent user experience. In more complex systems, guardrails also serve as a way to keep agents aligned with organizational policies and domain-specific constraints without overloading the main agent with validation logic. In practice, this means your agents can remain focused on their core tasks, while guardrails handle edge cases, policy enforcement, and safety concerns.

Both input and output guardrails use a similar pattern:

1. We must first define a guardrail function that returns a `GuardrailFunctionOutput` object. It can also take as input the context, the agent that triggered the guardrail, as well as the user's prompt/agent output. `GuardrailFunctionOutput` contains a `tripwire_triggered` Boolean, which indicates whether a guardrail tripwire has been executed.

2. Inside the guardrail function, we must include logic that determines whether our guardrail tripwire should be activated. This is where we can have hardcoded logic (i.e., if the user prompt contains the word "negative," we should trigger a tripwire and stop the agent) or agent-based logic (i.e., we create another agent whose sole job is to reason whether the tripwire should be triggered).

3. Finally, we must gracefully handle the tripwire (which raises a particular exception) and output something to the user.

We will look at input guardrails first and then move on to output guardrails.

Input guardrails

Think of input guardrails as the flight attendant at an airport gate, checking that only ticketed passengers enter the airplane and no one else. These guardrails act as the first line of defense so that only relevant user prompts are passed to your agentic system and nothing else. For instance, you might use an input guardrail to detect whether a user's request violates usage policies, or to check whether the request is something your agent is not supposed to handle. Preventing misuse of your agentic system can save you a ton of money as you can intercept queries before they run through your agentic system, saving you token and processing costs.

Let's bring back a customer service example that we created in a previous chapter, and add an input guardrail to it. For now, we will force the trigger of a tripwire based on something naïve, such as if the prompt contains the word "complaint" (or, really, it could be any word).

Create a new Python file called input_guardrail.py and run the following code. First, import the required modules and load your environment variables:

```python
# Required imports
import os
from dotenv import load_dotenv
from agents import Agent, Runner, function_tool, trace
from agents import GuardrailFunctionOutput,
InputGuardrailTripwireTriggered, input_guardrail, RunContextWrapper,
TResponseInputItem

# Load environment variables from the .env file
load_dotenv()

# Access the API key
api_key = os.getenv("OPENAI_API_KEY")
```

Next, we'll create a simple tool for checking the status of an order. This will serve as the agent's useful functionality:

```python
# Create a tool
@function_tool()
def get_order_status(orderID: int) -> str:
    """
    Returns the order status given an order ID
    Args:
        orderID (int) - Order ID of the customer's order
    Returns:
        string - Status message of the customer's order
    """
    if orderID in (100, 101):
        return "Delivered"
    elif orderID in (200, 201):
        return "Delayed"
    elif orderID in (300, 301):
        return "Cancelled"
```

Now, let's define our guardrail. This function checks whether the user's prompt contains the word "complaint" and, if so, it triggers a tripwire:

```
# Create a guardrail
@input_guardrail
def complaint_detector_guardrail(
    ctx: RunContextWrapper[None],
    agent: Agent,
    prompt: str | list[TResponseInputItem]
) -> GuardrailFunctionOutput:

    tripwire_triggered = False

    if "complaint" in prompt:
        tripwire_triggered = True

    return GuardrailFunctionOutput(
        output_info="The word Complaint has been detected",
        tripwire_triggered=tripwire_triggered,
    )
```

With the tool and guardrail ready, we can now define the agent. Notice how the guardrail is attached to the agent in the input_guardrails parameter:

```
# Define an agent
agent = Agent(name="Customer service agent",
              instructions="You are an AI Agent that helps respond to
customer queries for a local paper company",
              model="gpt-4o",
              tools=[get_order_status],
              input_guardrails=[ complaint_detector_guardrail])
```

Finally, we wrap it all up with a simple loop to interact with the agent. The guardrail will check every input before passing it through to the agent:

```
with trace("Input Guardrails"):
    while True:
        question = input("You: ")
        result = Runner.run_sync(agent, question)
        print("Agent: ", result.final_output)
```

Let's walk through the input guardrail functionality here, matching the pattern we laid out earlier. First, we defined a guardrail function (complaint_detector_guardrail) that accepts RunContextWrapper, the agent, and the user's prompt. This function must always return a GuardrailFunctionOutput object, which indicates whether a tripwire has been triggered.

Second, inside the function, we write the detection logic. In this example, we check whether the word "complaint" appears in the prompt. If it does, the tripwire_triggered flag is set to True, and the guardrail reports back that it has been tripped. Note that this is very simple guardrail logic. Traditionally, here, you would want more sophisticated logic to (for example) scan for policy violations or malicious input.

Finally, when the tripwire is triggered, the SDK raises an InputGuardrailTripwireTriggered exception. This interrupts the normal flow of execution, preventing the agent from processing the request and instead surfacing the error. For now, the error is not handled, so it does not produce a great customer experience, but it still achieves our desired result.

Let's try it out. Run the program, and enter the following message:

```
You: What's the status of my order? My order ID is 200
Agent: The status of your order with ID 200 is: Delayed. If you have any
further questions or need assistance, please let me know!
```

The tripwire has not been triggered as the user prompt does not contain the word "complaint." Let's try again and purposely trigger the tripwire:

```
You: I have a complaint
InputGuardrailTripwireTriggered error
```

Here, we can see that the system raises an InputGuardrailTripwireTriggered error and halts execution. Now, let's modify our script to more gracefully handle the tripwire exception. We can do this by adding the following to the end of the code:

```
...
with trace("Input Guardrails"):
    while True:
        try:
            question = input("You: ")
            result = Runner.run_sync(agent, question)
            print("Agent: ", result.final_output)
        except InputGuardrailTripwireTriggered:
            print ("The tripwire has been triggered. Please call us
instead to register complaints.")
```

Then, let's retry our previous prompt:

```
You: I have a complaint
The tripwire has been triggered. Please call us instead to register
complaints.
```

Here, we can see that the tripwire is still triggered and our agent execution halts, but the exception is gracefully handled and a nice message is displayed to the user.

We can also see the input guardrail in the **Traces** module:

< **Traces** / **Input Guardrails**   □ trace_c9943226b6ca4a0...

⌄ ⚠ Customer service agent   0 ms

     ⊘ complaint_detector_guardrail   0 ms

Figure 8.2: Input guardrail in Traces module

> **Note**
>
> It's important to note that input guardrails are only executed for the first agent in a multi-agent system. This means they act as the initial gateway for the entire workflow, screening user input before it flows downstream into other agents.

In this example, the logic to trigger the input guardrail tripwire was fairly basic. For example, the tripwire would fail to be triggered if the customer had used a word other than "complaint" or had asked about something else entirely. Instead, the pattern here is to use another agent (run on a simpler and more cost-effective model) to assess whether the tripwire has been triggered. In this way, the cheaper agent can assess whether the user prompt is viable before sending it to the more expensive multi-agent system.

Let's update our previous example and make the guardrail logic more sophisticated. We will create another agent whose sole purpose is to determine whether the user prompt is relevant to customer service. If not, it will trigger the tripwire.

Create a new Python file called input_guardrail_agent.py and run the following code. First, let's import the required packages and set up our environment:

```python
# Required imports
import os
from dotenv import load_dotenv
from agents import Agent, Runner, function_tool, trace
from agents import GuardrailFunctionOutput,
InputGuardrailTripwireTriggered, input_guardrail, RunContextWrapper,
TResponseInputItem
from pydantic import BaseModel

# Load environment variables from the .env file
load_dotenv()

# Access the API key
api_key = os.getenv("OPENAI_API_KEY")
```

Next, we'll create a simple tool for checking the order status. This is the same as in our earlier examples, but now it will serve as part of our customer service workflow:

```python
# Create a tool
@function_tool()
def get_order_status(orderID: int) -> str:
    """
    Returns the order status given an order ID
    Args:
        orderID (int) - Order ID of the customer's order
    Returns:
        string - Status message of the customer's order
    """
    if orderID in (100, 101):
        return "Delivered"
    elif orderID in (200, 201):
        return "Delayed"
    elif orderID in (300, 301):
        return "Cancelled"
```

Now, let's define a Pydantic model that the guardrail agent will use to indicate whether the prompt is relevant to customer service or not:

```
class GuardrailTrueFalse(BaseModel):
    is_relevant_to_customer_service_orders: bool
```

With this model, we can now create the guardrail agent. Its only job is to decide whether the user prompt is relevant to customer service and order-related issues:

```
# Create a guardrail agent
guardrail_agent = Agent(
    name="Guardrail check",
    instructions="You are an AI agent that checks if the user's prompt is
relevant to answering customer service and order related questions",
    output_type=GuardrailTrueFalse,
)
```

Next comes the guardrail function itself. This function runs the guardrail agent and triggers the tripwire if the prompt is irrelevant:

```
# Create a guardrail
@input_guardrail
async def relevant_detector_guardrail(
    ctx: RunContextWrapper[None],
    agent: Agent,
    prompt: str | list[TResponseInputItem]
) -> GuardrailFunctionOutput:

    result = await Runner.run(guardrail_agent, input=prompt)

    tripwire_triggered = False

    if result.final_output.is_relevant_to_customer_service_orders ==
False:
        tripwire_triggered = True

    return GuardrailFunctionOutput(
        output_info="The word Complaint has been detected",
        tripwire_triggered=tripwire_triggered
    )
```

Finally, let's define our main customer service agent, attach the guardrail, and run it inside a simple loop:

```python
# Define an agent
agent = Agent(name="Customer service agent",
              instructions="You are an AI Agent that helps respond to
customer queries for a local paper company",
              model="gpt-4o",
              tools=[get_order_status],
              input_guardrails=[relevant_detector_guardrail])

with trace("Input Guardrails"):
    while True:
        try:
            question = input("You: ")
            result = Runner.run_sync(agent, question)
            print("Agent: ", result.final_output)
        except InputGuardrailTripwireTriggered:
            print ("This comment is irrelevant to customer service.")
```

Let's examine what we've changed here. First, instead of using a hardcoded keyword check, we now rely on another agent (guardrail_agent) to evaluate the user's input. This agent is configured with clear instructions to determine whether a prompt is relevant to customer service and order-related queries, and its output is typed using a Pydantic model (GuardrailTrueFalse).

Second, in the relevant_detector_guardrail function, we asynchronously invoke guardrail_agent with the user's input. The result is then inspected: if the agent indicates that the prompt is not relevant, we mark the tripwire_triggered flag as True. This makes the guardrail much more flexible, since it can handle a wide range of phrasing or intent, rather than relying on a single keyword match.

Overall, this pattern is far more robust and scalable because it allows you to use lightweight, inexpensive models for filtering and validation, while reserving the more capable (and costly) models for handling actual customer interactions.

If we run the program and ask about something irrelevant to customer service, it halts execution and tells us that this comment is not related to customer service:

```
You: What's the meaning of life?
This comment is irrelevant to customer service
```

Note

One small but important adjustment here is that the guardrail function is defined as `async`. This is necessary because the guardrail itself is invoking another agent asynchronously (`Runner.run`). In practice, this means you'll need to use asynchronous guardrail functions whenever they call out to other agents.

Now that we have a good handle on input guardrails, let's switch our focus to output guardrails instead.

Output guardrails

Output guardrails serve a similar purpose, but instead of validating what goes into your agent system, they validate what comes out. Think of them as the flight attendant making sure passengers disembark in an orderly fashion and that nothing unsafe leaves the plane. In practice, output guardrails act as a last checkpoint before the agent's response is returned to the user. They enable your agentic system to enforce constraints such as format compliance, sensitive data redaction, or ensuring that the output stays within policy guidelines.

In our customer support scenario, imagine we want to ensure the agent's final response always includes a valid delivery order status statement (for example, "Your order #5474 is out for delivery and will arrive tomorrow."). If the agent outputs something irrelevant (such as an apology without status details, or worse, a hallucination), we would want the system to intercept it before it reaches the customer.

Much like input guardrails, output guardrails are implemented as functions that return a `GuardrailFunctionOutput` object, with logic that determines whether a tripwire has been triggered. If the output is invalid or unsafe, the tripwire stops the response from reaching the user. One difference is that, since the output can be a structured object (if the agent has `output_type` defined), the guardrail function receives that output object.

Let's go through an example. Create a new Python file called `output_guardrail_agent.py` and run the following program. We first import the required modules and load our environment variables:

```
# Required imports
import os
from dotenv import import load_dotenv
from agents import Agent, Runner, function_tool, trace
```

```
from agents import GuardrailFunctionOutput,
OutputGuardrailTripwireTriggered, output_guardrail, RunContextWrapper
from pydantic import BaseModel

# Load environment variables from the .env file
load_dotenv()

# Access the API key
api_key = os.getenv("OPENAI_API_KEY")
```

Next, we define simple Pydantic models for our outputs:

```
class MessageOutput(BaseModel):
    response: str


class GuardrailTrueFalse(BaseModel):
    is_relevant_to_customer_service: bool
```

This agent checks whether the main agent's response is valid for customer service:

```
# Create a guardrail agent
guardrail_agent = Agent(
    name="Guardrail check",
    instructions="You are an AI agent that checks if the agent response is
relevant to answering a customer service question and not hallucinating",
    output_type=GuardrailTrueFalse
)
```

We then write the function that enforces the guardrail logic:

```
# Create a guardrail
@output_guardrail
async def relevant_detector_guardrail(
    ctx: RunContextWrapper[None],
    agent: Agent,
    output: MessageOutput
) -> GuardrailFunctionOutput:

    result = await Runner.run(guardrail_agent, input=output)
```

```
    tripwire_triggered = False

    if result.final_output.is_relevant_to_customer_service == False:
        tripwire_triggered = True

    return GuardrailFunctionOutput(
        output_info="",
        tripwire_triggered=tripwire_triggered
    )
```

Here, we define a deliberately "hallucinating" customer service agent to show how the guardrail catches invalid output:

```
# Define an agent
agent = Agent(name="Customer service agent",
              instructions="You are an AI Agent that outputs random song
lines and poems", # to force model to hallucinate and trigger the output
guardrail
              output_guardrails=[relevant_detector_guardrail])
```

Finally, we run the agent in a loop and catch cases where the guardrail is triggered:

```
with trace("Output Guardrails"):
    while True:
        try:
            question = input("You: ")
            result = Runner.run_sync(agent, question)
            print("Agent: ", result.final_output)
        except OutputGuardrailTripwireTriggered:
            print ("The agent system did not produce an output. Please try
again")
```

In this example, we have created an output guardrail. We decorated the `relevant_detector_guardrail` function with `@output_guardrail`, which means this guardrail runs after the main agent generates its response. Inside the guardrail, we asynchronously invoke the guardrail agent with the agent's output. If the result indicates that the response is invalid, the guardrail halts execution by raising an `OutputGuardrailTripwireTriggered` exception.

If the tripwire fires, the exception is caught, and instead of displaying the agent's hallucinated or irrelevant response, we show a safe fallback message to the user: "The agent system did not produce an output. Please try again."

If we run the program, it will trigger the output guardrail no matter what we type in as we have configured the agent to hallucinate purposely:

```
You: what's the status of my return?
The agent system did not produce an output. Please try again
```

Output guardrails can be tailored to a wide variety of scenarios. They might be used to guarantee that every response contains a clear and valid order status, to verify that results conform to a specific schema, or to automatically remove sensitive details such as personally identifiable information. By applying these checks at the very end of the pipeline, you can ensure that responses meet the exact standards your application demands.

Think of output guardrails as a final safety net. Even if earlier components of the system behave unpredictably, these guardrails provide assurance that the content ultimately returned to the user will be safe, compliant, and aligned with business requirements.

Logging, tracing, and observability

Managing agents does not only mean implementing guardrails; it also means having a good observability infrastructure to fully understand what your agent is doing. As we have seen in previous chapters, OpenAI Agents SDK comes with the powerful **Traces** module, which records the sequence of events (model calls, tool calls, handoffs, guardrail triggers, etc.) during an agent's run.

Tracing is automatically enabled for all agent runs and can be accessed via the OpenAI dashboard (as we have seen throughout this book). This provides an out-of-the-box solution for debugging and monitoring, which captures a rich set of events. These recorded events are stored as spans within an overall trace for the run. It is useful to understand the difference between traces and spans:

- **Trace:** Represents one full execution flow of your agent system. It's like a timeline of everything that happened from start to finish for a given user prompt. All the events related to one run are grouped under this trace.

- **Span:** A single event or operation within the trace that has a start time and end time. Spans can be nested and can also contain additional property data that is useful for debugging.

Think of a trace as the complete play-by-play of one user request, and spans as the individual steps in that play-by-play.

The trace and span model is powerful: it means you can trace through a complex sequence and see which operations took how long, and how they relate. For example, you could see that the whole trace took 3.2 seconds, out of which 1.5 seconds were the LLM thinking, 0.5 seconds were a database tool call, and so on.

The **Traces dashboard** provides a visual sequence of these events, which can be expanded to see details such as the prompt or the tool inputs/outputs. This is useful during development to step through what the agent did internally.

Let's go through an example. Create a new Python file called basic_trace.py and run the following program:

```python
from agents import Agent, Runner
from dotenv import load_dotenv

load_dotenv()

# Create an agent
agent = Agent(
    name="QuestionAnswerAgent",
    instructions="You are an AI agent that answers questions in as few
words as possible"
)

result = Runner.run_sync(agent, "Where is the Eiffel Tower?")
print(result.final_output)
```

Without writing any additional code, the SDK automatically does the logging for us in the **Traces** module. If we open the **Traces** dashboard, we can see the trace and the corresponding spans:

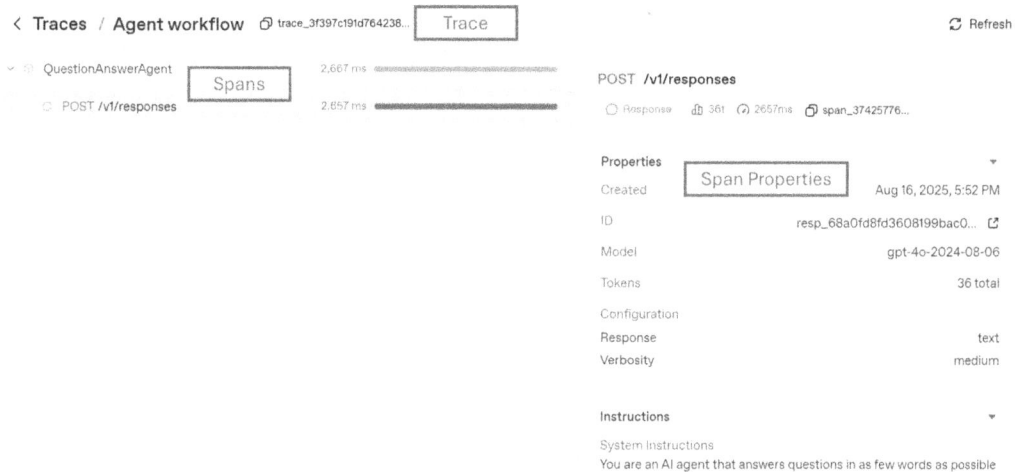

Figure 8.3: Spans in the Traces module

Now, let's add more sophistication to our logging and observability with custom traces, custom spans, and grouping traces and spans together.

Custom traces and spans

Traces can be given custom properties (such as a custom name) with the use of the `trace` function. Anything (code execution, agent runs, etc.) within a trace invocation will be logged under that trace. Let's go through an example. Create a new Python script called `custom_trace.py`, and type in the following code:

```
from agents import Agent, Runner, trace
from dotenv import load_dotenv

load_dotenv()

# Create an agent
agent = Agent(
    name="QuestionAnswerAgent",
    instructions="You are an AI agent that answers questions in as few
words as possible"
)
```

```
with trace("Henry's Workflow"):
    result = Runner.run_sync(agent, "Where is the Eiffel Tower?")
    print(result.final_output)
```

Here, we have given the trace a custom name of "Henry's Workflow." This will enable us to find the trace more easily in the **Traces** module:

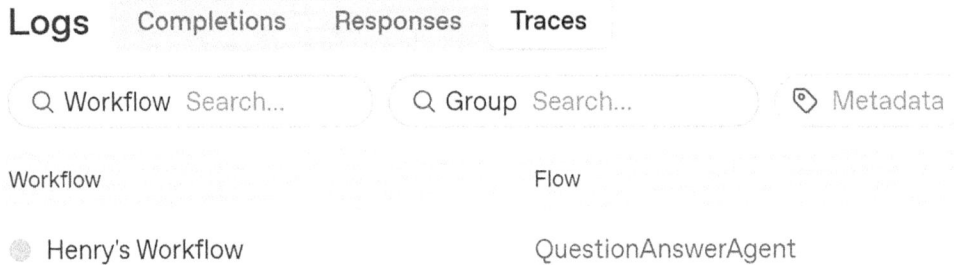

Logs   Completions   Responses   **Traces**

Q Workflow Search...   Q Group Search...   ◇ Metadata

Workflow   Flow

⬤ Henry's Workflow   QuestionAnswerAgent

Figure 8.4: Logs in the Traces module

> Note that you can also use `traces.start()` and `traces.finish()` but it's not recommended.

As we have discussed before, spans are automatically created for things such as agent handoffs and tool calls, but it may be useful to create your own custom spans to log something particular in your multi-agent system. The benefit here is not only the logging, but you also get to see how long the span takes.

To create a custom span, we can simply use the SDK's `custom_span` function. Let's create a new Python file called `custom_span.py` and run the following program:

```
from agents import Agent, Runner, trace, custom_span
from dotenv import load_dotenv
import time

load_dotenv()

# Create an agent
agent = Agent(
```

```
    name="QuestionAnswerAgent",
    instructions="You are an AI agent that answers questions in as few
words as possible"
)

with trace("Henry's Workflow"):
    with custom_span("Task 1"):
        time.sleep(5)
    with custom_span("Task 2"):
        result = Runner.run_sync(agent, "Where is the Eiffel Tower?")
    with custom_span("Task 3"):
        time.sleep(5)
    with custom_span("Task 4"):
        time.sleep(5)
```

In this example, we created five custom spans, each with a different name. Currently, the custom span only either performs an agent run or sleeps for five seconds. Because of these custom spans, we can see the logging related to these in the **Traces** dashboard:

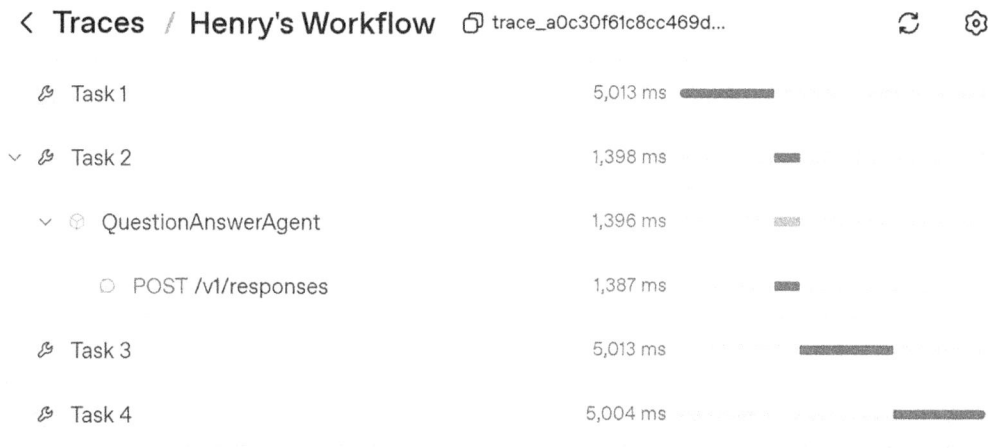

    ‹ Traces / Henry's Workflow   ⧉ trace_a0c30f61c8cc469d…

⚙ Task 1	5,013 ms	
⌄ ⚙ Task 2	1,398 ms	
⌄ ⦿ QuestionAnswerAgent	1,396 ms	
○ POST /v1/responses	1,387 ms	
⚙ Task 3	5,013 ms	
⚙ Task 4	5,004 ms	

Figure 8.5: Tasks in Traces modules

You can place the custom spans in various places in your agent system. This helps with breaking down complex workflows into smaller, measurable steps. By strategically adding spans, you can pinpoint exactly where time is being spent and identify any bottlenecks in the process. For example, if a workflow involves multiple tool calls and reasoning steps, spans allow you to quickly see which step is slowing things down or causing errors.

Grouping multiple traces and spans together

You may want to combine multiple agent runs together into one trace. By default, if you call Runner.run twice separately, that would generate two separate traces, but semantically, you might consider them part of one workflow. We can use the trace() context manager to tie them together.

Create a new Python file called multiple_agents_in_one_trace.py and run the following program:

```python
from agents import Agent, Runner, trace, custom_span
from dotenv import load_dotenv
import time

load_dotenv()

# Create an agent
agent = Agent(
    name="QuestionAnswerAgent",
    instructions="You are an AI agent that answers questions in as few
words as possible"
)

with trace("Henry's Workflow"):
    with custom_span("Task 1"):
        result = Runner.run_sync(agent, "Where is the Statue of Liberty?")
    with custom_span("Task 2"):
        result = Runner.run_sync(agent, "Where is the Eiffel Tower?")
    with custom_span("Task 3"):
        result = Runner.run_sync(agent, "Where is the Notre Dame?")
    with custom_span("Task 4"):
        result = Runner.run_sync(agent, "Where is the Burj Khalifa?")
```

In the **Traces** module, all of these runs will now be part of one trace (as opposed to separate traces).

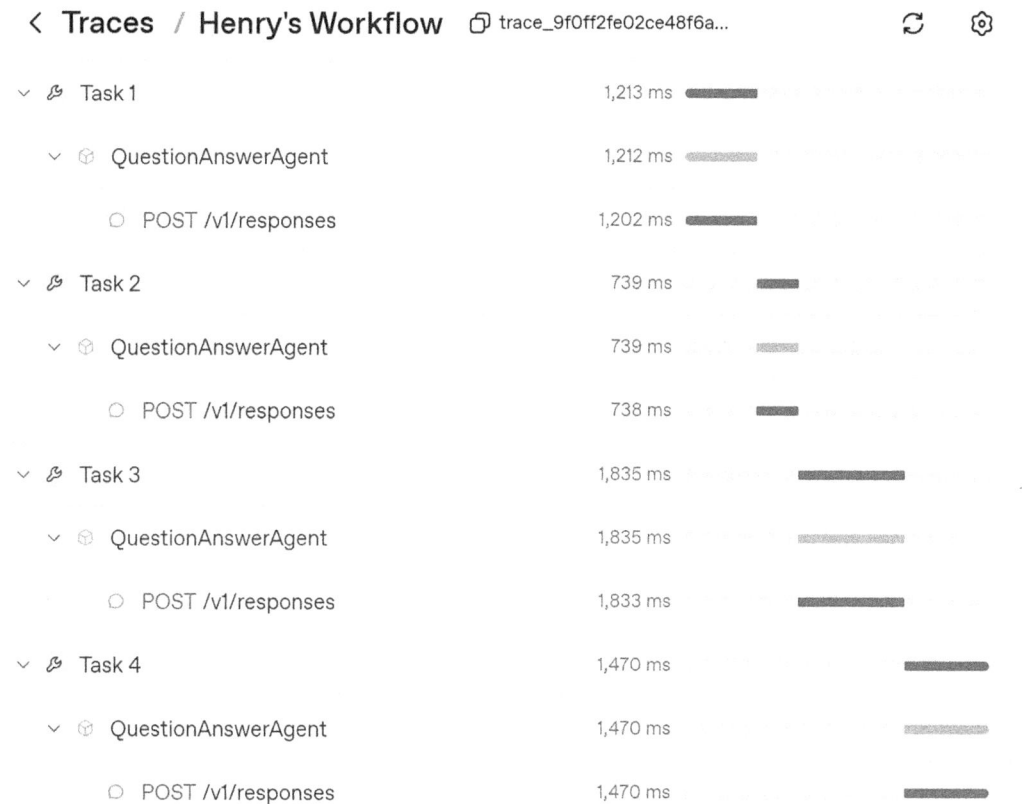

‹ **Traces** / **Henry's Workflow**   ⬁ trace_9f0ff2fe02ce48f6a...   ⟳   ⚙

⌄ ⌕ Task 1	1,213 ms	▬▬▬▬
⌄ ⬡ QuestionAnswerAgent	1,212 ms	▬▬▬▬
○ POST /v1/responses	1,202 ms	▬▬▬▬
⌄ ⌕ Task 2	739 ms	▬▬
⌄ ⬡ QuestionAnswerAgent	739 ms	▬▬
○ POST /v1/responses	738 ms	▬▬
⌄ ⌕ Task 3	1,835 ms	▬▬▬▬▬
⌄ ⬡ QuestionAnswerAgent	1,835 ms	▬▬▬▬▬
○ POST /v1/responses	1,833 ms	▬▬▬▬▬
⌄ ⌕ Task 4	1,470 ms	▬▬▬▬
⌄ ⬡ QuestionAnswerAgent	1,470 ms	▬▬▬▬
○ POST /v1/responses	1,470 ms	▬▬▬▬

Figure 8.6: Several tasks in the Traces modules

This can also occur between different Python programs by passing a unique `trace_id` into the traces call. Create a new Python file called `multiple_agents_in_one_trace_2.py` and run the program three times to simulate three calls and see it visible in the **Traces** module:

```python
from agents import Agent, Runner, trace, custom_span
from dotenv import load_dotenv
import time

load_dotenv()

# Create an agent
agent = Agent(
```

```
    name="QuestionAnswerAgent",
    instructions="You are an AI agent that answers questions in as few
words as possible"
)


with trace("Henry's Workflow", trace_id="A1B2C3"):
    with custom_span("Task 1"):
        result = Runner.run_sync(agent, "Where is the Statue of Liberty?")
```

Because we have passed a `trace_id` argument, we can now run the program separately as many times as we want and it will still be grouped together under one trace in the **Traces** module:

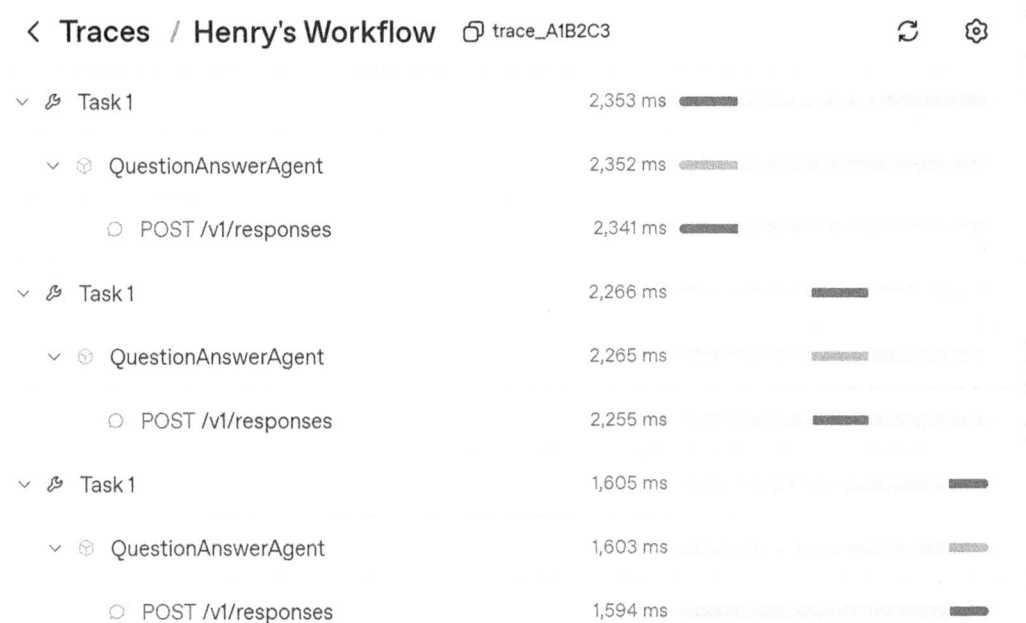

Figure 8.7: Tasks under the same trace ID in the Traces module

This can be beneficial for long-running or distributed workflows where different pieces of the process are executed at different times or even on different machines. By assigning the same `trace_id` value, you can stitch together activity from multiple sessions into one cohesive trace, making it easier to see the full life cycle of the workflow.

Like traces, spans can also be grouped together. Spans can even be nested. Suppose you have an agent workflow that does two primary things: research and text generation. Each piece can have its own set of agents and tool calls. With custom spans, these activities can be grouped together so that they appear "combined" within the **Traces** module.

Create a new Python file called nested_spans.py and run the following program:

```python
from agents import Agent, Runner, trace, custom_span, function_tool
from dotenv import load_dotenv
import time


load_dotenv()


@function_tool
def get_fun_facts():
    return "The Eiffel Tower is in Paris"


@function_tool
def clean_up_poem(poem_string: str):
    return poem_string.upper()


# Create the research agent
research_agent = Agent(
    name="Research",
    instructions="You are an AI agent that performs research",
    tools=[get_fun_facts]
)


# Create the text generation agent
text_generation_agent = Agent(
    name="Text Generation",
    instructions="You are an AI agent that pertakes research that's
performed and writes a poem",
    tools=[clean_up_poem]
)


with trace("Henry's Research Workflow"):
    with custom_span("Research Task"):
        result = Runner.run_sync(research_agent, "The Eiffel Tower")
    with custom_span("Text Generation Task"):
        result = Runner.run_sync(text_generation_agent,
            result.final_output)
    print(result.final_output)
```

This groups together the research and text generation tasks separately.

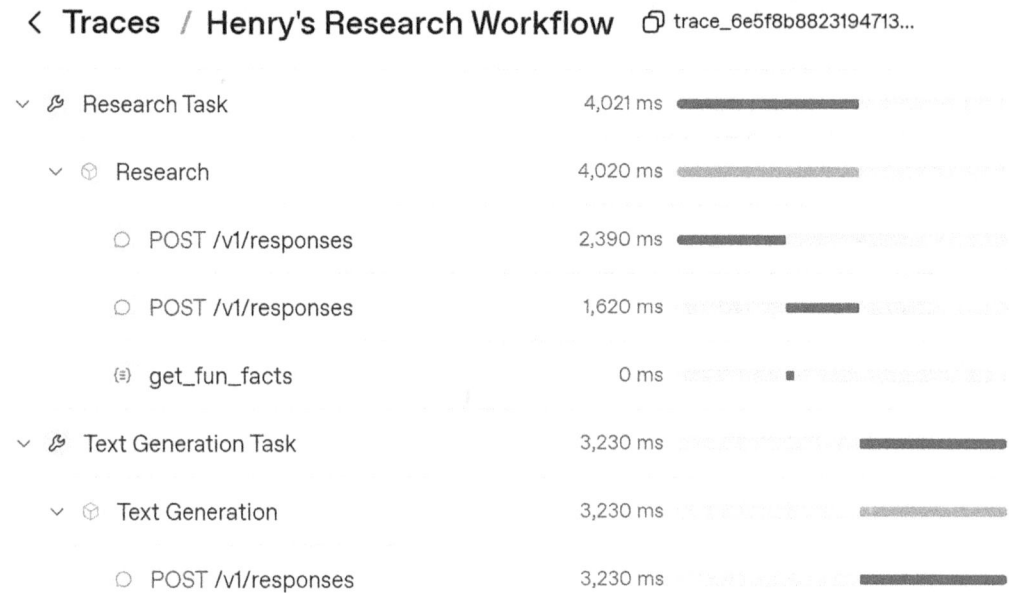

‹ **Traces** / **Henry's Research Workflow**   ⬚ trace_6e5f8b8823194713...

⌄ 🔧 Research Task	4,021 ms	
⌄ ◈ Research	4,020 ms	
○ POST /v1/responses	2,390 ms	
○ POST /v1/responses	1,620 ms	
⧈ get_fun_facts	0 ms	
⌄ 🔧 Text Generation Task	3,230 ms	
⌄ ◈ Text Generation	3,230 ms	
○ POST /v1/responses	3,230 ms	

Figure 8.8: Traces grouping multiple objects together

This means you can find those tasks more easily and see how long they take, which is useful for debugging and management.

Disabling traces

Sometimes, you may want to disable tracing. This can be due to regulatory requirements to not retain any logs or data, or perhaps there is sensitive material that you do not want to store in your logs. In that case, you can disable the tracing by placing the following piece of code at the top of your Python script, which sets the OPENAI_AGENTS_DISABLE_TRACING environment variable:

```python
import os
os.environ["OPENAI_AGENTS_DISABLE_TRACING"] = "1"
```

Agent testing

Another important aspect of agent management is testing, which is essential to confirm that it performs as intended and remains dependable over time. This becomes even more critical when the agent is connected to broader workflows or exposed directly to end users. The challenge is that agents often behave unpredictably and are non-deterministic (the same input can produce different outputs), which makes agents harder to validate than traditional software. Fortunately, OpenAI Agents SDK does offer structured methods to bring rigor and consistency to the testing process.

There are two important types of testing that we will discuss:

- **End-to-end testing**: Does the full agentic system perform as expected?
- **Unit testing**: Does one component of the full agentic system perform as expected?

So, let's get started!

End-to-end testing

End-to-end testing evaluates where the agentic system produces desirable outputs. For our customer support agent, an end-to-end test might involve simulating an actual user question and seeing whether the agent returns a helpful answer, uses the right tools, or performs a handoff appropriately.

Traditionally, this involves defining an input and an expected output, and verifying that our system produces the expected output. With agentic systems and their non-determinism, however, this proves to be difficult, but not impossible. One way is to have a human verify that the agentic system produced a desirable output. Another, more automated way is to have an LLM (or even another agent) determine whether the agentic system produced a desirable output.

Let's write a simple script to conduct an end-to-end test for a customer service agent that we have written previously: a customer service agent that returns the order status given an order ID. Create a new Python script called `test_end_to_end.py` and write the following code. We'll begin by importing required modules and loading environment variables:

```
# Required imports
import os
from dotenv import load_dotenv
from agents import Agent, Runner, function_tool
from pydantic import BaseModel
```

```
# Load environment variables from the .env file
load_dotenv()

# Access the API key
api_key = os.getenv("OPENAI_API_KEY")
```

Next, we define a tool that simulates returning an order status when given an order ID:

```
# Create a tool
@function_tool(
        name_override="Get Status of Current Order",
        description_override="Returns the status of an order given the
customer's Order ID",
        docstring_style="Args: Order ID in Integer format"
)
def get_order_status(orderID: int) -> str:
    """
    Returns the order status given an order ID
    Args:
        orderID (int) - Order ID of the customer's order
    Returns:
        string - Status message of the customer's order
    """
    if orderID in (100, 101):
        return "Delivered"
    elif orderID in (200, 201):
        return "Delayed"
    elif orderID in (300, 301):
        return "Cancelled"
```

Now, we wrap this tool into a simple customer service agent:

```
# Define an agent
agent = Agent(name="Customer service agent",
              instructions="You are an AI Agent that helps respond to
customer queries for a local paper company",
              model="gpt-4o",
              tools=[get_order_status])
```

Let's test the agent by asking for the status of order 200:

```
# Run the Control Logic Framework
result = Runner.run_sync(agent, "What's the status of my order? My Order
ID is 200")

# Print the result
print(result.final_output)
```

We know this agent leverages function_tool to return the order status. Now, let's build some end-to-end tests for this agentic system. This starts with defining an input and an expected output for each scenario. Then, we will write a script that iterates through each scenario, runs the agentic system with the input, and then compares the agentic system output with the expected output.

At the bottom of the script, add the following code. For proper end-to-end testing, we'll define multiple scenarios with inputs and expected outputs:

```
# create Scenario class
class Scenario(BaseModel):
    scenario: str
    input: str
    expected_output: str


list_of_scenarios  = [
    Scenario(
        scenario="Delivered example",
        input="Hi there, could you check my customer order? It's 101",
        expected_output="The order is delivered"
    ),
    Scenario(
        scenario="Delayed",
        input="My order ID is two hundred, why has my package not been
delivered yet?",
        expected_output="The order is delayed"
    ),
    Scenario(
        scenario="Order does not exist",
        input="What's the status of my Order? Its number is 400",
        expected_output="No status or order can be found"
    )
]
```

We need a simple output type (True/False) and a dedicated testing agent to evaluate results:

```python
# create output type
class OutputTrueFalse(BaseModel):
    test_succeeded: bool


# create testing agent
testing_agent = Agent(name="Testing agent",
             instructions="You are an AI Agent that tests expected
outputs from desired outputs of an agentic AI system",
             output_type=OutputTrueFalse)
```

Finally, loop through each scenario and check whether the agent produces the expected result:

```python
# Run test
for scenario in list_of_scenarios:
    print(f"Running scenario {scenario.scenario}")
    result = Runner.run_sync(testing_agent, f"Input: {scenario.input} |||
Expected Output: {scenario.expected_output}")
    print(result.final_output)
    print('---')
```

If we run this program, it will iterate through each scenario and perform end-to-end testing (with an agent or LLM performing the comparison for us):

```
Running scenario Delivered example
test_succeeded=True

---
Running scenario Delayed
test_succeeded=True

---
Running scenario Order does not exist
test_succeeded=True

---
```

Now, if we make changes to the agentic system, we can simply re-run it and it will perform the same tests.

Since all the tests succeeded, this indicates the agent successfully used the tool and included its result in the response. If the test failed, it could mean the agent didn't call the tool (perhaps a prompt issue) or formatted the answer unexpectedly. In a real scenario, you would analyze failures to improve the agent (maybe adjust instructions or tool implementation).

Unit testing

Unit testing evaluates the performance of a specific behavior or component of a system. For an agentic system, this could mean ensuring certain tools are being called, certain agents are being handed off correctly, certain guardrails are triggered, and so on. To do this, we can leverage the SDK's result and context objects and inspect them to ensure certain expectations are being met.

Let's go through an example, adding on to the previous example's script. Let's assume we want to test that function_tool is actually being called when we call the agent. To do this, we can inspect the result object and verify that the function_tool get_order_status function is, in fact, being called. Add the following code to the preceding script:

```python
from agents import ToolCallItem

# Run a unit test to check if the function_tool was called
result = Runner.run_sync(agent, "Please provide me the status of order 101")

# Inspect items in the result
items = result.new_items

print("Tool calls made during this run:")
for item in items:
    if isinstance(item, ToolCallItem):
        print(f"- {item.raw_item.name} was called")

# Assert that get_order_status was called
if any(item.raw_item.name == "get_order_status" for item in items if
isinstance(item, ToolCallItem)):
    print("get_order_status was called as expected")
else:
    print("get_order_status was not called")
```

In this snippet, we make a simple query to the customer service agent and then inspect the new_ items attribute of the result object. This lets us see exactly which tools the agent decided to invoke. By checking that the get_order_status tool appears in this list, we can confirm that the agent's control logic is working as intended. In this case, we do confirm that get_order_status is called:

```
Tool calls made during this run:
- get_order_status was called
get_order_status was called as expected
```

Unit tests such as this are valuable because they give you confidence in specific aspects of your agent's behavior. Rather than only validating final outputs, you can check intermediate steps such as whether the right tools are called, whether the correct agent handoff occurred, or whether a guardrail was triggered. This level of granularity makes it easier to pinpoint issues and ensures your system remains reliable as you continue to iterate.

Summary

In this chapter, we focused on how to manage, monitor, and validate agentic systems built with OpenAI Agents SDK. We began with visualization, learning how to generate graphs that show the flow of agents, tools, and handoffs, making system architecture easier to understand and debug. We then introduced guardrails, both input and output, which act as protective layers to enforce policies and prevent unsafe or irrelevant interactions. From there, we explored the **Traces** module, which records traces and spans of each run, giving you detailed insight into how your agents behave internally. Finally, we looked at testing, including end-to-end and unit testing approaches, to systematically verify agent reliability despite their inherent non-determinism.

Together, these capabilities form the foundation of agent management. They enable you to not only build powerful agentic systems but also keep them safe, observable, and dependable as they scale. In the next chapter, we will take everything we have learned so far in this book and apply it to build full end-to-end real-life agentic systems.

Subscribe for a free eBook

New frameworks, evolving architectures, research drops, production breakdowns—AI_Distilled filters the noise into a weekly briefing for engineers and researchers working hands-on with LLMs and GenAI systems. Subscribe now and receive a free eBook, along with weekly insights that help you stay focused and informed.

Subscribe at https://packt.link/80z6Y or scan the QR code below.

Part 3

Build AI Agents

Part 3 is the capstone. Here, you will assemble an end-to-end agentic system using OpenAI Agents SDK, not as isolated features but as a coherent application. You will take the components introduced earlier (tools, memory and retrieval, sessions, model and context management, guardrails, multi-agent orchestration, etc.), and integrate them into production-shaped applications and workflows with clear inputs and outputs.

This part contains the following chapter:

- *Chapter 9, Building AI Agents and Agentic Systems*

9

Building AI Agents and Agentic Systems

Up to this point, we've constructed various parts of AI agent systems in isolation. We've built simple agents, extended their abilities with tools, added memory and knowledge bases, orchestrated multiple agents together, and learned how to manage models and guardrails. Now, in this final chapter, we're going to put all of these pieces together. The goal is for you to design full, end-to-end agent solutions that leverage everything you've learned throughout this book.

Here is what you will learn as part of this chapter:

- *Building a customer service employee AI agent*: First, we will build a virtual customer service assistant that integrates secure database queries, knowledge base lookups, and input guardrails, and even hands off to a retention specialist agent when needed. This case study will show how to combine tools and multi-agent handoffs in a single coherent system.

- *Orchestrating an automated multi-agent workflow*: Next, we will orchestrate a multi-agent workflow to automate personalized customer outreach. One agent will gather information (from databases, past chat transcripts, and web searches) and pass it to a second agent, who composes a custom email. This example demonstrates how agents can collaborate sequentially to perform complex tasks from end to end.

By the end of this chapter, you'll know how to apply OpenAI Agents SDK to build real-life AI agent systems from scratch. We will unify everything we have learned in the previous chapters, including tools, memory, sessions, and multi-agent orchestration. This final project brings together everything you've learned, preparing you so that you can create your own powerful AI agents in the real world.

Technical requirements

Please follow the detailed steps outlined in *Chapter 3* to set up your environment.

Throughout this book, practical examples and complete code from each chapter have been made available in this book's GitHub repository at https://github.com/PacktPublishing/Building-Agents-with-OpenAI-Agents-SDK.

You are encouraged to clone the repository, reuse and adapt the provided code samples, and refer to them as needed while progressing through this book.

Building a customer service employee AI agent

Our first case study covers an AI-powered customer service chatbot for a fictitious company called *PaperCo*. This company supplies paper products to business customers.

The AI agent that we will build will act as a virtual customer service employee, handling customer questions, complaints, and order inquiries. It will integrate multiple advanced features that we have previously discussed:

- A function tool to query order statuses from a database
- A vector search tool to find information in company policy documents
- An input guardrail to ignore irrelevant user prompts
- Hand off to a specialized sub-agent (a retention agent) if the user expresses intent to cancel their service

All these components work together to create a robust, interactive chatbot that can both retrieve factual data and manage the conversation flow intelligently. The following diagram shows how this works:

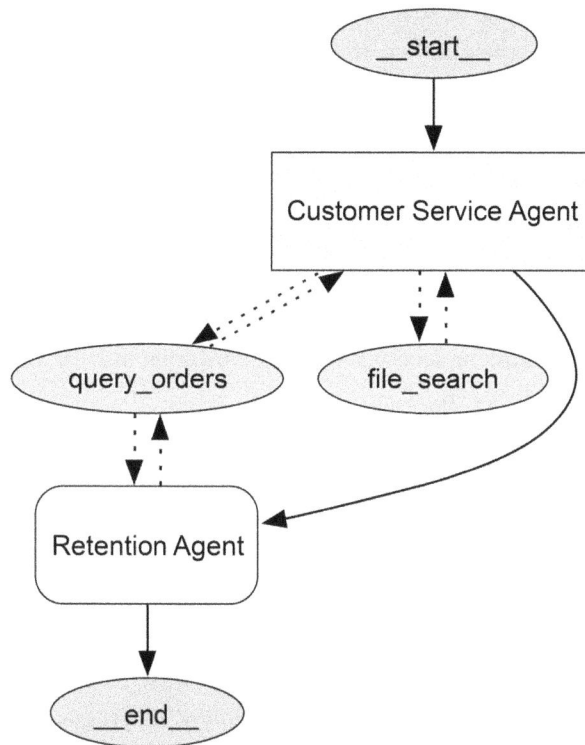

Figure 9.1: Agent visualization

Let's go through each component of our AI agent:

- **Order database and query tool**: A SQLite database of orders and a function tool (query_orders) that the agent can call to look up order statuses. The tool enforces that the customer provides an authorization key before retrieving order information (so that information can remain secure).

- **Knowledge base search tool**: A file-based vector search tool (file_search) that lets the agent retrieve answers from a customer service policy document (for general FAQ-type questions or company policy information).

- **Input guardrail (relevance checker)**: A guardrail agent that examines user queries and blocks those that are not related to customer service (to prevent off-topic requests). Guardrails are not present in the preceding diagram.

- **Retention agent**: An agent that specializes in "retention" scenarios. If a customer says they want to cancel their service, this agent takes over the conversation. It handles the situation with empathy and attempts to retain the customer (even offering incentives).

- **Main customer service agent**: The primary agent (`"Customer Service Agent"`) that the user interacts with (i.e., the entry point). It uses the aforementioned tools and guardrail, and it knows when to hand off to the retention agent. This agent maintains conversation state across turns using a session, so it can handle multi-turn dialogues.

Together, these pieces form a complete picture of how an AI agent can act as a capable customer service employee. In the following sections, we will dive deeper into each component, exploring how to implement them step by step.

Setting up the database

First, we need some data for the agent to work with. For our example, we'll create a small SQLite database for storing order information, and we will preload it with some sample orders.

The following setup script creates a SQLite database file and populates an orders table with some fake order records. It also defines a couple of test query functions to verify the data.

Create a new Python file called setup.py and run the following program:

```python
import sqlite3

# Set up SQLite DB
conn = sqlite3.connect("paper_data.db")
cursor = conn.cursor()

# Delete orders table if it exists
cursor.execute("DROP TABLE IF EXISTS orders")
# Create orders table
cursor.execute("""
CREATE TABLE IF NOT EXISTS orders (
    order_id INTEGER PRIMARY KEY,
    authorization_key TEXT,
    order_status TEXT
```

```
)
""")
# Insert fake order data
orders_data = [
    (1001, "154857", "shipped"),
    (1002, "154857", "processing"),
    (1003, "958542", "delivered"),
    (1004, "445720", "cancelled"),
]
cursor.executemany("INSERT OR IGNORE INTO orders (order_id, authorization_
key, order_status) VALUES (?, ?, ?)", orders_data)
conn.commit()
conn.close()
```

In this code, we used Python to create a new SQLite database file named paper_data.db and an orders table. Then, we inserted four sample orders, each one associated with a customer authorization key.

Setting up a vector store

The next step is to create a vector store that will contain our customer service information that the agent can query. To do this, follow these steps:

1. Go to OpenAI Platform at https://platform.openai.com/ and log in. Ensure you log in using the same account you used when generating the API key.

2. Select **Dashboard** from the top right, select **Storage**, and toggle to **Vector stores**.

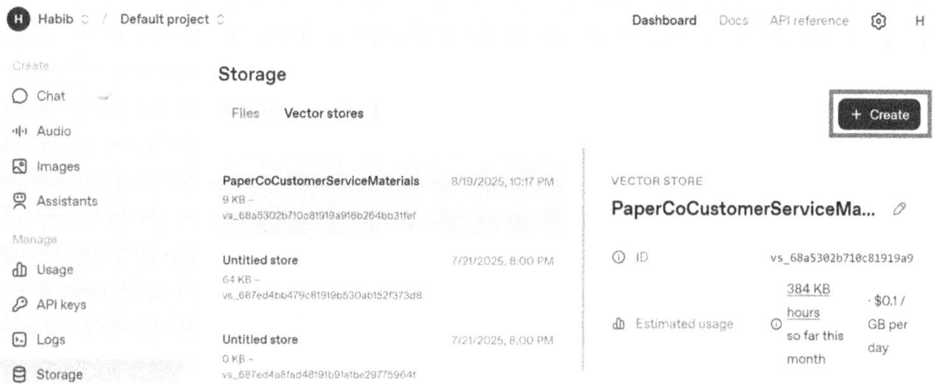

Figure 9.2: Vector stores

🔍 **Quick tip:** Need to see a high-resolution version of this image? Open this book in the next-gen Packt Reader or view it in the PDF/ePub copy.

📗 **The next-gen Packt Reader** is included for free with the purchase of this book. Scan the QR code OR go to `https://packtpub.com/unlock`, then use the search bar to find this book by name. Double-check the edition shown to make sure you get the right one.

3. Select **Create** to create a new vector store. Type in a vector store name – for example, `Pa perCoCustomerServiceMaterials`.

4. Scroll down and add a file to the vector store by selecting + **Add files**.

5. Upload the **PaperCoCustomerServiceMaterials** file (which can be found in this book's GitHub repository under *Chapter 4*). Name it `PaperCoCustomerServiceMaterials.docx` and select `user_data` for the **Purpose** field. Then, select **Attach**.

6. The `.docx` file we uploaded has now been successfully added to our new vector store, and all the related operations to enable RAG (such as producing embeddings, etc.) are complete.

7. Copy and save the vector store ID for the new vector store that you just created. The ID will be present at the top right of the vector page.

Figure 9.3: The Storage page

In this section, we set up a vector store that contains the customer service materials that will be used by our AI agent to answer questions.

Creating a function tool to query data

The next step is to create a function tool that the agent can use to query the orders database. As we learned previously, OpenAI Agents SDK enables us to create a tool by wrapping a Python function. In our case, we will define a function called query_orders that executes a SQL query on the orders table and returns the results. This function will be decorated with @function_tool so that it becomes an agent-accessible tool. Importantly, our query_orders tool will enforce that the query only returns results for orders that match a given authorization key (to prevent the AI from accessing orders it shouldn't).

Create a new Python file called agent.py and type in the following code:

```python
from agents import (
    Agent, Runner, SQLiteSession, trace,
    function_tool, FileSearchTool
)
import sqlite3
from agents import (
    GuardrailFunctionOutput, InputGuardrailTripwireTriggered,
    input_guardrail, RunContextWrapper, TResponseInputItem
)
from pydantic import BaseModel
from dotenv import load_dotenv
from agents.extensions.visualization import draw_graph


load_dotenv()


@function_tool
def query_orders(sql_query: str, authorization_key: str):
    """
    Executes the given SQL query on the orders table and returns the
result.
    You must provide the authorization_key.
    Table: orders
        order_id INTEGER PRIMARY KEY,
        authorization_key TEXT,
        order_status TEXT
    Only rows matching the provided authorization_key will be accessible.
```

```
        """
        db_path = "paper_data.db"
        try:
            conn = sqlite3.connect(db_path)
            cursor = conn.cursor()
            # Wrap the user's query as a subquery filtered by authorization_
    key
            sub_query = f"(SELECT * FROM orders where authorization_key =
    {authorization_key}) a"
            filtered_query = sql_query.replace("orders", sub_query)
            cursor.execute(filtered_query)
            result = cursor.fetchall()
            conn.close()
            return result
        except Exception as e:
            return f"Error querying orders.db: {e}"
```

Here, we defined query_orders with two parameters: sql_query (a string containing the SQL query the agent wants to execute) and authorization_key (a string that should match the customer's authorization key). The function connects to paper_data.db and executes a SQL query.

Within the function, something clever happens to enforce the authorization check: it takes the incoming SQL query and replaces any reference to the orders table with a subquery that filters by the provided authorization_key parameter.

In other words, if the agent tries to run a query such as SELECT * FROM orders WHERE order_id = 1003, the function will transform it into SELECT * FROM (SELECT * FROM orders WHERE authorization_key = 958542) a WHERE order_id = 1003. This way, the query will only return the result if the order has a matching authorization key, effectively preventing unauthorized data access.

> **Note**
>
> While using authorization_key to filter queries is a helpful teaching example, it should not be considered best practice for production systems. Hardcoding or directly passing authorization keys in queries introduces risks, such as SQL injection vulnerabilities or key leakage. In real-world agentic systems, you would typically store and validate authorization credentials through a secure authentication and authorization layer (e.g., OAuth, API tokens, role-based access control).

Creating a vector store search tool

Aside from specific order inquiries, our customer service chatbot should also handle general questions. For example, a user might ask, "What is your return policy?" or mention something that requires company guidelines to be referenced. To enable the agent to answer such questions accurately, we will use `FileSearchTool`, an OpenAI-housed tool that can search a vector-store index of documents. We have already created a vector store that contains a document that lists customer service-related information.

Add the following code to `agent.py`. This will instantiate `FileSearchTool` with the ID of the vector store so that the agent can query it:

```
file_search_tool = FileSearchTool(
    vector_store_ids=['<Enter your vector store ID here>']
)
```

The agent will now be able to search the vector store to answer questions.

Creating an input guardrail

We will also add an input guardrail to ensure that our agentic system isn't misused. If a user asks something completely unrelated (e.g., "Tell me a joke"), our chatbot shouldn't try to answer. To handle this, we will include an input guardrail that will intercept the user's question and determine whether it is related to customer service.

We'll implement this by creating a lightweight classifier agent (guardrail_agent) whose sole job is to examine the input and output a Boolean flag indicating whether the query is relevant to customer service. Then, we'll use the @input_guardrail decorator to plug this check into our main agent. If the guardrail determines that the user prompt isn't relevant, it will raise an InputGuardrailTripwireTriggered exception, which we can catch to handle the off-topic query gracefully.

Let's define the guardrail agent and the guardrail function. Add the following code to the agent. py script:

```
class GuardrailTrueFalse(BaseModel):
    is_relevant_to_customer_service: bool


# Create a guardrail agent
guardrail_agent = Agent(
    name="Guardrail check",
```

```
    instructions="You are an AI agent that checks if the user's prompt is
relevant to answering customer service and order related questions",
    output_type=GuardrailTrueFalse,
)

# Create a guardrail
@input_guardrail
async def relevant_detector_guardrail(
    ctx: RunContextWrapper[None],
    agent: Agent,
    prompt: str | list[TResponseInputItem]
) -> GuardrailFunctionOutput:

    result = await Runner.run(guardrail_agent, input=prompt)

    tripwire_triggered = False

    if result.final_output.is_relevant_to_customer_service == False:
        tripwire_triggered = True

    return GuardrailFunctionOutput(
        output_info="",
        tripwire_triggered=tripwire_triggered
    )
```

The relevant_detector_guardrail function will run asynchronously before the main agent processes the user's prompt. In simpler terms, when a user says something, the guardrail agent analyzes it. If the guardrail agent determines that the query is not relevant, a "tripwire" is triggered to stop the main agent from responding normally.

Creating a retention agent

Next, we need to set up a retention agent. This is a specialized agent that deals with customers who indicate they want to cancel an order or are dissatisfied.

We'll define the retention agent as a separate Agent instance with its own instructions. Add the following code to the agent.py file:

```python
retention_agent = Agent(
    name="Retention Agent",
    instructions=(
        "You are a retention agent. Your goal is to encourage the customer
not to cancel their service, "
        "understand their pain points, and empathize with their situation.
If the customer insists on cancelling, "
        "you may offer up to $100 credit on their account as a retention
incentive."
    ),
    tools=[query_orders],
)
```

Our retention agent will be polite, empathetic, and, if needed, offer credit (up to $100) to persuade the customer not to cancel their service.

Creating a customer service agent

At this point, we have all the pieces we need to create our main customer service agent. This agent will incorporate everything that's been mentioned so far (tools, guardrails, and handoffs). Add the following code to the agent.py file:

```python
customer_service_agent = Agent(
    name="Customer Service Agent",
    instructions=(
        "Introduce yourself as the complaints agent."
        "Handle any customer complaints with empathy and clear next
steps."
        "Use the file_search_tool to get general answers to questions"
        "For specific order related queries, you the query_orders
function_tool"
        "To use the query_order tool, you will need the user's
authorization key"
    ),
    tools=[query_orders, file_search_tool],
    input_guardrails=[relevant_detector_guardrail],
    handoffs=[retention_agent]
)
```

Let's break down these parameters:

- name and instructions: We name the customer service agent "Customer Service Agent" and instruct it to behave as a complaints agent. The prompt we give it is quite detailed, and we give it guidance on when to use certain tools and handoffs. We also explicitly mention the need for an authorization key when using query_orders.

- tools: We pass query_orders and file_search_tool. This means the agent's LLM can choose to call these as functions during its reasoning.

- input_guardrails: We attach relevant_detector_guardrail. This means every user input to this agent will run through that guardrail function. If the guardrail determines the input isn't relevant, it will prevent the agent from continuing as normal.

- handoffs: We include retention_agent in a list. By doing this, we are effectively creating a multi-agent system. OpenAI Agents SDK can perform a handoff if the conversation requires a retention specialist.

At this point, our customer service agent is fully defined. It has the tools it needs to fetch information, a guardrail to keep it on track, and a backup agent for specific scenarios. Now, let's build the runner for our agent system.

Building the runner

In a practical application, we would deploy this into a chat interface. Here, we'll simulate an interaction loop in our terminal. We'll use a SQLiteSession object to maintain conversation state (so that the agent remembers context between turns), and we'll use the Runner.run_sync() method to process user inputs in a loop. We'll also handle the guardrail-triggered exception to inform the user if they ask something out of scope.

Add the following code to agent.py:

```
# Create a session
session = SQLiteSession("session")
last_agent = customer_service_agent

with trace("Customer service agent"):
    while True:
        try:
            question = input("You: ")
            result = Runner.run_sync(last_agent, question, session=session)
            print("Agent: ", result.final_output)
```

```
        last_agent = result.last_agent
    except InputGuardrailTripwireTriggered:
        print ("This comment is irrelevant to customer service.")
```

We are now ready to start simulating our agentic system.

Testing the agent

Let's test the agent and start simulating our agentic system. First, we will try to ask the agent about something not related to customer service to verify that it trips the guardrails successfully:

```
You: What's 5 + 15?
This comment is irrelevant to customer service.
```

Now, let's ask the agent a question about our order. Notice that it actively asks us for an authorization key:

```
You: What's the status of my order? It's 1002
Agent: To check the status of your order, I'll need your authorization
key. Could you please provide that?
You: Sure, it's 154857
Agent: Your order with ID 1002 is currently in the "processing" status. If
there's anything else you need or if you have any concerns, feel free to
let me know!
```

At this point, let's try asking a general customer service-related question and verify that it can perform a vector search:

```
You: How much do I need to order to qualify for the bulk discount?
Agent: To qualify for a bulk discount, you need to place an order over
$500. This qualifies for a 5% discount which is applied automatically. If
you need any further assistance, feel free to ask!
```

Finally, let's demand that the agent cancel our account and observe the handoff to the retention agent. We'll also see that it sends us a retention offer:

```
You: I want to cancel my account
Agent: I'm sorry to hear you're considering canceling your account. Could
you let me know what's prompting this decision? I'd love to help resolve
any issues or concerns you might have. If there's something specific
bothering you, maybe I can assist or find a suitable solution for you.
You: It's just too expensive
```

```
Agent: I understand how important it is to manage expenses. To help with
that, I can offer you a $100 credit on your account, which can ease the
cost a bit. Would that work for you?
```

All our tests succeeded. With that, we have built a fully functioning AI agentic system that acts as a customer service employee through a chatbot. This example showcases a full-fledged agent employing multiple advanced features in concert. The main agent can retrieve factual data, search documents, maintain context, and even delegate to a specialized agent, all while ensuring it stays within its domain.

To wrap up this section, let's step back and reflect on what we've just built. You've seen how a customer service agent can combine multiple components (tools for querying structured data, vector search for retrieving policy documents, guardrails for keeping the system on track, and handoffs to specialized agents) into one cohesive solution system. This example is important because it demonstrates how different features of OpenAI Agents SDK can be orchestrated together to create a realistic, business-ready agent that doesn't just answer simple queries but also manages context, enforces security, and adapts to customer needs.

In the next section, we'll continue to build on this foundation and use an AI agent to automate a workflow for *PaperCo*.

Orchestrating an automated multi-agent workflow

Our second case study showcases how AI agents can be used within workflow automation. Our company, *PaperCo*, wants to periodically send personalized follow-up emails to its customers, catching up on their interests and subtly promoting a new product offering. Instead of manually researching each customer and crafting an email, we can build an agent system to do this automatically.

This workflow will involve two agents working in sequence:

- **Customer research agent:** This agent gathers information about a customer – including basic details from a database, recent conversation transcripts (to recall their interests or any personal information they mentioned), and even current news related to those interests (via a web search)
- **Email creation agent:** This agent takes the compiled information from the research agent and generates a short, personalized email for the customer, while also mentioning the new product offer

The following diagram shows how these components fit together:

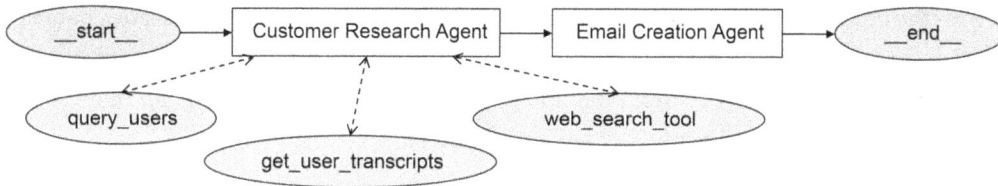

Figure 9.4: Diagram of workflow components

Let's go through each component:

- **User database and query tool**: A SQLite database of customer details (name, email, location, etc.) and a query_users tool function to retrieve a customer's information by ID.

- **Customer transcript data and retrieval tool**: A JSON file that contains past conversation transcripts for customers, and a get_user_transcripts tool to extract those transcripts for a given user. These transcripts contain personal interests mentioned by the customer in previous chats (such as their favorite sports or foods).

- **Web search tool**: A tool that enables the agent to perform a web search to find recent news or information (web_search_tool). The agent will use this to find something current related to the customer's interests (e.g., if the customer loves a sports team, the agent might find a recent game result or news about that team).

- **Customer research agent**: An agent that uses the aforementioned tools to compile a "customer profile" or briefing. It will output a summary or collection of relevant information that can be used to personalize an email.

- **Email creation agent**: An agent that takes the research output and generates an actual email. It will be configured to produce a structured result (with fields such as subject and body), and it will incorporate the personalized touches (interests or news) alongside a marketing message (e.g., the new *PaperCo* offer). The agent will also use another GPT model that is more geared toward personalized writing.

We will also create a simple loop (the orchestration workflow) that goes through a list of customers, runs the research agent for each, then feeds the result to the email agent before saving the generated emails.

Together, these components form a complete workflow that transforms scattered data into a polished, personalized customer email. In the next section, we will begin by setting up the customer database, which serves as the foundation for the research agent's work.

Setting up a customer database

As with the first example, we'll start by setting up some data. To do so, we'll create a database called `customer_details.db` that contains a users table that stores basic customer information (e.g., name, email, location, business type, and phone number). The setup script for this example will create the database and populate a few sample users.

Create a new Python file called `setup.py` and run the following code to set up the database:

```python
import sqlite3
# Set up SQLite DB
conn = sqlite3.connect("customer_details.db")
cursor = conn.cursor()

# Create users table for customer details
cursor.execute("""
CREATE TABLE IF NOT EXISTS users (
    user_id INTEGER PRIMARY KEY,
    first_name TEXT,
    last_name TEXT,
    email TEXT,
    location TEXT,
    business_type TEXT,
    phone_number TEXT
)
""")
# Insert fake user data
users_data = [
    (1, "Emily", "Clark", "emily.clark@example.com", "New York", "Retail",
"555-1234"),
    (2, "Michael", "Nguyen", "michael.nguyen@example.com", "San
Francisco", "E-commerce", "555-5678"),
    (3, "Sophia", "Patel", "sophia.patel@example.com", "Chicago",
"Wholesale", "555-8765"),
    (4, "David", "Martinez", "david.martinez@example.com", "Houston",
"Manufacturing", "555-4321"),
]
cursor.executemany(
```

```
      "INSERT OR IGNORE INTO users (user_id, first_name, last_name, email,
  location, business_type, phone_number) VALUES (?, ?, ?, ?, ?, ?, ?)",
      users_data
  )
conn.commit()
conn.close()
```

Each has an email and a basic profile. These details might be used to tailor the email to the customer or at least fill in the recipient fields.

Setting up the transcripts JSON

We'll also need a JSON file called `customer_transcripts.json` that contains some historical conversation transcripts for each customer. These transcripts are basically logs of prior support chats that include some personal conversations where customers mention their hobbies or preferences (these are the kind of details that can make an email feel personalized).

Create a new file called `customer_transcripts.json` and copy the contents of this file from this book's GitHub repository:

```
{
   "conversations": [
      {
         "user_id": 1,
         "date": "2024-06-01",
         "transcripts": "Hi, I have a question about my order...
  (conversation with support agent)... I'm a big fan of the New York
  Knicks... (more chat)..."
      },
      {
         "user_id": 2,
         "date": "2024-06-02",
         "transcripts": "Can I change my delivery address?... I'm a sushi
  fan... also I love the San Francisco Giants... (more chat)..."
      },
      ...
   ]
}
```

Each conversation log contains user_id, a date, and a combined transcript of a conversation. In this example, we can see that user 1 mentioned being a New York Knicks (basketball team) fan, whereas user 2 talked about loving sushi and being a San Francisco Giants (baseball team) fan.

Creating function tools to retrieve data and search the web

With the data in place, we need to create tools that our agent can use to get that data. We will create two function tools:

- query_users: To run a SQL query on the users table and get user information
- get_user_transcripts: To load the transcripts JSON and extract all transcripts for the given user, returning them as one big string

Create a new Python file called agent.py and type in the following code to create these two function tools:

```python
from agents import (
    Agent, Runner, SQLiteSession, trace,
    function_tool, WebSearchTool
)
import sqlite3
from pydantic import BaseModel
from dotenv import load_dotenv
from agents.extensions.visualization import draw_graph
import json


load_dotenv()


@function_tool
def query_users(sql_query: str):
    """

    Executes the given SQL query on the users table and returns the
result.
    Table: users
        user_id INTEGER PRIMARY KEY,
        first_name TEXT,
        last_name TEXT,
        email TEXT,
        location TEXT,
```

```
            business_type TEXT,
            phone_number TEXT
        """

    db_path = "customer_details.db"
    try:
        conn = sqlite3.connect(db_path)
        cursor = conn.cursor()
        cursor.execute(sql_query)
        result = cursor.fetchall()
        conn.close()
        return result
    except Exception as e:
        return f"Error querying users: {e}"


@function_tool
def get_user_transcripts(user_id: int) -> str:
    """
    Extracts and returns all transcripts for the given user_id from
    customer_transcripts.json as one long string.
    """
    json_path = "Chapter9/WorkflowAutomation/customer_transcripts.json"
    try:
        with open(json_path, "r", encoding="utf-8") as f:
            data = json.load(f)
        transcripts = [
            conv["transcripts"]
            for conv in data.get("conversations", [])
            if conv.get("user_id") == user_id
        ]
        return "\n\n".join(transcripts) if transcripts else ""
    except Exception as e:
        return f"Error reading transcripts: {e}"
```

The query_users function is straightforward: it connects to customer_details.db, executes whatever SQL query is passed in (expecting that query to target the users table), and returns the fetched results. This is similar in spirit to the query_orders tool we made earlier.

The `get_user_transcripts` function opens the JSON file containing transcripts, finds all conversation entries matching the given `user_id`, and joins them into one big string. Essentially, if a customer has had multiple prior conversations, all those transcripts are aggregated. Once again, we decorate both functions with `@function_tool` to expose them as tools for the agent.

We will also use an OpenAI-hosted tool to enable our agent to perform web searches. Add the following code to the `agent.py` file to create that tool:

```
web_search_tool = WebSearchTool()
```

At this point, we have everything we need to start building the agents.

Creating the customer research agent

Now, let's create our first agent in this workflow. This agent's job is to produce a comprehensive context for the email and then produce a report containing the following information:

- The customer's basic details (name, location, etc.)
- A summary of personal interests or notes gleaned from the transcripts
- A summary of one or two current news items or facts related to those interests

Let's create the agent. Add the following code to `agent.py`:

```
customer_research_agent = Agent(
    name="Customer Research Agent",
    instructions=(
        "You are an AI agent that performs research on customers to create
a customer profile."
        "Given a customer ID, you should create a customer report that:"
            "- retrieves customer details"
            "- reads previous customer transcripts on the customer
interests, to be used to personalize emails"
            "- summarized latest news (search the web) on things related
to their interests they've noted in the transcript"
    ),
    tools=[web_search_tool, query_users, get_user_transcripts]
)
```

In this agent, the instructions are critical. Here, we explained its role and then bulleted out the specific tasks needed. We also included all the tools that we created.

Creating the email creation agent

This agent will take the output from the research agent as its input and generate an actual email. To ensure the email is well structured (and easy to send), we'll have this agent produce a JSON object with specific fields: the recipient's email, the sender's email, the subject, and the body of the email (we can produce the body in HTML).

We'll use a Pydantic model to define the expected output schema for the email (for things such as the To field, the Subject field, etc.). Let's define the model by adding the following code to agent.py:

```python
class EmailOutput(BaseModel):
    to_email: str
    from_email: str
    subject: str
    html_email: str
```

Now, we can create the email agent and tell it to use this output type:

```python
email_creation_agent = Agent(
    name="Email Creation Agent",
    instructions=(
        "You are an AI agent that generates emails to keep in touch with
customers of PaperCo."
        "Your goal is to create an email given the information that you
have been provided from another agent"
        "Use the information in a subtle way, like you're trying to share
with them a news story related to their interests or a personal feature"
        "The goal of the email is to be personable and catch up with them,
and also to let them know about our newest offer on Paper Products"
        "The newest offer in Paper products includes a premium
subscription plan where all their orders are 10 percent off"
        "The email should be very concise, just a few sentences, and to
the point"
    ),
    output_type=EmailOutput,
    model="gpt-4.1-2025-04-14"
)
```

In this agent, we set output_type to EmailOutput so that the agent will try to output JSON that fits the EmailOutput schema. The SDK will parse the model's output through Pydantic, so we will directly get an EmailOutput object in Python as the result (with nicely accessible fields).

For example, imagine that the research agent discovers that a customer named Sarah recently talked about her love for sustainable office supplies. The email creation agent may output something like this:

```json
{
  "to_email": "sarah@example.com",
  "from_email": "support@paperco.com",
  "subject": "A quick note on eco-friendly supplies",
  "html_email": "<p>Hi Sarah,</p><p>We saw that sustainability is
important to you, so we thought you'd enjoy this recent article on eco-
friendly office trends. We're also excited to share that our new premium
subscription plan gives you 10% off all orders, including our recycled
paper line.</p><p>Best,<br>PaperCo Team</p>"
}
```

This shows how the agent doesn't just spit out plain text, but instead structures the output into a well-defined JSON object that's ready to send. This way, developers can plug it directly into their email delivery system without extra parsing or formatting.

We also manually adjusted the model to GPT-4.1. Crafting a good email that seamlessly blends personal touches with a promotional offer might need a more capable model (such as GPT-4) to do well, so we explicitly chose a GPT-4 variant that is better at personalized writing.

Orchestrating the workflow

Finally, we need to tie the two agents together in a script that runs the workflow for each customer. To do so, for each user ID, we will do the following:

1. Run `customer_research_agent` with the user ID as input. This will return some result containing the profile/news summary.

2. Take the result from the research agent and feed it as input to `email_creation_agent`.

3. Get the final email output (which will be an `EmailOutput` object).

4. Save that output to a file.

Add the following code to `agent.py`:

```python
for user_id in ["1", "2", "3", "4"]:
    with trace(f"Workflow automation agent for user: {user_id}"):
        result = Runner.run_sync(customer_research_agent, input=user_id)
        print(result.final_output)
```

```
        email = Runner.run_sync(email_creation_agent, result.final_output)
        print(email.final_output)
        # Write email to a new JSON file with title equal to the user_id
        with open(f"{user_id}.json", "w", encoding="utf-8") as f:
            json.dump(email.final_output.dict(), f, ensure_ascii=False,
                indent=2)
```

Here, we iterate through user IDs 1 to 4 (the ones we inserted into the users table). For each, we wrap the operations in a trace, which will help us see the actions in the logs for that specific user's run in the **Traces** module. Now, we have everything we need to start testing this workflow automation.

Testing the workflow

Let's run the program and observe what happens. Here, we will go through the results for user 1. The first thing to note is that customer_research_agent creates a report about that customer by compiling their user information and summarizing their previous call transcripts. We can see this happen in the **Traces** module:

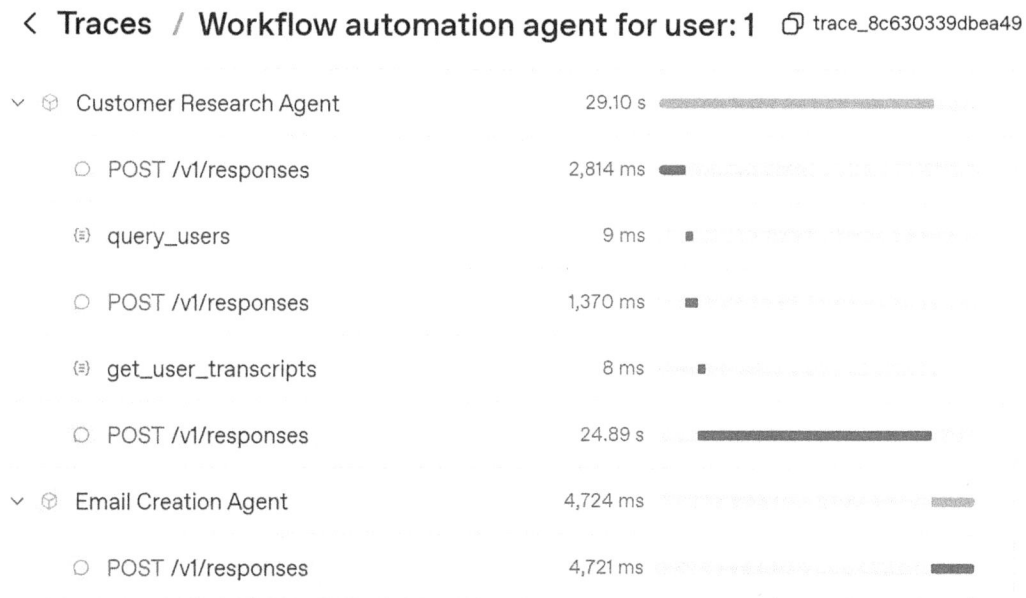

Figure 9.5: The Traces module for this workflow

The output of this agent is the following report:

```
Customer Profile: Emily Clark


Personal Information:


Name: Emily Clark
Email: emily.clark@example.com
Location: New York
Business Type: Retail
Phone Number: 555-1234
Customer Interests:
Based on previous interactions, Emily has expressed a strong interest
in basketball, particularly as a fan of the New York Knicks. She enjoys
playing basketball recreationally with friends and has recently purchased
new sneakers for the court. Additionally, she has a preference for
pepperoni pizza, especially after playing basketball.


Recent News Related to Interests:


Mikal Bridges' Contract Extension:
On August 1, 2025, Mikal Bridges agreed to a four-year, $150 million
contract extension with the New York Knicks. The deal includes a player
option for the 2029-30 season and a trade kicker, making Bridges
ineligible for trade for six months. By accepting a slightly reduced
salary compared to his maximum extension, Bridges has provided the Knicks
with additional salary cap flexibility to strengthen their roster. Since
joining the Knicks in 2024, Bridges has been instrumental in the team's
success, helping them reach their first Eastern Conference Finals in 25
years. (reuters.com)


Appointment of Head Coach Mike Brown:
In July 2025, the New York Knicks appointed Mike Brown as their new head
coach following their first conference finals appearance in 25 years.
Brown, 55, brings a wealth of experience from previous coaching roles
with the Cleveland Cavaliers, Los Angeles Lakers, and Sacramento Kings.
He emphasized the importance of relationships, trust, and accountability
within the team and is eager to lead the Knicks to their first NBA
championship since 1973. (reuters.com)
```

```
Karl-Anthony Towns' Impact:
Since being traded to the New York Knicks on October 2, 2024, Karl-Anthony
Towns has made significant contributions to the team. Notably, on October
29, 2024, he scored 44 points and grabbed 13 rebounds in a 116-107 victory
over the Miami Heat. This performance marked the highest point total by
a Knicks center since Patrick Ewing in 1995. Towns' addition has been
pivotal in the Knicks' recent successes. (en.wikipedia.org)
```

Then, the report is fed into the next agent (`email_creation_agent`). This agent takes the report and creates a personalized email before producing an `EmailOutput` object. This object is then saved to a file called `1.json`, as shown here:

```json
{
  "to_email": "emily.clark@example.com",
  "from_email": "hello@paperco.com",
  "subject": "Big Knicks News & Exclusive PaperCo Offer!",
  "html_email": "<p>Hi Emily,</p><p>Exciting times for Knicks fans—Mikal
Bridges just signed a new contract extension, and Coach Mike Brown is
now at the helm! With games heating up and sunny weather ahead, it's the
perfect season for basketball.<p><p>As you gear up for fall, we wanted to
share our newest PaperCo premium subscription: enjoy 10% off every order,
making your retail supply runs even easier. Let us know if you'd like to
learn more!</p><p>Stay energized and Go Knicks!<br/>The PaperCo Team</p>"
}
```

By doing this, we had two agents collaborate to create a personalized outreach email for this customer to upsell them on an offer. There are many ways to extend this workflow. For instance, you could use a tool that enables the agent to automatically send the email via a **Simple Mail Transfer Protocol (SMTP)** tool. You could also create another agent to decide which customers to target. The possibilities are endless once you know how to mix and match tools and agents in this way.

Summary

In this final chapter, we built two comprehensive agent-driven solutions that brought all your skills together. First, we developed a customer service chatbot for *PaperCo* that combined multiple advanced capabilities. It used a database tool for order lookups (with authorization checks), a knowledge base search for FAQs, an input relevance guardrail, and a handoff to a dedicated retention agent for cancellation requests. Next, we created a workflow automation system to personalize customer outreach emails. In that case study, a research agent gathered each customer's details and interests (via database queries, transcript retrievals, and web searches), then handed off to an email agent that generated a tailored message with a new product offer.

Looking back on your journey throughout this book, you started by understanding what AI agents are and why they matter. You learned the foundations of OpenAI Agents SDK, set up your environment, and built simple agents from scratch. From there, you expanded your agents' capabilities with tools and protocols, provided them with memory and retrieval mechanisms, explored multi-agent handoffs, and practiced managing models and context. You also learned how to monitor, secure, and govern your systems so that they behave reliably in production. Each of these steps prepared you for the complex, end-to-end systems you assembled in this final chapter.

The key takeaway is that you now possess a complete toolkit for building agents that can handle meaningful, real-world tasks. You can design agents that don't just respond to a single prompt but integrate with data sources, remember context, collaborate with other agents, and operate safely within defined policies. This skillset empowers you to move beyond experimentation and into practical deployment, whether you are automating repetitive business workflows, creating specialized assistants, or innovating entirely new applications.

Most importantly, you should recognize that this is only the beginning. The field of agentic systems is evolving rapidly, and the knowledge you've gained puts you at the forefront of this transformation. With OpenAI Agents SDK as your foundation, you are equipped to explore new architectures, integrate emerging tools, and push the boundaries of what AI agents can achieve. The possibilities are vast, and the next generation of intelligent systems will be shaped by builders like you.

Happy AI agent building!

Unlock this book's exclusive benefits now

UNLOCK NOW

Scan this QR code or go to `https://packtpub.com/unlock`, then search for this book by name.

Note: Keep your purchase invoice ready before you start.

‹packt›

Subscribe to our online digital library for full access to over 7,000 books and videos, as well as industry leading tools to help you plan your personal development and advance your career. For more information, please visit our website.

Why subscribe?

- Spend less time learning and more time coding with practical eBooks and Videos from over 4,000 industry professionals
- Improve your learning with Skill Plans built especially for you
- Get a free eBook or video every month
- Fully searchable for easy access to vital information
- Copy and paste, print, and bookmark content

At www.packtpub.com, you can also read a collection of free technical articles, sign up for a range of free newsletters, and receive exclusive discounts and offers on Packt books and eBooks.

Other Books You May Enjoy

If you enjoyed this book, you may be interested in these other books by Packt:

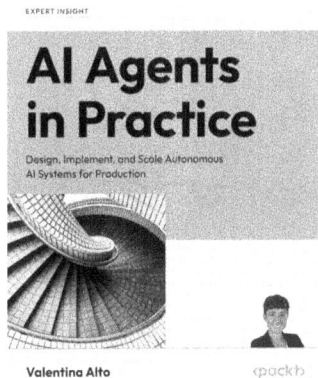

AI Agents in Practice

Valentina Alto

ISBN: 978-1-80580-135-1

- Build core agent components such as LLMs, memory systems, tool integration, and context management
- Develop production-ready AI agents using frameworks such as LangChain with code
- Create effective multi-agent systems using orchestration patterns for problem-solving
- Implement industry-specific agents for e-commerce, customer support, and more
- Design robust memory architectures for agents with short- and long-term recall
- Apply responsible AI practices with monitoring, guardrails, and human oversight
- Optimize AI agent performance and cost for production environments

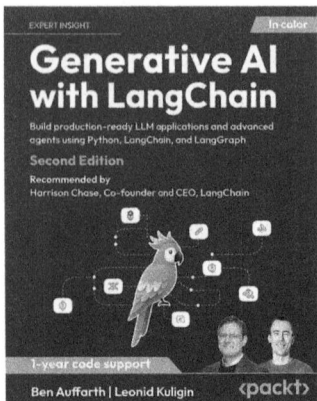

Generative AI with LangChain, Second Edition

Ben Auffarth, Leonid Kuligin

ISBN: 978-1-83702-201-4

- Design and implement multi-agent systems using LangGraph
- Implement testing strategies that identify issues before deployment
- Deploy observability and monitoring solutions for production environments
- Build agentic RAG systems with re-ranking capabilities
- Architect scalable, production-ready AI agents using LangGraph and MCP
- Work with the latest LLMs and providers like Google Gemini, Anthropic, Mistral, Deep-Seek, and OpenAI's o3-mini
- Design secure, compliant AI systems aligned with modern ethical practices

Packt is searching for authors like you

If you're interested in becoming an author for Packt, please visit authors.packtpub.com and apply today. We have worked with thousands of developers and tech professionals, just like you, to help them share their insight with the global tech community. You can make a general application, apply for a specific hot topic that we are recruiting an author for, or submit your own idea.

Share your thoughts

Now you've finished *Building Agents with OpenAI Agents SDK*, we'd love to hear your thoughts! Scan the QR code below to go straight to the Amazon review page for this book and share your feedback or leave a review on the site that you purchased it from.

https://packt.link/r/1806112000

Your review is important to us and the tech community and will help us make sure we're delivering excellent quality content.

Index